T0330258

Propaganda and Zionist Education

Propaganda and Zionist Education

The Jewish National Fund 1924–1947

Yoram Bar-Gal

Ⓡ University of Rochester Press

First published 2003 by the University of Rochester Press
Transferred to digital printing 2017

University of Rochester Press
668 Mt. Hope Avenue, Rochester, NY 14620, USA
www.urpress.com
and Boydell & Brewer Limited
PO Box 9, Woodbridge, Suffolk IP12 3DF, UK
www.boydellandbrewer.com

ISBN-10: 1-58046-138-7
ISBN-13: 978-1-58046-138-2

Library of Congress Cataloging-in-Publication Data

Bar-Gal, Yoram.
    Propaganda and Zionist education : the Jewish National Fund, 1924–1947 /
Yoram Bar-Gal.
        p. cm.
Includes bibliographical references and index.
ISBN 1-58046-138-7
1. Jewish National Fund. 2. Propaganda, Zionist. 3. Zionism. I. Title.
    DS149 .B3235 2003
    320.54'095694'090412—dc21   20030006708

A catalogue record for this title is available from the British Library.

Originally published in Hebrew as *An Agent of Zionist Propaganda: The Jewish National Fund 1924–1947.* © 1999, the University of Haifa Press.

Designed and typeset by Straight Creek Bookmakers.
Cover design by Mauro Design.
Cover photograph by Y. Schweig, 1942. Photo Archive JNF-KKL, Jerusalem.

Contents

Figures and Table

Preface

My father, who emigrated from Poland to Israel in the early 1930s and settled in a workers' neighbourhood near Haifa, died in December 1995. After his death we found in his house boxes full of letters and documents. One box contained a large collection of tree-planting certificates sent by the Jewish National Fund (JNF) in honour of the birthdays that my brother and I had celebrated during the 1930s and 1940s. The sight of these illustrated certificates brought back to my memory many of our childhood experiences, at school and in the youth movements. There had been stamp collecting, the weekly donation dropped into the Blue Box, 'flower days' in the streets, collecting empty bottles and newspapers, donating days of work in kibbutzim, harvest ceremonies, and more. This was not exclusively our experience, for many people in Israel and Jewish people throughout the world had experienced these things as children and young people. These were experiences created by the Jewish National Fund in its work of collecting donations for the redemption of the land.

From the distance of many years I began to ask questions. If the JNF was a Zionist organisation established in 1902 for the economic purposes of buying national land in Eretz Yisrael (the Land of Israel), why did it become so involved in the fashioning of Zionist education? Why did it create a variety of educational projects for all those years? Who was responsible for them? What were the practical and educational results of collecting bottles or the weekly donation? What was the significance of the different symbols the JNF circulated, in particular the Blue Box? These and other questions led to the writing of this book. It attempts to expose the tip of the iceberg of the JNF's work in Israel and the Diaspora in the areas noted. The organisational responsibility for carrying out these activities lay with the Propaganda Department, as it was called, which was one of the four divisions of the institution. Later on sub-departments within this department, namely Newspapers and Schools and Youth developed, and they all worked together under the heads of the Propaganda Department.

The book discusses the work of the departments dealing with propaganda, newspapers, and youth in the head office of the JNF from 1924 to 1947. It has been written from both a historical and a social scientific perspective. To date, hardly any research has been conducted on these aspects of propaganda and the Zionist socialisation of the JNF, which formed our collective memory and stamped its impress on the Hebrew culture of Israel, in the wider sense of the term. The research is based on archival material mainly assembled in the Central Zionist Archives in Jerusalem, and also on materials located throughout the world. From all these a picture took shape of the methods inspired by the JNF's propaganda department.

Careful study and cross-referencing of the information in the documents of the period under review allows us to study the institutional motives that drove the JNF functionaries to such intensive activity, its effects felt by every child who received a Zionist education in those days. The JNF devoted considerable resources to this work, presumably motivated by the politics and struggles within the Zionist movement. The study identifies a small group of people, from the fields of education and propaganda, who saw Eretz Yisrael as a product they had to market to different segments of the population using persuasive techniques common at that time.

There is no intention to discuss the complex theoretical issues emerging from the subjects discussed in this book, although from time to time, comments are made when necessary. Accordingly, I would like to make certain things clear, particularly the frequent use of the word *propaganda*. This has been an emotionally charged term since the Second World War.[1] Indeed propaganda is one of the expressions of the art of persuasion, that is, an organisational or institutional effort to convince others and make them believe (or not believe) in certain truths or to make them perform certain actions or stop them from performing other actions. Some define propaganda as a form of communication which attempts to change attitudes and opinions of others. Thus there is a common basis for propaganda and other forms of mass persuasion such as education or advertising and public relations. At the beginning of the twentieth century propaganda became one of the conventional means of spreading doctrines and ideas, largely owing to the development of the means of communication ranging from written and photographic journalism through cinema to radio broadcasting. From the First World War on means of propaganda were widely used by organisations such as independent states or political movements, and they reached their zenith in the totalitarian and fascist regimes in the following years. In these regimes (such as the Soviet Union and Nazi Germany) propaganda and education could hardly be distinguished: both were directed towards specific goals and left the individual no freedom of opinion. As a result the term *propaganda* developed a negative connotation.[2]

The JNF personnel in that interwar period, who had grown up in those same European countries, absorbed the concepts and ideas which appeared and crystallised at that time. For them *propaganda* was not a negative concept at all but positive, and they used it prolifically. They believed that they could persuade the masses of the Jewish people to contribute money to buy national territory in Eretz Yisrael. Their work, which arose out of this basic belief, they called *means of propaganda* and the methods of distribution they called *propaganda work*. This idea blended well into the educational philosophy which was dominant in some of the Zionist educational institutions, namely education in values, and it was even evident in other concepts, called in those days *the time of education* or *the educator's moment*. In this educational philosophy values such as physical work, the love of nature, public service, pioneering, and defending the homeland were formed and fostered.[3]

In time, after the rise and fall of the totalitarian regimes, criticism of the individual's duty to the collective began to be heard. Education in values was censured as a form of indoctrination. Similar criticism was voiced by various intellectuals in Israel such as the writer Yizhar Smilansky, who applied the terms advertisement and propaganda when he spoke about determining the limits of education. He said, 'It is good and fitting to tell the truth and talk about "propagandising" values or to "advertise them" . . . and not to mislead people about "educating towards values". Propaganda and advertising are not at all inappropriate means of distributing products or ideas, but nowhere is education these things'.[4]

But if for Smilansky the line between education and indoctrination was clear, for at least some of Israel's educators it was not easy to identify. Zvi Lavi wrote, 'Unfortunately the borders between education and indoctrination are neither as clear nor as unambiguous in educational practice as they are on the theoretical level. It is impossible to carry out a normal process of education and utterly to avoid any trace of indoctrination'.[5] Clearly, the above argument is not only relevant to Israeli society but is part of the public debate over the essential nature of education and the goals of a democratic culture that is trying to find different ways and didactic methods to grasp both ends of the stick: the development of freedom of individual opinion on the one hand, and the fostering of collective responsibility on the other.

From the viewpoint of the people at work in the JNF's propaganda department in those years the argument about the line separating education in values and propaganda was irrelevant. As will be demonstrated in several places in this book, for them the means justify the ends. Their involvement in formal and informal education was intense, as they tried to achieve organisational advantages with the aid of the Hebrew education network. The JNF functionaries succeeded in imparting to the Zionist public the feeling that the good of their organisation was the good of the nation. For many long years they operated a multifaceted international organisational network, created personal life experiences, and established common cultural concepts which affected millions of children receiving Hebrew education. In this way the staff of the JNF propaganda department contributed to the formation of the collective memory of the Zionist experience in Israel and the Diaspora. The people of this department created their own language, enfolded children and young people in a pervasive network of images, had them participate in weekly and annual ceremonies, and thus strengthened the myths which were developed at that time. This book is an attempt to disclose the work methods of one of the important agents of the formation of our collective memory, one that gave meaning to the concept of being Israeli.[6]

The book has a three-part structure. The first part, covered by chapter 1, presents different historical reviews of the JNF that attempt to touch upon the wider issues that form the background to my research. This section describes events which took place between 1924 and 1947 and to which the JNF had to respond with various propaganda methods. A number of principles that guided the institution in its propaganda work during the period under study are likewise discussed. This propaganda work was aided by a special organisational structure, characterised by a reciprocal relationship between the centre in Jerusalem and the different branches in the Jewish Diaspora. This organisational structure also contained other organisations such as The Teachers' Council for the JNF and youth movement centres in Eretz Yisrael and the Diaspora, which assisted in the distribution of propaganda.

In the second part (chapters 2 through 5), I present what the JNF considered the most important of the many means of propaganda it produced. Each of these is presented in a separate chapter and demonstrates a different kind of propaganda.

The Blue Box (chapter 2): the symbol of the organisation which became a Zionist icon. This section discusses the factors that influenced its design and its production in Eretz Yisrael. Then a description follows of the work with the boxes in propaganda and of the collection of donations for the organisation. In the conclusion of this chapter I discuss the importance of the donations collected to help redeem the land.

Stamps (chapter 3): Stamps were another means used for propaganda purposes. These were miniature posters making political and social statements, principally designed for schools. At this time the JNF was very active in distributing them to other institutions and organisations, too, and it introduced the practice of the obligatory stamp which characterised the activist attitude of the institution during that period.

Books, games, and toys (chapter 4): These are examples of direct means of propaganda aimed at children and young people and not intended for collecting funds. The JNF succeeded in publishing close to a hundred monographs during this time, but on the other hand it failed to distribute them in any mass way. An analysis of the editing process of the monographs shows the heavy-handedness of the social and political censorship of JNF publications.

Filmstrips, films, and lectures (chapter 5): The JNF exploited technological developments in mass media for its own purposes. Although the organisation made some attempts, at great cost, to produce real films, most of the visual propaganda was through means that were simpler to operate and distribute, as well as cheaper to produce. A review of the decision-making process in the production of visual propaganda is followed by consideration of the simpler means that allowed the production of the slides and filmstrips which accompanied the propaganda lectures. These slides were mainly directed to the adult population and brought the sights and scenes of Israel to the Diaspora.

The third part (chapters 6 through 8) is different from the first two in that it presents a critical cross-sectional analysis of the significance of the propaganda and of the messages conveyed by the materials produced by the JNF in the years under study. The concepts I apply originate in critical approaches used in the social sciences and which, among other things, claim that cultural systems in the broadest sense (language, art, science, myth, religion, and so on) exist to serve stability and social solidarity, to move people to desirable action, and to safeguard the ruling elite. At the centre of this approach is the organisation—the JNF as a social/political/economic institution, operating in different environments and developing special ways to survive as an organisation. Three aspects are considered:

The Blue Box rituals (chapter 6): These were the methods devised by the JNF to inculcate the idea of contributing to the fund. They involved the development of different practices in the Hebrew education network introduced into various ceremonies. These became part of the annual routine of schools and served as the basis for ceremonies still held today in the Israeli education system.

Propaganda in JNF maps (chapter 7):The political statements made by JNF maps, which appeared on the Blue Box and various publications, carried much significance. The way the JNF dealt with the different challenges and political struggles of that time while simultaneously fighting internal Zionist battles over its public image are discussed.

The JNF's regional imagery (chapter 8): This became an inseparable part of Israeli symbolism. Several human and landscape symbols arose out of the creative milieu of the propaganda department of the JNF. I attempt in this chapter to explain the way an agrarian philosophy and regional preferences become explicit when one analyses the different means of propaganda. In first place here was the sanctification of the *Emek*, the Jezreel Valley, as Zionism's finest regional achievement; all this arose as part of a process of robbing other areas in Palestine of their legitimacy.

Acknowledgements

This study could not have been accomplished without the assistance I received from all the staff and librarians in the Central Zionist Archives in Jerusalem. All were most painstaking during the constant search into the different JNF files, which allowed me the use of documents, photographs, and publications. Special thanks go to the JNF, especially the Jerusalem-based Institute for Research into the History of the JNF, Land and Settlement, headed by Dr. Gabi Alexander. They not only assisted with the material but also furnished me with moral support that helped me complete the study. My gratitude is also expressed to the staff of the photographic archives of the JNF who retrieved the pictures for the book which made its publication possible. Other archival materials were also made available to me by the National Office of the JNF in New York; I thank them for this.

The architect David Tartkower provided me with interesting material from Tel Aviv on the subject of games from that period: many thanks. The people of the Spielberg Hebrew Film Archive in Jerusalem also deserve special thanks for furnishing me different films produced by the JNF; especially Mr. Hillel Trister for exchanging information on this subject. I wish particularly to thank Professor Yossi Katz, who also provided me with interesting material that helped the research.

My thanks go to the Research Authority of the University of Haifa, which extended support in many ways at the beginning of the research. I am deeply indebted to my colleagues who read various chapters: Professor Arnon Sofer and Professor Stanley Waterman. I thank Dr. Josef Goldstein for comments from his personal experience in the education system. Special thanks to my brother, Professor David Bargal, who religiously followed the current reports he received about the progress of the research and made useful comments on various chapters. Likewise the anonymous referees of the publishers who read the manuscript, for their comments that contributed to the re-writing process.

Finally I wish to express my gratitude, and especially my appreciation, to my wife Bruria and to all my family and close friends. They shared with me the uncertainty, enthusiasm, and excitement that accompanied the process of writing, and for several years were swept along by it into remote periods of time.

Chapter 1

The Historical Background to JNF Propaganda

Historical Background to the JNF's Activities between 1924 and 1947

Seeking Direction after the First World War

After the First Zionist Congress met in Basel in 1897 the question of financing the future activities in Eretz Yisrael was raised. Accordingly a fund for the collection of contributions and the purchase of land for Zionist settlement was established in 1901 and was called *Hakeren hakayemet leyisrael,* rendered The Jewish National Fund in English. During that period a migration from Eastern Europe to Palestine of Jewish immigrants of socialist ideology, known as the Second Aliya (migration), began. These immigrants saw cooperative rural settlement on national land as a central principle of their activity. These immigrants, led by David Ben-Gurion, had deep political convictions and became the political elite that dominated the Jewish community in Eretz Yisrael as well as gaining control of the institutions of the World Zionist movement during the 1920s and 1930s. The political domination of the Second Aliya made their political principles the official policy of the Zionist movement, with the emphasis on 'national land' and cooperative rural settlements in Eretz Yisrael (see Table 1.1).

Together with this one must note that after the First World War and the arrival of other waves of immigration (the Third and Fourth Aliya) the urban population grew, especially in the Tel Aviv area. Some of these immigrants brought with them a capitalistic outlook and believed in the purchase of private land and individual, rather than cooperative settlement. As a result, during the 1920s and 1930s private Jewish settlement grew in the country. Together with this, the political activity of the Revisionist right, who challenged the socialist control of the Second Aliya, also grew in the Zionist movement. The right wingers, however, did not manage to upset or change the political structure of the Zionist institutions or change the socialist ideology that dominated them.

The First World War brought about the transfer of the centre of organisation and activity of the Zionist movement from Central and East-

Table 1.1

General Course of Events

1882 – 1884　-　Jews of the First Aliya settle in Eretz Yisrael.

1897　-　1st Zionist Congress.

1901　-　5th Zionist Congress; resolution to establish the JNF.

1902　-　Beginning of JNF collection of contributions; stamps and donations.

1904　-　Start of the Second Aliya to Eretz Yisrael.

1906　-　JNF purchases its first agricultural land.

1907　-　Arthur Ruppin presents the Zionist Settlement Program in Eretz Ysrael.

1909　-　Establishment of the city of Tel Aviv, first as a Jewish neighbourhood of Jaffa.

1914　-　Outbreak of First World War; JNF Head Office moves to The Hague.

1915　-　Balfour Declaration: 'The establishment in Palestine of a national home for the Jewish people'

1919 – 1923　-　Third Aliya arrives in Eretz Yisrael.

1920　-　The Zionist Organization's London conference; establishment of Keren Hayesod; JNF's mission is defined as purchasing national land in Eretz Yisrael.

1920 - 1931　-　Weizmann president of the Zionist Organization.

1920 – 1921	-	Decision to purchase land in Jezreel valley; establishment of Nahalal and Ein Harod.
1922	-	JNF Head Office is moved to Jerusalem.
1923	-	13th Zionist Congress authorizes JNF to engage in land preparation (afforestation and swamp drainage); Ussishkin is elected JNF president.
1923	-	Borders of Mandatory Eretz Yisrael are finally determined.
1924	-	Julius Berger is appointed head of JNF Propaganda Department.
1924 – 1928	-	Fourth Aliya arrives in Eretz Yisrael; expansion of Tel Aviv.
1925	-	14th Zionist Congress debates the purchase of 'national' or 'private' land. Intensification of private enterprise's purchase of private agricultural and urban land.
1926	-	Establishment of JNF Department for Youth and Schools, headed by Nathan Bistritski.
1927	-	Establishment of the Teachers Council for the JNF.
1928	-	Purchase of land in the Hefer valley (Emek Hefer) and in Haifa Bay area by the JNF.
1929	-	Establishment of the extended Jewish Agency.
1929 – 1931	-	Extensive afforestation by the JNF in Jezreel Valley and Judean Hills.
1933	-	Revisionist right wing, led by Jabotinsky, leaves the

Zionist Organization.

1933 – 1935 - Purchase of land in Beth Shean valley and

Jordan valley by the JNF; Rise of the Nazis in Germany

and Fifth Aliya arrives in Eretz Yisrael. Private capital

flows into Eretz Yisrael.

1936 – 1938 - Clashes with the Arabs; Peel Commission's Partition

Plan; the 'Tower and Stockade' period.

1939 – 1945 - Second World War; death of Ussishkin

(1941); purchase of land in northern Negev.

1947   - The UN decision on the establishment of the State of

Israel.

ern Europe to the English-speaking world, namely Britain and the USA. After the war, in February 1919, the World Zionist Congress met in London and discussed future settlement activity and questions of land in Eretz Yisrael, development strategies, and different organisational matters. The discussions on these subjects also involved the annual conference, which convened in London a year later, in July 1920. This conference was especially important since practical decisions were made there. These, together with ideological-political decisions, carried repercussions of great significance for the future of the JNF.

In the first place, prior to the First World War the JNF had spread its work over a variety of different areas, beyond its declared goals; nevertheless, decisions on them were made by the Zionist Federation during the second half of the first decade of the century. The JNF did not deal only with the purchase of land and the collection of money for this, but also with the establishment of settlements, support of the settlers, the founding of educational institutions, and so on.[1] Because of the criticism expressed at various conferences about this additional activity, at the London conference the roles of the JNF were redefined and reconfirmed thus:

1. To purchase land in Eretz Yisrael, through contributions by the nation, as the property of the Jewish People.
2. To lease such land for cultivation and construction.
3. To provide for the settlement on JNF land of people with no capital.
4. To find ways to engage private capital in the purchase of land.

Secondly, at that time the fate of all the development plans in Eretz Yisrael was contingent on the mobilisation of additional investments, and it was clear that after the war such money would come mainly from American Jews. The representatives of American Jewry, headed by Judge Louis Brandeis (1856–1941), came to the London conference and, in the spirit of capitalism and individualism, proposed a different approach to settlement and land ownership in Eretz Yisrael, and regarding the structure and operational methods of the Zionist movement. The following points in the American proposals are noteworthy:

1. No settlement activity should begin until the infrastructure was prepared (by draining swamps, finding water, etc.).
2. Fundraising must precede practical activity.
3. Preference should be given to private enterprise.

The approach and policies proposed by the Brandeis Group were not unacceptable to the delegates at the London conference. The conference did, however, resolve to establish a new institution whose role was to collect money for the migration and settlement of Jews—in Eretz Yisrael. This was Keren Hayesod (the Foundation Fund). It also decided that at least 20 percent of the money collected by Keren Hayesod would be handed over annually to the JNF. Moreover, the formulation of the goals of Keren Hayesod contained a statement that it would not assist private enterprise. In this setting a crisis developed with the Brandeis Group, which held the key to the mobilisation of massive funds in North America. In 1921, at the National Zionist Conference of the USA in Cleveland, Chaim Weizmann (1874–1952) announced the establishment of Keren Hayesod, an act that led to the resignation of Brandeis from the leadership of the Zionist movement and to the rise of a new leadership that accepted the authority of the centre in London.[2]

Thirdly, during this post-war period the Zionist Executive decided to send a re-organisation committee to Eretz Yisrael to study requirements and to organise Zionist activity more efficiently. The committee recommended a reduction in the flow of money for 'non-productive' goals such as education, and non-involvement in any investments before all financial obligations were securely covered. This was the background to the Thirteenth Zionist Congress held in Karlsbad (January 1921). There the proposals of the London conference concerning Keren Hayesod and the JNF were eventually accepted, as were the decisions to purchase land in the Jezreel Valley and to establish the settlements of Nahalal, Eyn Harod, Tel Yosef, and Kfar Yehezkel by the same methods as the ones that had been used up to that time.

Finally, in those years immediately after the First World War the political issue concerned the Zionist movement. Parallel to seeking new organisational methods and definitions of goals for the Zionist Federation, its leaders were obliged to become involved in the political activity arising out of the Balfour Declaration and the establishment of the British Mandate for Palestine. At a meeting between Weizmann and Balfour on 4 December1918 a decision was made concerning the formation of a mission that would demand recognition of the historical rights of the Jews to Eretz Yisrael, and the granting of a mandate to the British government for the country, based on the assumption that this would lead to the establishment of a national home for the Jewish people.[3] Consequently, on 24 April 1920 the San Remo Conference authorised the grant of a mandate for Palestine to Britain. In that same whirlpool of events, the clashes of interests of different powers and movements determined the fate and borders of Eretz Yisrael. Each power was bent on establishing its own sphere of influence, as evident in the San Remo agreements and in other agreements during the 1920s (see Figure 1.1).[4]

In view of this background one can understand that the political battlefield was most favourable for Menahem Ussishkin's activity as president of the JNF from 1923 until his death in 1941.[5] Ussishkin worked for the extension of the tasks of the JNF beyond just the purchasing of national land but also their preparation (afforestation and swamp drainage). In order to achieve more political and organisational power many of the JNF's resources were diverted to cultural and educational areas in a process in which the legend of the *halutz* (pioneer) and the fundamental features of Israeli culture were created. Ussishkin's (and the JNF's) approach were consistent with the ideology of the major Zionist institutions until the territorial question, involving the partition of Eretz Yisrael between Jews and Arabs (the Peel Commission), was raised in the second half of the 1930s. Ussishkin moved to the right of the line drawn out by David Ben-Gurion and Chaim Weizmann, and became a supporter of *Eretz yisrael hashlema* (the entire Eretz Yisrael) in present-day terminology. The outbreak of the Second World War, and more especially Ussishkin's death (1941), restored the JNF to the political consensus. This was accomplished by means of the new leadership, carefully chosen, with due regard for political correctness, to include representatives of the liberals, the workers, and the religious. The activities and approach of the JNF from 1924 to 1947 are covered in greater detail and depth in the following sections.

The Organisation of the JNF and the Background to Its Policies from the 1920s to the Mid-1930s

As noted, at the London conference in 1920 the guidelines for JNF activities after the First World War were formulated. The transfer of the JNF Head Office from Holland to Jerusalem was decided at the Thirteenth Zionist Congress in Karlsbad. Decisions were also made on organisational changes, the appointment of a new directorate, and the establishment of different committees; Menahem Ussishkin was elected head of the directorate. In September 1922 the office indeed was moved to Jerusalem, and the JNF concentrated on the purchase of land, conceding the other aspects of settlement to the new fund, Keren Hayesod. The struggle between these two bodies over areas of authority was an issue at the Thirteenth Zionist Congress in Karlsbad, 1923.The JNF position was adopted since its tasks were not limited to the purchase of land but included 'preparation of the land'.[6]

The information and propaganda policies of the JNF were undoubtedly influenced by these events. By the organisation's twenty-fifth anniversary year (1927) its share of the total amount of land owned by Jews in Eretz Yisrael was still relatively small. Of the total of twenty million dunams of land administered by the British Mandatory government and that were in the area of the Jewish National Home, the Jews in mid-1927 owned only a million dunams, These were divided between different owners: 80 percent was privately owned and 20 percent was national lands of the JNF.[7] In terms of regional distribution, the JNF was somewhat better off. More than a third of the land it owned was in the Jezreel Valley and more than 20 percent was in the Akko Valley.[8] Hence all land purchases in the central regions were seen as an impressive achievement, justifying the existence and policies of the JNF. During this period Canadian Jewry came to its rescue with a contribution of a million dollars, making possible the purchase of 50,000 dunams in the Sharon area (Emek Hefer) and in the Haifa Bay area (Emek Zevulun). These purchases were vital to the JNF in their power struggles within the Zionist Federation, expressed at the Fifteenth Zionist Congress at Basel (1927) as at earlier ones.

At the beginning of the 1930s two British investigation committees published their findings: the Shaw Commission of Inquiry report in January 1930 and the Hope-Simpson Report on Immigration, Land and Settlement, at the end of that year. These reports censured the land and settlement policies of the Zionist movement, including those of the JNF, and this forced the latter to modify its propaganda—for external as well as internal purposes. Despite the discord with the British the internal Zionist criticism of the fund's policies did not disappear. In these same years, following the rise of Nazism in Germany the Fifth Aliya reached Palestine, creating a rise in land profiteering and in prices. The financial resources of the fund had to compete in a land market of limited supply and high prices, which reduced the fund's land purchases.

The propaganda activities of the JNF in the period under review were also influenced by the struggles within the Zionist movement and its institutions, for the JNF as an organisation needed legitimation for its approach and activities. Until the late 1920s it was not entirely clear what the desirable strategies in the area of land purchase were. At about the time of the creation of the Jewish Agency in 1929 criticism of the JNF, which proposed to limit the Agency's authority and activity, was published in a report drawn up by American Zionist and non-Zionist circles. Accordingly, some of the JNF's variegated propaganda was presumably for internal consumption, with a twofold aim: to accumulate power and resources in order to survive within the Zionist organisation and to win the support of the Jewish-Zionist public throughout the world as part of its survival strategy.

JNF Activities and the Background to its Policies from the Mid-1930s till after the Second World War

The second half of the 1930s were affected by the Arab anti-Jewish riots in Eretz Yisrael (known in Israeli history as the *me'ora'ot*), as well as by a rise in tension over the division of the territory in Eretz Yisrael. In 1937, close to the opening of the Twentieth Zionist Congress in Zurich, the report of the Peel commission was published, proposing the partition of Palestine. Eretz Yisrael. Quite naturally, it sparked fierce debates in the Zionist movement and among the public in Eretz Yisrael on acceptance or rejection of the partition plan. The JNF found itself at the centre of this controversy owing to the personal involvement of Ussishkin, as noted earlier, then Chairman of the JNF directorate, who took a stand against Chaim Weizmann, who generally favoured partition. Ussishkin opposed the plan; in today's parlance he would be described as belonging to the political right. Between 1936 and 1945 the political, economic, and security events in Eretz Yisrael apparently proved beneficial for the JNF:[9]

1. There was a drop in the investment by private enterprise in the country, so the demand for land dropped.
2. The deteriorating situation of Arab landowners increased the supply of land for sale.
3. A Zionist settlement strategy became crystallised.

The circumstances enhanced people's understanding of the importance of land acquisition; the twentieth Zionist Congress of 1937 concerned itself with the necessity of purchasing land and charged the JNF with responsibility for the vigorous and rapid redemption of new areas of land as a solid foundation for the establishment of the Hebrew homeland. The success of this policy was plain. In 1937 JNF lands accounted for 31 percent of all Jewish-owned land in Eretz Yisrael, an area of about 400,000 dunams. Ten years later the total area of JNF land exceeded 800,000 dunams, being 48 percent of Jewish-owned land in the country.[10]

In the thirteen years from the *me'ora'ot* to the end of the Second World War the JNF doubled its land holdings, with priority going to acquisitions in particular regions. This priority arose out of the Peel Commission report, which determined that certain areas in Eretz Yisrael (mainly Beth She'an and the Negev) would be outside the territory of the Jewish State. The political events, the security situation, and the organised activities of the Zionist institutions in settlement and land purchase seemingly led, among other things, to a relaxation of the tension among the various Zionist organisations. The JNF saw itself as an inseparable part of the *Homa Umigdal* (Stockade and Tower) method of settlement, which became an important symbol for the organisation. The JNF presented its participation in the settlement process as an important achievement for its status and prestige in the Zionist movement. This expression is clearly seen in a resolution adopted by the 21st Zionist Congress held in August 1939 in Geneva: 'The 21st Congress applauds the miraculous efforts of the JNF in its success at redeeming more than a hundred thousand dunams of land during the years of Arab incidents that made possible the heroic project of new settlement and acted as a foundation for the establishment of forty new sites'.[11]

When the delegates to the 21st Congress convened they had no idea that within days events would start to unfold that would transform the face of the world, particularly the Jewish world and within it the Zionist movement especially. The Second World War, which caused the annihilation of East European Jewry, in fact destroyed the popular foundation of the JNF, which depended on this Jewry. As we shall see, in the 1920s and 1930s the JNF Head Office directed the main thrust of its propaganda, publicity, and information at the Jews of Eastern Europe and the Hebrew schools in that area. The faithful core of JNF operatives had been formed there in a deep-rooted and extensive organisation that pervaded all levels of Jewish society. Reliance on Eastern European Jewry, Karsel argues, although it won popularity for the JNF, did not yield large contributions to it.[12]

The Second World War resulted in a shift of the Zionist movement's power centre as a whole, and of the JNF in particular, to the English-speaking Diaspora. This Jewry assisted with a massive flow of contributions for the purchase of land and the establishment of settlements. The setting for this marked rise in donations was the restrictions listed in the White Papers (1937, 1939) and the unchanging ideology ascribing vital importance to rural settlement for producing the territorial profile of the state in the making.[13]

The years of the Second World War were therefore fruitful for the activities of the JNF, in terms of the financial resources it mobilised and the political contribution it made, which justified its approach. The circumstance at the time demanded that land acquisition be augmented by settlement activity, which the JNF resumed after being prevented from engaging in it since the 1920s following the establishment of Keren Hayesod.

The JNF's reward for taking on this role was the erasure of all the years when it had been cut off from real settlement activity and had concentrated principally upon the acquisition and preparation of land. Throughout the war the Head Office in Jerusalem continued, as well as it could, to keep its propaganda channels open. It produced and distributed propaganda material in Eretz Yisrael and overseas on the subjects of land problems, the country's ability to absorb immigration, and the JNF's political aims in the struggle against the land transfer regulations, alongside its relentless solidification of the map of land settlement. This reached its zenith with the acquisition of land for the establishment of eleven settlements in the Negev just before the UN General Assembly's resolution on the partition of Palestine and the creation of a separate Arab and Jewish state (29 November 1947).

The Character, Organisation, and Deployment of JNF Propaganda

The Propaganda and Its Patterns

A historical survey gives us to understand that the JNF maintained ongoing contacts with the world outside the organisation in several spheres, which obliged it to construct a large and widespread propaganda network.

In the internal Zionist sphere the JNF had to defend the areas of its activity against the invasion of other external organisations. It had to justify its ideological and practical path and preserve its assets in light of the dilemmas presented by other factors in the Zionist movement.In the internal Jewish sphere the JNF saw itself as the spearhead of the Zionist movement and as the standard-bearer of the idea of Eretz Yisrael. The propaganda in this sphere was the breath of life for the JNF since the contributions were its source of survival.

The importance of the non-Jewish sphere for the JNF was relatively small, and it left this area of activity to other Zionist factors regarding propaganda and information.

Throughout the whole period under review, propaganda was an inseparable part of the JNF's work. Emmanuel Haroussi (1950), who analysed the work of Zionist propaganda, wrote the following about it:

> The inclusion of the mechanism of propaganda within the general activity is a kind of obligatory requirement. Propaganda is an organisational function of the movements' entire leadership, and there should be no separation between 'practical' action and the action of 'propaganda'. One depends upon the other.[14]

Haroussi indicated two principal types of propaganda, direct and indirect. In direct propaganda the symbol and the slogan were the primary tools, but these were insufficient for the JNF to 'conquer hearts'. So it emphasized the second approach, indirect propaganda, which was 'the education of the masses'.

To understand Haroussi's retrospective evaluation of JNF propaganda one must go back to the beginnings of the organisation at the start of the twentieth century, and to the importance the founders accorded to propaganda activity. The early historiography of the JNF shows that immediately after the Fifth Congress the popular form of collecting funds was decided: stamps and the Blue Box. These constituted the heart of the propaganda method that spread throughout the Jewish world during the first decade of the twentieth century. After the establishment of Keren Hayesod the links between the collection of money and propaganda needed redefinition and a fresh characterisation. According to the JNF, 'the donation in its purest form' was a highly efficient means for the accrual of money for the Zionist movement. Donation of this sort strengthened national consciousness, so one should consider this, not the collection of funds, as the success of Zionist propaganda. This was so since the main purpose of collecting donations was 'to win over the person'—meaning to bring the masses closer to Zionism.

The staff of the Head Office in Jerusalem periodically defined the aims of propaganda and determined the content, which would disseminated by various means. For example, in 1924–1925 the slogan 'Hunger for Land' was chosen, its financial significance being an attempt to raise £500,000 to buy 100,000 dunams—thus doubling the area of land owned by the JNF.[15] At the same time the JNF aspired to being an institution that would change norms and conduct, and 'prepare hearts' for Zionist work through the idea of redeeming the land. Accordingly the JNF tried to raise interest in redeeming the land by stimulating a sense of identification in the Jews in the Diaspora with the settlement project.

The JNF's propaganda approach led it to operate in two domains simultaneously: the private domain, or the individual's home; and the public domain, or public buildings and the thoroughfares of a town. In these domains a variety of propaganda methods were used:

1. Means for collecting funds: boxes, stamps, the Golden Book, donations of trees.
2. Printed matter: books, magazines/newspapers/bulletins, diaries, and journals.
3. Audio-visual aids: magic lantern slides, filmstrips, films, records.
4. Personal contacts: emissaries, volunteers, delegates, and committee members.

These methods and the entry into the private and public domains were part of the propaganda strategy adopted by the JNF staff in their attempt to imitate commercial propaganda/advertising:

Commercial propaganda essentially aspires to achieve the same goal we are trying to achieve, and that is to arouse as many people as possible for a known purpose to do something that they would not have done without the propaganda; for example: buy some given product, prefer a certain well-known firm. . . . We also wish to cause the large Jewish multitudes to remember the JNF at all times.[16]

Accordingly the Head Office recommended the following:

We must inundate the Jewish public with slogans and pictures, to rivet their attention, to create an atmosphere of unrest . . . [to distribute the pictures and slogans] in every place a Jew sets foot in: in communal centres, lodges, places of business, society and union centres, the offices of charity organisations, mutual aid societies, rabbinical offices, libraries, theatres, bath houses and rest houses, shelters, hospitals, pharmacies, clinics, synagogues, seminaries, schools, doctors' waiting rooms, restaurants, hotels, pensions . . . leave no place where there is no illustrated poster with a clear and brief text. . . .[17]

Together with the conventional methods of propaganda, personal, direct contact between the propagandist and his target population was stressed by the JNF staff. *Propagandistim*—in the Hebraised rendering—set out from Eretz Yisrael for the Diaspora for periods of several months to help with the work. They were carefully chosen and also received 'special education' in the form of seminars and courses on propaganda, part of which was visits to JNF land holdings and explanations from different experts before leaving for overseas.[18]

Personal contact between the organisation's emissary and the public was not the only important means of propaganda; mass propaganda also began to be applied during that same period. The organisation's propaganda staff world-wide, being residents of major cities, were exposed to the innovative methods used in propaganda, and they adopted them all wherever possible. With mass propaganda beginning to flourish throughout the Western world, aided by a variety of technological advances, not surprisingly the JNF workers adopted these methods. For example, in first half of the 1920s in Warsaw they began to use the 'phonograph', recording speeches of leaders and intellectuals in Yiddish and Polish. In the USA and Britain at that time they were already using the 'radiophone' to disseminate the speeches of different leaders.[19]

Basic Assumptions of JNF Propaganda

There is insufficient room to describe and analyse the wide range of methods and means the JNF employed in its propaganda. Below we concentrate on just some of the important operational means as they appear in eyewitness reports. However, considering the propaganda means used as a whole over the years, it seems that the JNF Head Office staff (see Figure

1.2) adopted certain basic assumptions in the field of propaganda, as follows.

Publicity. Information about the fund-raising activities and collection of donations should be public, not kept within the internal framework of the heads of the organisation. It should spread through organisational network and out to the entire Jewish public.[20] Publication of donors' names and the amount of their donations were introduced for different social and organisational purposes. First, it allowed donors and volunteers to be assured that their contributions did, in fact, get to their designated local, national or international objectives. Secondly, it served as a kind of acknowledgement by the organisation to the donors and enhanced their social prestige. The listing of contributions from important bodies and people, with the constant addition of more names, evinced the existence of a special social group, of which the contributor was a member. The publicity had the power to intensify the desire to imitate, and to also allow the ordinary person to join this social group working for a national goal. The organisation, for its part, won greater identification with its goals and increased the sums contributed and also its overall prestige in the Jewish-Zionist world. These were extremely important achievements in light of the organisation's struggle for survival. This publicity was expressed in many forms, one being the use of competition as a method of increasing propaganda and collecting funds—competitions between individuals, between schools, and between communities—and they all received ample publicity.

Total commitment. The JNF adopted the approach that it was bound to work for the total commitment of the community and the individual to the organisation's goals. It aspired to see its contributors as a 'large popular army distinguished by the Blue Box as members of one huge society whose daily concern was the redemption of the land of the homeland'.[21] The organisation constantly strove to enter additional social sectors, such as women, children, young people, and the ultraorthodox, while developing the appropriate means of propaganda. Total commitment to the JNF and its goals had to be internalised and carved into a personal scale of values and into the norms and behaviours of different individuals and groups. An expression of this approach can be found in a famous speech by Ussishkin at the Second Conference of Teachers in Eretz Yisrael (1929). Turning to the teachers he said, 'It is not the child who gives to the JNF, but the JNF that gives to him: it gives him a noble foothold and ideal for all his life. . .don't collect *prutot* (pennies) for the JNF: win the children's souls for the building of the nation'.[22] The goal of total commitment was stressed not only externally by the organisation, but also internally, re-flected in the constant demand for voluntary work and the personal commitment of the volunteers.

One of the expressions of total commitment was the creation of the 'voluntary tax', a self-imposed tax whereby individuals undertook to contribute a share of their monthly salaries to the JNF or to raise a regular contribution in some other way.[23] Various organisations as well as individuals assumed this tax, which over the years took on different forms. The atmosphere generated among the public in Eretz Yisrael of total commitment of the individual to the JNF sometimes led to instances of informing on people and blacklisting those who deviated from their commitments—as we shall show later.

Centralization. In their daily operations, the departments of the Head Office in Jerusalem tried to function as a world headquarters. The JNF organisational structure gave the national offices some freedom of action in a variety of areas, but the Head Office in Jerusalem functioned as the central junction for propaganda decisions and initiatives, which it tried to impose on the branch offices throughout the world. As the organising team in the field, the local workers, the wider public in the towns and villages, teachers and pupils, saw the Head Office as the address for their requests, reports, and ideas. For the organisation they provided feedback, and the JNF staff in Jerusalem treated their reports with the utmost seriousness.

The flow of information from the periphery to the Head Office was like oxygen for the organisation's staff, who greatly desired direct contact with the field. However, the information they received was not always entirely accurate. Centralisation in organising the propaganda made the means identical in goal, form, timing, and strategy throughout the Jewish world. Most of the propaganda material was translated into several languages and experience gained in one place was applied to other places. As a consequence a JNF culture arose, which was typical particularly of activities for young people and children. Although local activities in different countries were not negligible, the Jerusalem staff aspired to unify JNF operational propaganda strategy, and they encouraged this approach in a variety of ways.

Innovation. Propaganda policy and application reflected a conflict between the desire to preserve symbols and ideas and the desire to renew, refresh, and create the feeling of constant momentum for the organisation. On the one hand, signs of conservatism are evident, figuring in goals, methods, content and propaganda means; on the other hand the desire for constant renewal existed, especially in the variation of propaganda methods and approaches. The need to innovate in propaganda methodology was for a variety of reasons, such as struggles for public approval in different circles of influence, the desire to penetrate additional population sectors, or the need to increase income.

A factor in the process of renewing propaganda methods concerned the influence of German culture on the JNF Head Office in Jerusalem. From the 1920s to the mid-1930s there was a powerful symbiosis between the staff of the Propaganda Department in the Head Office and the

JNF centre in Berlin. That city was known at that time for its many propaganda innovations, in theory (the concept of mass persuasion methods) and in practice, namely the exploitation of different techniques in printing, photography, cinema, and so on.[24] The professionals who actively worked on or assisted in JNF propaganda may well have been influenced by their exposure to all this to apply those techniques and methods of propaganda and publicity to JNF concerns.

The Organisation of Propaganda and Its International Dissemination

JNF propaganda and money-raising activities throughout the world were supported by its organisational structure, which was determined by the institutions of the Zionist movement. At the top of the organisational pyramid was the executive, later called the directorate, whose meeting place until 1923 varied according to the political circumstances; but in that year Jerusalem was decided upon as its permanent venue. At the head of the organisation was the president of the JNF, the chairman of the directorate, and at this time, as noted earlier, Menahem Ussishkin held this position until his death in 1941 (see Figure 1.3). As Avraham Granot (Granowski) was appointed successor to Ussishkin only in 1945 (see Figure 1.4), the interim the directorate was run by a three-member committee. Ussishkin's character, ideas, and actions presumably influenced the organisation's policies work during the period under study.

The daily work of the organisation was carried out by the Head Office, which was responsible world-wide. In the early 1920s the work at the Head Office was divided into three administrative sections, namely Land, Propaganda, and Finances & Economics, and the heads of these sections constituted the management. After the move to Jerusalem the directorate restructured the Head Office as four sections: Land, Finance, Personnel, Propaganda, and Journalism.[25] Julius Berger was made head of the Propaganda division and Nathan Bistritski (Agmon) was his deputy. In 1926 the Department of Youth and Schools was established in the Propaganda Division and Bistritski was appointed to head it (see Figure 1.5). There was no real separation between the Propaganda staff and Youth Department staff; they worked together throughout the years and produced the propaganda material distributed to adults, young people, and schools.[26] When differences of opinion arose Julius Berger was forced to resign (1928), and three people ran the Propaganda Section (Department) during the 1930s in his place.

The distribution and organisation of JNF propaganda throughout the Jewish world is evident from the reports prepared by its head for the various congresses, such as the report prepared for the ninth Zionist Congress held in Köln.[27] Propaganda policy to involve all levels of the Jewish people, not only the rich. This, the department heads argued, would make it difficult to assess the effect of the propaganda through the simple method of reckoning the contributions made to the fund. The extent of the propaganda activities at this period was already large, as indicated by the array of contributions, collected from twenty-five different countries where liaison offices had been established in the first decade of the twentieth century. The geographic distribution of contributions does not necessarily reflect the geographical scope of the propaganda, but it does given an impression of the fund's international activity and of its regional development at different times. At that time the abundance of JNF publicity in the Jewish press was also obvious: over fifty journals regularly printed news, articles, and announcements by and about the JNF. In this period the Head Office and the national offices published hundreds of advertisements and posters in nineteen different languages.[28]

Despite the reduction in opportunities for international activities following the First World War, and the need to move the organisation's centre and central office from country to country, by 1920 JNF bureaux were to be found in over fifty countries across the globe. By the end of the JNF's second decade of existence it had expanded its activity in Europe and had penetrated new areas in North Africa and the Far East, under the auspices of the various colonial powers.

Between 1922 and 1927 the JNF's propaganda and information efforts bore fruit, with a rise in its income. The propaganda system began to operate more intensively and included a range of means, methods, and procedures. During those years emissaries were sent out by the Head Office, mostly senior executives, professional propagandists, and representatives of the settlements in the Emek. They conveyed the organisation's message, goals, and propaganda means from Jerusalem to the rest of the world. In the years following the transfer of the Head office to Jerusalem the JNF's basic patterns of activity turned it into an international, internal-Jewish organisation, so that interdependence between Eretz Yisrael and the Diaspora was created. Propaganda, learning, and teaching material was sent from Jerusalem, and on the other hand there was feedback, namely a flow of funds from the Diaspora to the Head Office.

The ties of the centre to the Diaspora were not uniform all over the world. Between the world wars an imbalance arose between the JNF propaganda effort and activity in Eastern and Central Europe and in Western Europe and North America. The staff of the Head Office were aware of this asymmetry, and in a report to the 21st Zionist Congress in Geneva (1939) they wrote:

> In recent years the JNF has expressed its opinion especially about Eastern and Central Europe. But it has been impossible to ignore the fact that, from a financial point of view, the West European and the English-speaking countries fulfil a crucial role in the JNF's operations, while regarding organisation and propa-

ganda they do not yet occupy the position they deserve in the framework of JNF work.[29]

Changes occurred in the disposition of the organisation's activities throughout the world following the Second World War. The destruction of Eastern and Central European Jewry reduced the number of centres of activity but the collection of funds was not affected: collection actually increased during the war years. During the forty years of the JNF's existence, from 1902 to 1945, altogether about £P10.5 million (Palestine pounds: *ly* in Hebrew) were collected—and 60 percent of this sum was raised during the five years of the war in the English-speaking World and in Eretz Yisrael. This situation was completely different from the past. Prior to the First World War, three quarters of the contributions had come from the European continent and one-sixth from the USA. Between the wars the share of North America and other areas such as South Africa rose. After the Second World War Europe's part was reduced radically, while 60 percent of all contributions were from the USA alone. In absolute terms the collection of funds during the war was of an entirely different order from that until 1940.[30]

Social Distribution and Entry into Schools

In addition to the broad geographic spread of the organisation one must note the social distribution of the JNF organisational—and propaganda activities. In the following we focus mainly on the activities in schools, but note that this began later than activities concentrated on other specific population sectors such as the ultraorthodox. The Head Office established a special unit for the above sector, expanded its activities in their communities, and organised propaganda with the aid of rabbis; the Blue Box was placed in synagogues, which served as places where JNF propaganda was disseminated. For example, in Lvov in 1925,

> In every synagogue a special representative of the JNF was appointed whose role was to stand next to the *bima* (prayer platform) while the Torah was being read and to encourage those called to read a portion to pledge something to the JNF. He had to remember who the people called to the Torah were and how much they had pledged, and to register them after the Sabbath or festival was over so as to claim the funds immediately.[31]

The Head Office in Jerusalem also published newspapers, journals, and magazines in different languages aimed at the ultraorthodox Jewish population.

At the beginning of the 1920s JNF personnel started to work with children and young people in various places, with as yet no clear policy developed for this population by the Head Office. For example, in 1924 the national office of Bulgarian Jewry published a bulletin for schools that outlined several principles of JNF activities with children. The propaganda had to begin as early as kindergarten; the basis of the propaganda had to be the building of Eretz Yisrael; the teachers had to be involved in JNF activity. The Head Office, which printed this report in its own paper, made the point that other countries should also adopt the example of Bulgaria in their activities with children.[32]

In the USA, too, there were activities for children in the schools. In 1923, for example, the Union of Hebrew Teachers of New York resolved at its annual conference, to support the introduction of JNF activity into schools.[33] A year later a JNF delegation left Eretz Yisrael to take part in a conference in New York attended by representatives of Jewish youth movements in the USA: Young Judea, Young Israel, Menora, and others. The conference resolutions called for bringing American young people closer to pioneering work in Eretz Yisrael, and appealed to the youth federations to join in fund-raising for the JNF. The outcome was the establishment of a Youth department in the JNF national office of the USA, which worked together with teachers and school principals to encourage JNF work in schools in Eretz Yisrael.[34]

One must assume that several factors caused the situation where an institution established to acquire and prepare land became involved in propaganda, education, and ideological socialisation, activities in the fields of society and culture.

Previous involvement in educational issues. In the first and second decades of its existence the JNF had been involved in various fields of activity in Eretz Yisrael, such as buying land and assisting in the construction of educational institutions in Haifa, Tel Aviv, and Jerusalem. At that time the JNF carried out propaganda for the collection of funds in the country in a variety of places and organisations. But fund-raising and the acquisition of land for educational institutes were apparently not the major reason for the organisation's entry into the area of education in the third decade of its existence; other factors are noteworthy.

Ussishkin's personality and the dispute over responsibility for education in Eretz Yisrael. Even at the beginning of the twentieth century while still in Russia (before being elected head of the JNF), Ussishkin was deeply involved in issues of Jewish youth and education. After arriving in Eretz Yisrael at the head of the Hovevei Zion delegation he influenced educators in the country to establish a teachers' union (*Histadrut Hamorim*) (1903). After being appointed head of the JNF he continued to take an interest in Hebrew education in Israel and was aware of the special problems. In the early 1920s the institutions of the Zionist Organisation were in dispute over continuing financial support for educational institutes in Eretz Yisrael, which had become mass establishments following the First World War. The representatives of the Yishuv (the Jewish settlement in

Eretz Yisrael)wanted the continued support of the Zionist movement as they wished to remove this financial burden from themselves and even give up educational autonomy. That meant reaching a compromise with the British Mandatory authorities. Ussishkin opposed any compromise over the educational autonomy of the Yishuv and proposed the establishment of a special fund to finance education. This proposal was rejected by the general executive committee of the World Zionist Organization. Immediately after this the department for Youth and Schools was established in the JNF.[35]Three years later, in a speech before the Second Teachers' Conference, Ussishkin declared that the JNF had three goals: the redemption of the land, the nationalisation of the land, and national education. He saw education as an inseparable element of the organisation's role, equal to the others.

The status of the JNF in the Zionist movement. The decision to establish Keren Hayesod in 1920 and to transfer various tasks to it reduced the JNF to a place of secondary importance as an institution carrying out Zionist policies in Eretz Yisrael. Limitations on fund-raising were also imposed on the JNF and they impaired its ability to collect large contributions. During those years the JNF tried to obtain additional powers from the Zionist Organization and, in fact, fought a war of survival against Keren Hayesod. This struggle constituted the chief motive for its propaganda and information activity, and the JNF executive made an emotional call for it 'to be once again the baby of the Zionist movement'.[36] Over time the JNF did acquire additional powers, but exclusively in the field of land preparation and water resources, not in the establishment of settlements and other projects.

The resolutions on expanding propaganda taken at the first JNF conference in 1921 were apparently the result of the clipping of its wings. In the following four years as well the JNF annual conferences in Eretz Yisrael continued to call for an increase in propaganda in schools, and they also requested the teachers' central body to allow the introduction of a discussion on JNF activities in schools.[37]Beyond the public debate over who was responsible for education, a feeling developed in the JNF leadership that to survive as an organisation and safeguard its position in the community and the Zionist movement they should exploit the education network as an area of additional activity—to which Keren Hayesod had no access.[38]

Local initiatives of schools and teachers. Among the factors that encouraged links between the JNF and the education network were teachers of Hebrew in the schools, seeking ways to manage Modern Hebrew. An outstanding example is Shlomo Schiller (1879–1925), who was a teacher and active in the JNF in Galicia still prior to his immigration to Eretz Yisrael. There he began to teach at the Jerusalem Gymnasia; he preached education for pioneering, and saw the JNF as an institution that could be the standard-bearer for this education. Accordingly, in 1925, he called on teachers to become active in the introduction of JNF activities into schools. What was new in this call was the demand to make the idea of 'the redemption of the land' central to Hebrew education. In consequence of this activity the Committee to Organise Youth and Schools was founded, and it ultimately led to the establishment of the Teachers' Council for the JNF.

National organisation—the Teachers' Council for the JNF. The combination of the foregoing factors apparently brought the JNF and the education network together at a point in time when both groups could only profit from it. The first organised meeting of the Teachers' Council for the JNF took place at Givat Hamoreh during Passover 1927, and it won the support of the JNF and the blessing of the Teachers' Union. At the conference it was decided to assist in the JNF's information programme, to distribute Blue Boxes to all the children, and to aspire to publishing learning materials about the geography of Eretz Yisrael. At first the JNF bureaucracy was not enthusiastic because it did not understand the significance of this historic meeting. This can be learned from the exchange of letters a few weeks after the conference in Givat Hamoreh between Eliezer Rieger (1896–1954), a functionary in the Teachers' Union, and Julius Berger of the JNF's Propaganda Department.. Rieger suggested that the Propaganda Department assume responsibility for contact with the schools and provide them with educational materials on subjects concerning Eretz Yisrael. Berger replied that it was not the task of the JNF Head Office, nor was the latter able, to implement such a proposal. Yet despite his reservations, the Youth Department was established in the JNF Head Office, and Nathan Bistritski was appointed its head. Its designated activities were to provide support for the Jewish schools affiliated to the Va'ad Haleumi (the National Committee of the Yishuv) and for other cultural institutions, and to publish educational materials for schools and youth movements. Close and ongoing cooperation arose between the JNF Youth Department and the Teachers' Council, which was even given financial support by the Youth Department.[39]

Note that the heads of the Teachers' Council for the JNF did not intend to help the JNF in its collection of funds in the schools, but saw the JNF as a symbol around which they could develop a curriculum for pioneering values (*halutziut*), as preached by Shlomo Schiller. They received ideological assistance in the formulation of their approach from Chaim Nahman Bialik (1873–1934), the 'national poet', who took part in the first conferences of the Teachers' Council. In his speeches Bialik called for the introduction of the subject of the country's land into Jewish education, not only in short-range material terms, but in the spiritual concepts of the eternal nature of the Jewish people and its ties to Eretz Yisrael. These concepts would be incorporated into the regular studies: Nature,

History, Arithmetic, or Geography. In fact, there was symbiosis between the Youth Department and the Propaganda Department of the JNF and the Teachers' Council. The two JNF bodies dealt with the development of educational means as well as study and information materials, while the Teachers' Council attended to their distribution and introduction into the schools.

Figure 1.1. Map of British Mandatory Palestine

Figure 1.2. JNF Head Office staff in Jerusalem, 1939. Standing, front row, from left: Y. Weitz, A. Granowski, M. Ussishkin, N. Bistritski, M. Ha'ezrachi (Photographer: A. Melavski. Source: Photo Archive JNF-KKL, Jerusalem)

Figure 1.3. Menahem Ussishkin in Zurich 1937 (Photographer: Dicker. Source: Photo Archive JNF-KKL, Jerusalem)

Figure 1.4. Avraham Granowski, 1929 (Photographer: Y. Schweig. Source: Photo Archive JNF-KKL, Jerusalem)

Figure 1.5. Nathan Bistritski, 1936 (Photographer: A. Melavski: Source: Photo Archive JNF-KKL, Jerusalem)

Figure 2.1. The old 'Blue Box', Poland, 1920 (Photographer: Y. Schweig. Source:
Photo Archive JNF-KKL, Jerusalem)

Figure 2.2. A paper-made pocket Blue Box, France, 1936 (Photographer: A. Melavski: Source: Photo Archive JNF-KKL, Jerusalem)

Figure 2.3. A girl collecting money, with the 'New Blue Box', 1942 (Photographer: Y. Schweig. Source: Photo Archive JNF-KKL, Jerusalem)

Chapter 2

'The Redemption of Our Country's Land': The Blue Box

The Production of the Blue Box

Among the first tools that were harnessed for the purposes of propaganda were those called in the organisation's jargon *means of collection,* meaning the box, stamps, and the Golden Book, whose primary purpose was to raise funds for the purchase of land in Eretz Yisrael. Over the years, and especially after the First World War, the borders between the monetary goals and the propaganda goals became blurred and the *means of collection* became, for all practical purposes, the central propaganda symbols of the organisation. Perceiving the box as a means of propaganda created a situation where responsibility for distributing and producing it were assigned to the staff of the organisation's Propaganda Department. Over the years the latter constructed an entire culture around it, with the objective of serving the interests of the JNF and Eretz Yisrael; they saw the Blue Box as a yardstick to gauge the organisation's activities throughout the world. After the Head Office moved to Jerusalem it became clear that the appearance of the box had to be refreshed and its manufacture had to be transferred to Eretz Yisrael as part of the propaganda effort and the reorganisation of the JNF. This is the subject of the present chapter.

The beginnings of the Blue Box are well documented.[1] The initiative to raise money for the JNF by means of a collection box, like the charity boxes commonly used in Jewish institutions, came from Chaim Kleinman, a bank clerk from Galicia, who made the suggestion in a letter written to the Zionist newspaper *Die Welt* in 1902; he wanted such a box to be placed in every Jewish household. During the period under study, JNF historiography attributed the first box to the organisation's founder, Herman Shapira, on account of a tin box he had placed in his house before the JNF was established.

Until the First World War the boxes were manufactured mainly in Germany; during the 1920s and 1930s other centres of production in Poland and Eretz Yisrael were added. By the end of the Second World

War an estimated two to three million boxes had been distributed throughout the world, although the exact number is not known. From the periodic reports of the JNF to various Zionist congresses, the volume of annual production until the beginning of the 1920s may be estimated at twenty to thirty thousand boxes. They were decorated with a printed text in the language of the target country: English for the English-speaking countries, German for Central Europe, and Hebrew and Yiddish for Eastern Europe.[2] From the second half of the 1920s, as Zionist activity in the Diaspora became greater, and as the settlements in Eretz Yisrael grew in size, the greater was the demand for the Blue Box. Production had to meet the demand for hundred of thousands of boxes annually.

One of the notable characteristics of the boxes until after the First World War was the variation in the design according to the countries and the different manufacturers. In 1903, for example, boxes made of wood were distributed in Russia and were decorated with the words *Keren kayemet leumit* (National Fund) or, in Yiddish, *Natzional Fund*; in the middle was the symbol of the Star of David, inside of which was the word *Zion*.[3] Such symbols had already appeared on the first stamps of the JNF, known as *Bul Zion* (Zion stamp). Other boxes, manufactured at the same time in Germany, had text in German and Hebrew; they were distinguished by the symbol of the Star of David being inside a circle.[4] During the second decade of the century simple white tin boxes with blue, green, and silver wording on them were manufactured in Germany. The graphics included the Hebrew slogan 'Eretz Yisrael for the People of Israel', with the Latin letters JNF above.[5] In the middle of the box was a drawing of the traditional Star of David next to drawn branches (palm trees?), and inside it the figure of a lion (the Lion of Judah). Inside the Star of David there were six more stars, and above the apex an additional large star (the 'Seven Stars').

Boxes from the second decade of the century in different countries such as Britain, Poland, Germany, and Eretz Yisrael had designs containing several common elements (see Figure 2.1). Their shape was rectangular, on top was a slot to drop coins in, and at the back there was a hook for hanging it up. The boxes were coloured blue and had three elements on the front: the name *Keren kayemet leyisrael* (Jewish National Fund), the Star of David, and above it a circle containing the organisation's initials (KKL or JNF). The uniformity of design of the boxes during this decade apparently came about because of centralised manufacture at a factory in Germany, which exported them to other countries according to the instructions of the JNF Head Office.[6]

Feelers about the production of the boxes in Eretz Yisrael were put out even before the First World War. In 1911 the Berlin office approached Arthur Ruppin (1876–1942), the representative of the Zionist Organisation in Jaffa, to examine the possibility of producing them there.[7] At that time nothing came of the talks, and only at the end of 1924 did the JNF directorate decide to order Blue Boxes from Alfred Zaltsman's factory in Jerusalem. This decision, which was made for ideological rather than economic reasons, was taken in the hope that about one hundred thousand boxes a year could be produced in Eretz Yisrael, a number that would satisfy world demand. Still, the Head Office in Jerusalem realised that they would have to go on ordering boxes in Germany and other countries until Zaltsman's factory could begin production and become the main supplier.

We recall that the JNF was an international Zionist organisation whose decisions were made by the directorate, the executive, and the Head Office, all of which bodies were transferred to Jerusalem at the beginning of the 1920s. Initially the executive was responsible for assembling information and resources from different parts of the world, making decisions, and relaying them to the offices of countries world-wide. In practice variations occurred according to local conditions and the period. On two occasions the Head Office twice collected the requests and sent out orders to go ahead, and it seemed to be in control of what occurred in the organisation throughout the world. At other times the national offices acted autonomously in certain things and clashed with the Jerusalem headquarters. These work relations affected the manufacture and distribution of the boxes throughout the Jewish world.

The concentration of information and the distribution of resources allowed the Jerusalem Head Office to gather current, but not always complete data on the volume of the distribution of the boxes and to report on them periodically in its magazine *Karnenu*. No ongoing statistics have been found concerning the production of the boxes in different countries, but the boxes that were produced give an indication of the size of production and distribution. For example, from 1926 to 1930 world distribution was seventy to one hundred thousand boxes a year. At the beginning of the 1930s there was a rise of thirty percent in the distribution of boxes produced in Zaltsman's factory and in factories in other countries.[8]

An example of the control by the Head Office control is evident in 1924–26, when Jerusalem ordered the shipping of boxes from Germany to the USA. The request was sent from New York to the Head Office, which ordered the boxes from the German factory and informed the New York committee about it. Prior to 1924, thirty thousand boxes had been sent from Germany to the USA, as stated in the Head Office's report on the organisation of work in the USA.[9] At the beginning of 1925 the JNF personnel in the USA increased their propaganda and began to cover the Jewish schools in Greater New York, a step that increased the demand for boxes. In anticipation of this operation the Head Office ordered a large number of boxes with simple locks from Germany. But a few weeks later, at the beginning of May 1925, complaints began to reach Jerusalem that these boxes could be easily opened with an ordinary pin. On receiving these letters the Jerusalem staff felt the need to apologise to the New York committee and explain why poorly made boxes had been sent from Germany. They explained their decision on the basis of the rising demand for boxes and the need to produce them quickly. At the end of 1925 the American Jews tried to obtain boxes directly from Germany, but when Jerusalem protested they resumed the connection through the Head Office. The latter ordered from Germany about ten thousand boxes for the USA every two months.[10]

A different example of decision-making that affected the production and distribution of boxes can be seen in Poland, which had the largest concentration of Jews in the world up to the Second World War and where the Zionist movement was very active. Until production began in Eretz Yisrael the national office in Warsaw received its boxes from Germany and local factories. In November 1925, about a year after Zaltsman took on the project, the Head Office in Jerusalem informed the national office in Warsaw that it had to stop ordering boxes from Polish factories and that from the beginning of 1926 they would be able to receive boxes made in Eretz Yisrael. The Head Office in Jerusalem even added the following in its letter to Warsaw:

> Re the quality of the boxes you produced in Poland: if we consider this according to the sample we received (the bottom of which fell out in transit) we cannot concur with what you say about their good quality. There is no doubt that the boxes from Eretz Yisrael are superior to them.[11]

In response the Warsaw national office informed Jerusalem that at that stage it had no need for additional boxes.

This was the start of a dialogue between Jerusalem and Warsaw about the production of the boxes that continued to the end of the 1930s. The Head Office tried to impose its authority to distribute the Eretz Yisrael products, while in Warsaw other decisions were being made. The national office in Warsaw often ignored letters since it had the feeling that the Head Office in Jerusalem could not function without it. Despite ordering boxes from Eretz Yisrael during the 1930s, they continued manufacturing boxes in Poland in various factories, including the Eilstein plant in Warsaw, which became an important producer during that decade making tens of thousand of boxes.[12]

Customs problems, import licenses, and commercial competition between European countries in the 1930s affected the production and distribution of the boxes. Early in1933 the Head Office examined the possibilities of distributing the boxes in the light of these problems. A memorandum drawn up on the question shows that production of boxes was continued in Germany for distribution in Germany, Austria, and Switzerland, which presented no import problems. For countries that disallowed imports from Germany, boxes could be exported from Eretz Yisrael. For other countries such as France, Italy, and Hungary the memorandum suggests local production because of the high customs dues that were imposed.[13] At the same time, boxes were already apparently being produced in the USA, but no clear picture about this production existed in Jerusalem, as is made clear in this memorandum.[14] During the following years Jerusalem recognised the manufacture of Blue Boxes in the USA and even encouraged their export to South Africa, which was an important Blue Box consumer (see Figure 2.2).[15]

Theory and Practice in Blue Box Work

The collection of funds using the box was based upon the assumption that the box itself would do the donation work. It was the box that was the instrument of contribution and represented the institution and its goals, while the role of the organisation's personnel was to distribute and empty the boxes so that they could continue to work efficiently. In a booklet produced by the Head Office at the beginning of 1921 the duality of the *means of collection* as both an important propaganda instrument and an instrument for raising funds was clearly recognised. Under the heading 'The Value of the JNF Box' the following was written:

> The box donation is important since it is given through the goodwill of the donor more than it is collected by the collector. The box itself is a kind of eternal fundraiser in the house, the synagogue, the clubhouse, and so on, and it is always ready and available to receive a gift to the JNF at any time, on any day, in any circumstance: a celebration, mourning, games, visits, spare cash, and all sorts of other occasions. What the collector does once a month, or once a year, or from time to time, the box does constantly, every minute.
>
> The box introduces the JNF into the Jewish home in its everyday life and across generations. It does its ethical work with great and small, with family and strangers in the house. It performs constant and perpetual propaganda work for the JNF wordlessly, and when the day comes to empty it, it provides an opening for the JNF representative to enter the house. It gives him the opportunity to discuss things with the householders, to explain things to them both orally and through propaganda literature and JNF certificates, and to provide them with a summary of the important news about its projects since he is their regular representative.[16]

The above clearly reflects the approach that no division existed between the box as a fundraising instrument and its being an instrument for doing 'its ethical work . . . with the family', constantly engaged in propaganda work for the JNF and allowing the organisation's representative to enter the houses of Jews for additional public relations purposes. The directors of JNF propaganda gave public expression to this approach in the Head Office's magazine, where they justified their activities, and not only from the point of view of what was good for the organisation. They were convinced that the JNF 'introduces real live content into the empty lives of the Diaspora Jews, brings the spirit of Eretz Yisrael closer, and presents them with idea of building the land in the present in preparation for a great future'.[17] They saw the box 'not only as a tin container for the collection of small coins' but as an educational propaganda instrument that, incidentally, established the JNF's patterns of operation as we can see from the case of the hiring of paid contractors to empty the boxes.

The dilemma over hiring paid workers as opposed to volunteers arose frequently over the years in different places. For example, in the USA at the beginning of the 1920s to employ paid distributors and collectors was normal practice.[18] The Head Office in Jerusalem criticised the New York office over its Blue Box work, writing that 'the question of the box in America is an organisation question'. Paying employees to collect funds resulted in insufficient money accruing to the JNF; therefore, the American office had to strive to change the basis of the work, through mustering groups of volunteers among the veteran activists and the youth (see Figure 2.3).[19]

The image of those who conducted the Blue Box work in the field also appeared in other publications. In its directions for the box campaign, written in 1936, the Head Office suggested that in each city there should be a 'Box Committee' headed by 'a man who, up till then, had excelled in organising the box work, not too young—since he would have to get the help of veteran activists'. At the head of the City Committee, the JNF's partner, an active member would be co-opted 'from every Zionist organisation (such as WIZO, Zionist youth groups, sports organisations) whose role would be to assist in the preparation of the work of the project in his own circle.[20] These directions show the diversity of considerations surrounding the choice of the activists that the Head Office proposed: not only their being loyal volunteers, who clearly knew what the JNF was about, but also their organisational membership. This membership was important to the success of the box campaign since its purpose was to obtain monetary undertakings from organisations as well as promises to place the JNF box in the house of every member or parent.

The basis for JNF Blue Box work was a clear and orderly procedure, which sought efficiently to organise the process of distribution and collection of the boxes and contributions along clear lines, and which relied on a large public of volunteers that included a nucleus of loyal and consistent activists. The system in general undoubtedly worked, and contributions collected from hundreds of thousands of boxes across the globe reached their destination, the Head Office in Jerusalem. But the correspondence and documents of that time yield a different view of that idyllic picture. Activities in the field on all levels of organisation—individual towns, whole regions, or certain countries, did not function as expected. Throughout the whole period under review the Head Office staff in Jerusalem corresponded with the periphery regarding the implementation of their instructions, the distribution of boxes, and the fall in contributions. The Head Office's sense of only partial control over the peripheral areas emerges from reports from the national offices, but also from various local reactions throughout Eretz Yisrael and the Diaspora, which arrived directly in Jerusalem (see Figure 2.4).

The complaints from the field to the Head Office concerned the following matters. Of hundreds of letters that were sent every year to the Jerusalem office a very high percentage dealt with the quality of the boxes, especially those made in Eretz Yisrael; the their poor quality harmed the 'box work'. For example, a letter reached the Head Office from the National Committee for Eretz Yisrael and Syria (1928) containing the following passage:

> We have to remark that we are receiving complaints from a lot of places about the fact that the door of the box opens with the smallest amount of pressure from the coins inside the box; these cases are especially frequent in schools since the children are used to shaking and rattling the boxes. Several schools have informed us that if they are not given stronger boxes they will have to stop taking them altogether.[21]

A similar impression arises from the content of other letters attesting to the relationship between the quality of the boxes and the work of the activists. The Latvian national office wrote to the Head Office in Jerusalem (1932) that the collectors were frequently unable to open the door of the box and had to force it, an act that left a bad impression on the box owners and even unnecessarily lengthened the time taken to empty the boxes: 'Such things happen (mainly) with women who empty the boxes . . . you must either be more exacting when you get the boxes from Zaltsman . . . or allow us to order boxes in those places where there is a guarantee that both the keys and the boxes will be made with more precision and quality (for example in Berlin or Warsaw)'.[22]

Other charges received by the Head Office about emptying the boxes mostly concerned the lack of regular activity. Despite the procedures that instructed workers to carry out the emptying of the boxes every month or at least every two months, instances existed where collectors did not appear for many months. The irregular collection was a major weakness in the box work, but it was not the only one. Another was apparent at the beginning of the process, namely the distribution of the boxes. This was obviously simpler than the collecting, and it was done routinely and in occasional special campaigns by the Head Office in Jerusalem. The flaw in the distribution was the inexact registration of the addresses to which the boxes were supposed to go, and the consequences of this were evident in the planning of the collection and the replacement of damaged boxes, as well as in the identification of potential sites for future distribution.[23]

The Head Office's principal information about the boxes was, of course, not based on letters or private complaints but on the periodic reports it required from the national committees. These reports were part of the internal bureaucratic dialogue that the centre and the periphery conducted. This correspondence shows that the system of reports and the collection of information provided the Head Office with a general picture of what was going on in regard to the box work. Even though the organisation's personnel did not manage to create a credible system of reporting it was possible for Jerusalem to follow what was happening in the periphery on the national level. The data received by the national committees were drawn from reports from the local committees, which themselves gave an account of the work of volunteers, the distributors and collectors. Clearly, information so gathered, even if it was current, was incomplete and not always credible. This was attested by members of the American Bureau of JNF, who said that they had no proper control over what was done with the boxes after they were sent to the different towns: reports and statistics were difficult to obtain.[24]

The Head Office staff were aware of the problematic nature of the information and understood its significance in terms of control over the *means of collection* sent to different countries. They knew the difference between the dispatch of boxes to the national committees and the amount of money collected. At the beginning of 1924, for example, a correspondence took place between New York and Jerusalem, in which the former requested the Head Office to order additional boxes from Germany for them. Jerusalem replied to the American national committee that there was hardly any increase in the income despite the fact that they had already distributed thirty thousand boxes, and requested that they should not 'leave the box in its present poverty'.[25] The widening gap between the distribution of the boxes and the collection of funds in the period under study propelled the staff at the centre in Jerusalem to conduct periodic campaigns and to hold detailed censuses to collect accurate information and to increase distribution and collecting.

In sum, the Head Office in Jerusalem enjoyed only partial ability to control and supervise the box work in the field. This work was based on volunteering, which despite the enormous motivation was apparently essentially amateurish. The Head Office attached great importance to the various reports, but it had no power to impose sanctions in order to receive them. The local and national committees were caught between the work of the volunteers in the field and the Head Office of the organisation, and they had no clear and ongoing picture of the box work in the field either (see Figure 2.5).

The Financial Value of the Box Contribution

The above discussion shows that in the period under study a gap sepa-rated theory and practice concerning the distribution and emptying of the Blue Boxes. Political events such as wars or international and regional economic problems clearly affected the box work, but factors in the ac-tual organisation itself also apparently widened the gulf between the goal and the results in this work. Such factors were the decision to transfer the manufacture of the boxes to Eretz Yisrael and their poor quality, the volunteerism of the collectors, and the competition with other means of raising and collecting funds.

At the same time, the publication of numbers and data about the box work became a central feature (almost an ideology) of the work of the JNF staff. As practical operatives they believed in quantitative proof—in numbers. For them the quantitative information, the numeric value itself, was significant, almost sacred. At every opportunity they were certain to present a plethora of figures to aggrandise their work. By means of the published data we can attempt to grasp the importance of the box work in terms of the amount of money collected through it for 'the redemption of Eretz Yisrael'.

The income to the JNF in general from various sources between the two world wars fluctuated, including the income from the boxes.[26] The Head Office staff, who constantly checked the box income, published occasional reports in the JNF magazine *Karnenu*; these mainly gave cur-rent information, usually showing a rise in the box income. In long criti-cal reviews, however, which appeared once every few years, they assessed that 'the main source of our income is not, today, as high as it should be and is much less than we had hoped for'.[27]

A more inclusive picture of the part played by the boxes in the total contributions can be seen from the following figures summarising the period 1918–37: general contributions 51.1 percent, boxes 17.2 percent, traditional projects 10.0 percent, the Golden Book 7.1 percent, tree do-nations 6.6 percent, stamps and telegrams 2.1 percent, other 5.8 percent.[28]

Hence, for two decades the share of the boxes was about one-sixth of the total income of the JNF; however, as a means of collection it yielded the highest income of all the traditional means of collection such as stamps or the Golden Book. In the years of the Second World War the opportunities for collecting money for the JNF obviously altered, and the share of the boxes in the organisation's total income fell to between seven and ten percent, a decline that was relative and absolute, owing to changes in exchange rates.

As for the long-term figures from 1902 to 1947, the share of the *means of collection* decreased in relation to the other sources of funds, and the proportion contributed by the Blue Box was correspondingly lower.[29] According to the data for the forty-five years of their existence, the boxes brought in a sum equivalent to £P 1.6 million (Palestine pounds) out of a total of £P 12 million, which was the JNF's revenue for that period. Accordingly it appears that the Blue Box's share from 1902 to1947 was only about one-eighth of the organisation's total income.

To estimate the total income from the boxes over the lengthy period of time the organisation existed and raised funds for Eretz Yisrael, additional data of fundraising in the USA for the Zionist cause are needed. These campaigns, especially the United Jewish Appeal (UJA), collected money centrally and divided it among the JNF, Keren Hayesod, and philanthropic Jewish organisations such as the JOINT. During the Second World War the UJA collected about $120 million, and the JNF received about one sixth of it. The various appeals raised the JNF's income considerably, and necessarily reduced the relative contribution of the traditional means of collection generally and of the box work in particular. Despite the publication of the amount of income allocated to the JNF by the UJA, the JNF staff feared they would lose their identity in the collection of funds, so they were unenthusiastic about the unification of the fundraising.[30]

As we know, the main goal for which the JNF had been established, and which was reaffirmed many times at Zionist Congresses, was 'the redemption of Eretz Yisrael', which meant the acquisition of land and its development for the Jewish People. The rate at which land was acquired was dependent upon the supply of land, its price, political factors, the amount of money available to the JNF, and so on. The acquisition of land was a most important motif in the JNF propaganda and was expressed through different slogans that emphasized the contribution of coins collected in the boxes for the redemption of land in Eretz Yisrael. We will, thus, try to examine how much land could be redeemed through the collection of coins in the boxes.

One must recall that in the period under discussion, the 1920s and 1930s, most of the capital that flowed to Eretz Yisrael was private Jewish funds. According to Ulitzur's calculations about one fifth (21 percent) of a total of £P 95 million that entered Eretz Yisrael during that period was 'national capital'(through the UJA and the JNF) and the rest (79 percent) came from the private sector.[31] Of the total sum the share of the JNF was £P 6.4 million from all its sources, including £P 0.59 million from contributions collected in Blue Boxes. Accordingly, of the total Jewish capital that flowed into Eretz Yisrael between 1918 and 1938, the share from the boxes was no more than one half a percent.

The contribution of the JNF to land acquisition in Eretz Yisrael was likewise insubstantial. By the end of the 1930s the amount of national land owned by the JNF in Eretz Yisrael was small compared with the amount owned by Jewish private factors.[32] Ulitzur estimated the sum that the JNF spent on the purchase and improvement of land, according to the balance sheets of the national funds between 1902 and 1937, was £P 3.7 million . In terms of land prices, the sum of £P 0.6 million obtained through the Blue Boxes in a period of almost 35 years until 1937 was enough to redeem 63,000 dunams.[33] In those years the JNF redeemed a total of 400,000 dunams; accordingly, the income from the Blue Boxes was sufficient for the redemption of about 16 percent, or one-sixth, of all JNF redeemed land. But out of the total land of Eretz Yisrael redeemed in that period (west of the Jordan river) the income from the Blue Boxes accounted for only 0.25–0.30 percent.[34] Recall that the large purchases of land by the JNF occurred during the 1940s, and by the time of the establishment of the state of Israel in 1948 these doubled the area of land owned by the Fund. But even including these figures the estimate of the JNF's contribution does not change significantly.

These figures attesting to the small part played by the Blue Box were not unknown to the heads of the JNF Propaganda Department or to the chiefs of the organisation. Still, they continued with their propaganda and information policies, which drew a direct link between the Blue Box and land redemption in Eretz Yisrael. This policy came into being because of their judgement, which retrospectively seems justified, that the Blue Box not only served as a direct *means of collection* of funds but was principally an excellent vehicle of propaganda for the Zionist idea as a whole and to strengthen the consciousness of the JNF operatives in particular.

The Blue Box became a symbol not only of the organisation but of Zionism as a whole and of the redemption of Eretz Yisrael in particular. Its unique design, in the national colours (blue and white) and the illustrations on it, especially the map, helped to make it an ever-present element at ceremonies and events concerning education in Zionist values throughout the world. The real, direct contribution of the Blue Box to the 'redemption of our country's land' was minuscule, but its symbolic value was enormous. Great appreciation should be accorded to its excellent work in the area of public relations, propaganda, and image making, which contributed inestimably to what the JNF and its heads will be remembered for.

Chapter 3

'To Touch the Land of Israel': Propaganda with Stamps

Continuity and Renewal

The conversion of an instrument for collecting funds into a means of propaganda in the JNF was not exclusive to the Blue Box. A similar process also took place with the first means of collection created by the JNF, the stamp. In retrospect, the stamps, like the Blue Box, did not become a permanent or considerable source of income for the JNF; still, the Head Office made sure that they were developed and used. There is a difference between these means: the box was a constant propaganda tool, for years enduring with the same conservative design, and it became the most important symbol of the organisation. By contrast, the stamps served as a propaganda tool whose initial design was conservative but later it had to be constantly and regularly renewed. The need for renewal arose out of the changes in the perception of the stamp's role and the relations between the Head Office in Jerusalem and the national offices, which were both competitive and complementary. Since its founding the JNF has issued several thousand stamps, some appearing once and others several times, of a range of colours and values. Between 1902 and 1947 the Head Office issued more than 250 stamps, which were distributed throughout the Jewish World.[1] At times competition ensued with stamps issued by national JNF committees, especially that of the USA, where an identical number of stamps were issued in the above period. The Polish national JNF committee was also active in issuing stamps, producing over one hundred by 1939. By contrast, the national committees in Germany, Britain, Austria, Brazil, and some other countries only issued several dozens of stamps, so they were apparently not in competition with those of the Head Office.

This chapter concerns several factors pertaining to the stamps and arising out of the historical material of the Propaganda Department in the Head Office in Jerusalem, which was the prime mover in their distribution. These factors are the designs on the stamps and the reasons for their choice, as well as the roles and uses that the JNF proposed for its stamps as part of its propaganda efforts.

Stamps were first used in Britain in 1840 as payment for postal services. The first bore the portrait of the young Queen Victoria. By the end of the nineteenth century the idea of using stamps had spread throughout the states of Europe and their colonies abroad, including the Middle East. The Ottoman empire and the Egyptian royal court adopted this innovation in the 1860s.[2] So postage stamps, even a century ago, symbolised the sovereignty of the ruler and the independence of his or her country. Britain, for example, continued to print the figures of British royalty on stamps issued in India until the 1930s, ignoring that subcontinent's own history and culture. The stamps reinforced the colonial stereotypes passed on by the educational system in Britain and in India itself.[3] In contrast to the stamps appearing in Europe and its colonies in the nineteenth and early twentieth centuries, in the Muslim east the sultans of the Ottoman empire did not issue stamps imprinted with their images, nor did the khedives of Egypt prior to the 1930s. Instead they issued stamps on which cultural symbols, historic monuments, typical landscapes, and the like appeared.[4]

Apart from payment for postal services, in the mid-nineteenth century stamps began to be used for tax purposes, charitable donations, and fundraising. During the American Civil War, in some places postage stamps were sold at a price several times higher than their face value, and the difference was allocated to the cost of care for the war-wounded. In 1905 in Russia stamps were similarly used to raise funds for children orphaned as a result of the Russo-Japanese war. From the beginning of the twentieth century, more especially after the First World War, the custom of issuing stamps by philanthropic institutions for fundraising purposes became regular practice. In contrast to postage stamps, fundraising stamps were used for local, specifically defined, organisational purposes, and the period during which they were sold was relative short.[5]

Against the background of these political-cultural conventions one can understand the decision taken at the Fifth Zionist Congress in Basel (where it was also resolved to create the JNF) to issue stamps that would symbolise the national renaissance and would be a source of income for the JNF, a tool for collecting contributions for the redemption of Eretz Yisrael, and a means of propaganda and information.[6] Just a few months after the establishment of the organisation the first stamp appeared in Vienna, the first location of the Head Office. This was what is known today as *Bul Zion* (the Zion stamp) on which was inscribed the word *Zion* inside a Star of David decorated with rays of the sun; between every two rows of stamps appeared *Juedischer National Fond,* the German title of the organisation. Zion stamps continued to appear in different versions for the next five years, as long as the Head Office remained located in Vienna.[7]

The trend of stamps appearing with a symbolic design, which was typical of the first period of the JNF, changed when the Head Office moved to Köln in Germany. At that time stamps began to appear which memorialised important people in the Zionist movement, in the first place Herzl and Nordau (1909). The JNF Head Office staff presumably were aware of the way postage stamps were designed in the European countries, where monarchs and princes and well-known views of capital cities were their typical motifs. They appeared in the design of stamps commemorating the founder of the Zionist movement, which began to come out at that time. The national offices of the JNF in various countries began to issue stamps in 1913; in Germany a series of stamps appeared with landscapes of Eretz Yisrael and another with the symbols of the twelve Israelite tribes. In Poland during the next three years a series of portrait stamps appeared, depicting the leaders of the Zionist movement and well-known rabbis of the previous century.

During the First World War, when the Head Office moved to The Hague in Holland, the ideas that had taken shape were adopted by the national offices and they began to issue stamps with new subjects: scenes from Eretz Yisrael and portrait stamps of the proponents of Zionism. Accordingly, the notions for the range of themes for stamps issued by the Head Office were devised just before the period we are dealing with, rather than at the time when the organisation first began. The relations between the Head Office and the national offices around the work of the stamp section were also patterned at this time; these were marked by cooperation as well as competition.

When the Head Office moved to Jerusalem in 1923, the stamp section became less active and the feeling developed that it might be necessary to close it. By the start of the1920s income from stamps had already fallen to fractions of a percent of the overall JNF income. Accordingly, in May 1923, the Propaganda Department sounded out all the national offices on four matters, two pertaining to the goal of issuing stamps ad their use, and two to technicalities. The various answers stressed that the chief value the different countries saw in the stamps was their propaganda; most agreed that their worth for fundraising was slight. However, the propaganda value justified the financial and organisational investment in the stamps.[8] On these grounds the Head Office decided to continue issuing stamps despite their low economic value. The stamps were seemingly not perceived by the JNF heads as a prestigious instrument for collecting funds, like the Golden Book, nor as an instrument for the masses, like the Blue Box. The development of this branch from the 1920s and various documents attest that the policy on the design and production of the stamps was mainly connected to their propaganda value among the youth. Yet the financial aspect of the stamps was not neglected, and the Head Office staff worked assiduously to promote the use of JNF stamps for collecting contributions in various institutions (se Figure 3.1).

Dialogue with Branches in the Diaspora

After the Head Office moved to Jerusalem, professional relations and the exchange of information among countries in respect of the stamps continued. From time to time the Jerusalem Head Office got successful ideas from one country which it conveyed to another. In 1926, for example, Leopold Schen, one of the JNF heads in Britain, suggested a programme to Julius Berger whereby money would be collected through stamps which would be stuck on special cards printed with JNF propaganda slogans (see Figure 3.2):

> . . . This was by means of stamp cards, on which they were to attach 25 separate stamps in a particular order, the cards containing propaganda sentences. We should like to give it publicity, and for that purpose I am writing to request you to send us a full description of the plan, if possible, together with the actual card which you designed. . . .[9]

Leopold Schen's suggestion was adopted in the form of the Contribution Booklet issued by the Head Office, which became popular in the following years and was distributed in schools in Poland and other countries. A child had to buy one hundred JNF stamps and glue them in this booklet; on completing her task she would receive a fine certificate attesting to that fact. The distribution of the Contribution Booklets also spread to the Zionist youth movements, which volunteered to work for the JNF.[10]

One of the problems of conducting ongoing propaganda with stamps among the youth was the tedium involved in their collection. A certain Bloch, from Warsaw, suggested some ideas to improve stamp work in schools:

> It would be better to print a bigger picture which would take up the whole page of six stamps, for example, a map of Eretz Yisrael, the University in Jerusalem, the Technion in Haifa, Merhavia, and so on. Thus each separate stamp would be no more than one sixth part of the general picture. Since there are six pages in each booklet we should print six different pictures and the stamps of the six pictures should be dispersed throughout the book. In this way the pupil will have to make an effort to find the right stamp for each page in order to attach them in the correct order to complete the desired picture.
>
> This work will no longer be purely mechanical, demanding no thought or study, and the pupil will have to attach the stamps several times to make a picture until he gets used to doing it quickly and accurately.[11]

Bloch also suggested printing 'a booklet for stamps with Hebrew letters where each stamp will be one letter of the Hebrew alphabet, presented artistically and in lively, attractive colours'. The child would be able to use these stamps for different purposes such as presenting her parents with a birthday gift of their names formed from the letters on these JNF stamps. Finally, he proposed changing the name 'Contribution Booklet', which he thought was too staid for the child, to a name with a lighter ring to it: 'My Contribution'.

The staff of the Propaganda and School departments of the Jerusalem Head Office accepted the ideas raised in Warsaw and responded quickly. Within three months a letter went out to the artist Aba Sapoznikov (Aba Elchnani), in Tel Aviv, with a request for the design of new stamps for the schools: a map of Eretz Yisrael and a map of Jerusalem, as well as a one with a montage of the life of children in Eretz Yisrael.[12] Sapoznikov quickly prepared sketches in the form of pictorial maps on which he highlighted the various elements as requested by the Head Office. In the discussion at the Head Office on the approval of the new detachable stamps, the most effective way of using them for propaganda purposes among children was considered. One suggestion was to divide the pictures into dozens of stamps in different shapes to increase the interest and excitement of collecting them. Similarly diverse proposals arose about additional matter to be printed on the pictorial maps to adapt them for propaganda purposes. Eventually it was concluded that each map would consist of twelve detachable stamps (see Figure 3.3). The designs were then sent to be made into master plates.[13]

Six months later a circular was sent to all the JNF offices containing examples of the new stamps and a statement that the design of the stamp booklet and the certificates of merit, which were an integral part of the project, were about to be changed. In an earlier publication the Head Office had announced this campaign with the special new stamps in its magazine *Karnenu*. It was noted that since the staff had become aware of the stamps' propaganda value for children and youth they were making efforts to improve them. As for the detachable stamps, 'this is the first time that the JNF is to print its stamps in Eretz Yisrael, where printing work has succeeded in attaining this level . . . this will therefore represent one further deed by the JNF to increase the trade in national products in Eretz Yisrael'.[14] As with the Blue Boxes, described in chapter 2, the decision on the new stamp designs involved a change in the place of production. This was aimed at encouraging industry in Eretz Yizrael beyond the symbolic and propaganda value of the transfer. The text on the stamps had to be specific for every country (owing to the different currencies), so Warsaw was chosen as the centre of operations and distribution. There the particular requirements for the stamps of each individual country would be handled.[15]

This pattern, namely requests by the national offices in the Diaspora for new propaganda material in the form of stamps and efforts in Jerusalem to meet them, recurred every few years. According to the reports sent to the Head Office, children very quickly lost interest in the stamps and booklets, causing Jerusalem constantly to devise new stimulating material. This phenomenon continued throughout the 1930s. Just before the Second World War the Warsaw JNF Schools Department sent the Jerusalem Head Office a letter containing the following: 'Since we have been using the cover of the booklet "My Contribution" unchanged for the last three years we wish to request a new drawing for the cover'. The letter also suggested preparing a new series of stamps on the theme of flora and fauna in Eretz Yisrael. It reported much satisfaction with the stamps depicting the landscape of Eretz Yisrael and the new settlements.[16]

In the period under discussion the feeling apparently developed that the Head Office did not have a long-range policy for stamps. Complaining about this, a report from the Propaganda Department warned that tens of thousands of stamps produced by the JNF were lying discarded 'in a cemetery for old stamps in the Head and national offices'.[17] Among others, blame was placed on the national offices, which did not help the Head Office to distribute the stamps or pass on ideas and reports, but even competed with it. They produced their own stamps, an activity seen as a threat to the exclusive authority of the Head Office. The Head Office's response to the competition from the national offices and to the children's boredom was the production and re-styling of new, more complex stamps, while still taking into consideration the needs of propaganda, education, and the perpetuation of the organisation.

The national committees in Tel Aviv, Warsaw, and New York were highly influential in making the stamps a JNF means of propaganda among children and youth. Their input guided the methods of using the stamps (for certificates and study purposes), contributing to their graphic design and determining which motifs would be used. This influence is attested by the JNF's information material from the same period, as evident from the following extract:

> The JNF, knowing the soul of the Jewish child in the Diaspora, prepared several series of stamps for him. The certificate was to bring the Diaspora child closer to the far-off homeland, to its nature and landscape, to its world of plants and animals, to endow him with initial concepts, in a pliable way, through what he saw, of the new reality in the homeland and from the work of its sons. . . Thus he would acquire some sort of notion of that far-off homeland, about which he dreamed and which he was being trained and educated to build.[18]

Despite the importance of the education and propaganda involved in the stamp production there were occasional attempts to renew their use for collecting funds; from the mid-1930s was an increase in their use for collecting indirect 'taxes'. The belief in the total commitment of the Zionist public to JNF concerns, and the desire of the JNF leadership to gain access everywhere for the purposes of propaganda and fundraising, led them to greater use of institutional contributions for the JNF. A popular method in the 1930s was the 'stamp tax': public and private bodies undertook to buy stamps as a form of self-taxation and of JNF fundraising; the Eretz Yisrael national committee in Tel Aviv was especially highly involved in these activities.

The 'Stamp Mitzvah': Propaganda and Indirect Taxation for the JNF

During the 1920s and early 1930s the monetary value of the stamps increasingly diminished, and their educational and propaganda value reciprocally rose. These changes are evident from the weighty correspondence on stamp matters between the Propaganda Department and schools. Still, the Propaganda Department remained in charge of the annual issue of the stamps, and even exerted pressure to increase their use for raising money from different organisations. The increase in money collection with the aid of the stamps was also of concern to the head of the Schools Department, Nathan Bistritski, who dispatched a circular on the subject to all the major youth federations and youth emissaries from Eretz Yisrael. Bistritski's appeal demonstrates belief in the total commitment of the public Zionist institutions, and even individuals, to JNF interests.[19] He stressed the idea of attaching the stamp as 'an obligatory mitzvah' for Zionist youth, who should act as 'examples and pioneers for others to emulate'. The demand to attach JNF stamps was not only addressed to Zionist youth federations in the Diaspora. Staffs of the national offices were also charged with ensuring the attachment of stamps to the many and varied documents—stationery of the different organisations, theatre tickets, membership cards, and all community payments—at a rate of one percent. All these projects 'will stimulate everyone's interest in the JNF and Eretz Yisrael', according to the Head Office.[20]

The JNF operatives were not satisfied with imposing the stamp mitzvah just on public institutions of the Zionist movement but they approached other public institutions as well. By 1936 they had already persuaded several national institutions in Eretz Yisrael to print JNF stamps on their letterheads, among them the Histadrut (General Workers' Federation), political parties, and the Hebrew University in Jerusalem.[21]

In the opinion of the JNF staff, the stamp mitzvah was not only necessary for secular Zionist circles but was also an obligation for religious people. In this case they tried to apply their approach of 'total propaganda'. This can be learnt from a fascinating document issued by the

Head Office on the distribution of stamps to ultraorthodox circles. This document reveals the rationale and the conventional formulation of the reasons for distributing JNF stamps; but in addition it shows the all-embracing nature of the demand:

> We ask you to make all efforts to distribute these stamps among the 'Mizrahi', 'Torah V'Avoda', and 'Bnei Akiva' circles and amongst ultra-orthodox circles in general. One must try to make sure that the Rabbinical offices and the Rabbis attach these stamps to every letter, judgement, certificate, and so on, which they issue. . . One must also clarify whether it is possible to introduce the custom of attaching a JNF stamp to invitations to weddings, circumcisions, bar mitzvah celebrations, festive parties, and so on, as well. . . .[22]

The call to increase the propaganda among the ultraorthodox shows how much the JNF operatives aspired to gain entry into every corner of every walk of life to show their presence and to collect funds. The appeal attests to the development of fundraising patterns in one country, their adoption by the Head Office, and their transmission to other countries. This circular, like others, always set forth splendid examples worthy of imitation ('synagogues in the USA', 'Schools in Eretz Yisrael') and the mood generated by such documents was one of optimism, conveying a message of progress and momentum.

The optimistic messages emanating from the Head Office's messages to the national offices on expanding the stamp section concealed an on-going struggle between different bodies and the JNF centre regarding this obligation, including public organisations and institutions in Eretz Yisrael as well. The request to attach stamps was made to many institutions, such as banks, commercial companies, political organisations, and various cultural bodies. In March 1937 the Head Office sent to the Eretz Yisrael national committee a list of all organisations that had agreed to pay the stamp tax and attach JNF stamps to their stationery. The list includes dozens of educational and cultural institutions, political parties, banks, social organisations, and kibbutzim located throughout the Yishuv (the Jewish population of pre-state Eretz Yisrael).[23] Practically every institution engaged in wide-ranging contacts with a broad public and considerable correspondence was the target of an appeal from the JNF staff; those that refused were approached again and again.[24]

In sum, despite the campaigns and propaganda about the stamps, throughout the whole period under discussion income from them was very low—about one percent of the total income of the JNF, not counting the real costs of work and distribution. Clearly, fundraising was not the only aspect that the JNF leadership deemed important when they pressured different bodies into appending JNF stamps to their papers. Other motives apparently lay behind the stamp mitzvah activity, concerned with strengthening the standing of the JNF among the Zionist public: it was a struggle for JNF survival.[25] The obligation to stick stamps on various documents exposed the adult public to the JNF's current propaganda and kept the organisation's activity in the public consciousness. The stamp was a kind of conspicuous statement about the presence of the institution in every place at all times, a factor which made it stand out above other Zionist institutions whose public propaganda was modest. The JNF Head Office seemed to grasp that the stamps were not only bits of paper with drawings on them, which served as a pastime or game for children. They were political and cultural statements aimed at the Jewish public, and they broadcast this message: 'See how important the JNF is, and how important its projects are'.

Content of the Stamps

The content of the stamps reflects the processes involved in the decision making: the flow of knowledge and ideas between the centre in Jerusalem and the periphery, political developments in Eretz Yisrael and in the world, and the changing needs for which the stamps were issued. Among the preferred content of the stamps was personalities and scenes from Eretz Yisrael (buildings, settlements, or plant and animal life); less frequent were symbolic stamps or stamps showing elements connected with their place of issue in the Diaspora.[26]

Here, then, we consider the motives that determined the stamps' content during the period under study. Obviously, no single factor determined this content since there were stamps and even whole series whose appearance met complex demands. But we can attempt to identify some of the main motives behind the determination of the stamps' contents: inspirational stamps, stamps in honour of the JNF itself, stamps for didactic purposes, stamps for school certificates, and stamps for political protest.

Inspirational stamps. This name refers to themes of two seemingly contrary types: those commanding broad consensus and those for particular use.

The first type involved stamps intended for a mixed audience, with no particular elements, such as stamps with classic content (which were printed several times): Star of David stamps and Herzl stamps. These spread a Zionist-Jewish message easy for the masses to identify with. The combination of two types of content (Zionist and Jewish) produced stamps with very strong symbolic messages, for example, the 'Herzl on the Rhine' stamp, designed by the artist A. M. Lilian (1874–1925). It portrayed the father of political Zionism standing on a bridge over the Rhine in Basel and seeing, in his mind's eye, the nation's masses flocking to Zion, the eternal capital of the Jewish people, with the Sun of Hope shining above.[27]

Many elements figured in the design of this stamp: past and present, man and place, Diaspora and Eretz Yisrael, leader and people, light and hope. Presumably, the making of such stamps was expected by the propaganda personnel of the JNF to inspire the hearts of the masses of the Jewish people. This group also deserves credit for stamps of a range of celebrities who formed part of the Zionist ethos, such as Baron Edmond de Rothschild (1845–1934), whose commemoration on stamps was preceded by a special decision of the JNF directorate.[28]

Other stamps that may be included in this category are those intended to commemorate Jewish heroism. This motif had become the foremost subject in the fashioning of the Zionist ethos, and it is not surprising that the JNF saw it as an important element for commemoration in stamps. In most cases the stamps appeared as part of a general commemoration process of the entire Yishuv, for example, after the Second World War (commemorative stamps, the Jewish Brigade, the Warsaw Ghetto Revolt). The Tel Hai episode and its hero Yosef Trumpeldor (1880–1920), who became one of the outstanding symbols of the ethos of heroism in Eretz Yisrael, were given special attention for commemoration (see Figure 3.4).[29] Tel Hai became a major symbol for exemplary behaviour and identification by youth in Eretz Yisrael and the Diaspora, so the issuing of a stamp to commemorate it was expected to inspire. The Head Office contributed its share to the commemoration of the event by issuing several 'Trumpeldor' stamps (in 1927, 1936, and 1945), in which the slain warrior appears as a national-military hero who defended his country and the freedom of its people. On the margin of the stamp the legend 'Jewish National Fund' of course appeared, so hearts were inspired for the institution through this model of heroism.

The second type of stamp, intended for particular purposes, varied in content, using celebrities, places, or symbols. This group contains stamps which appeared in order to inspire the religious community, as can be seen from the following excerpt from a memo sent out by the Head Office: 'Among the special means that the JNF Head Office uses to bring the ultraorthodox closer to the JNF's work of redeeming Eretz Yisrael, and to expand our activities among these circles, is the important issuing by the Head Office at this time of a series of stamps which have a distinctly religious character. . . .' The six-stamp series depicted famous rabbis as well as the Western (Wailing) Wall, Kfar Hassidim, and Tirat Zvi. Like the 'Herzl' stamp, this series contained combined messages of Zionism-Judaism, past and present, place, and leader, but here they were directed at the religious sector.

The issuing of special stamps might have upset a certain balance in the stamps' aim to inspire hearts, a danger of which the Head Office was aware. So when an additional series was suggested, namely stamps of the new settlements, the staff were at pains to point out that they proposed settlements 'of all parties, as well as a *moshav* [private holdings] of the middle class German immigrant settlement (Shavei Zion) and a Youth Aliya settlement (Alonim)'. The proposal also envisaged settlements from a variety of regions in Eretz Yisrael.[30]

Stamps in honour of the JNF. This motif concerned the wish to celebrate through stamps the JNF organisation, its leadership, its founders, and its range of projects. At first only a few stamps were issued with this goal in mind, among them those commemorating Herman Shapira (1917), which appeared with stamps bearing the likeness of other figures. After the First World War JNF stamps began to appear honouring the organisation's projects in Eretz Yisrael. The favourite subject at this stage was institutions established with the aid of the JNF, such as the Technion in Haifa and the Hebrew University in Jerusalem. Stamps bearing these motifs appeared several times in series along with others, such as ancient historical buildings: Absalom's Tomb and David's Tower (1927). The message was clear: the link between the JNF's projects and the well-known symbols of the past; just as the historical monuments were eternal evidence of the Jewish people so would the JNF projects be also. Stamps denoting the JNF's 'redemption of the land of Eretz Yisrael' may be included in this category, with depictions of the Jezreel, Hefer, Zevulun, and Jordan valleys. Other symbolic stamps in praise of the organisation showed tractors, trees, or ploughs, and as well as maps of Eretz Yisrael, which appeared frequently in different versions and were also issued for a range of didactic purposes. Alongside these, stamps commemorating the heads of the organisation continued to appear, and in 1940–41 the JNF brought out a series of stamps memorialising its presidents until that time.

Stamps for didactic purposes. When the staffs of the Head Office and national offices realised the importance of the stamps for their work with pupils, they embarked on the issue of series of stamps whose definitive goal was didactic. The formulation of the idea of detachable stamps, as well as the stamp booklet, which was one of the vehicles for these ideas, have already been described. Accordingly, series with larger numbers of stamps appeared, for example, the series of 'Aleph-Beth' stamps which enjoyed much publicity and appeared in 1940. Warsaw wrote about this to Jerusalem:

> The picture must be drawn by a master artist under the supervision of a teacher, a pedagogue. This series should be thoughtfully adapted to the needs of study. . . . In regard to the series itself, we draw your attention to the need for twenty-eight stamps. . . . Behind each letter should be a background portraying the landscape of Eretz Yisrael. One can arrange the letters so they can be used for several sentences or order them in such a way that some of the letters look like one big picture. For example, Jerusalem: the sequence of letters will depict the City of Jerusalem as well. . . .[31]

In Jerusalem the Head Office accepted the idea, and an internal memorandum noted that this series of stamps had three goals: it would serve as an 'aid in the study of the homeland through the collecting'; it would be 'an aid to learning [Hebrew] reading' if used in younger classes as a game with stamps; and it would increase the amount of money collected in schools. The stamps would be designed like the earlier landscape stamps, and 'on the background of the landscape a large letter would be printed— the initial letter of the name of the site depicted on the stamp'.[32]

Didactic series with a large number of stamps and ideas appeared in the USA in 1938, under the encouragement of the Council of Hebrew Teachers working for the JNF in New York. These series included stamps each showing a part of a disassembled map. The most famous of these was the series called 'Do You Know?' It consisted of ninety-nine stamps, on which appeared distinct JNF propaganda themes: landscapes of Eretz Yisrael, personalities, and the like (see Figures 3.5 and 3.6). These stamps were placed in a booklet, providing the answers to a quiz for youth on Eretz Yisrael and the JNF. The rationale for the appearance of these didactic stamps is formulated in the foreword to the booklet:

> You have to teach about Eretz Yisrael, which is our only hope. In these bad days ships sail across the sea carrying miserable, wandering Jews, men and women, the old and the sick running away from the evil hatred, and every shore closed to them. And only one hope exists for these Jews in the whole sea of trouble, and the name of that country is Eretz Yisrael. But will you recognise that country?[33]

That year another booklet for collecting stamps appeared in New York called The Galilee Album in which stamps with pictures of animals, plants, and even a disassembled map of the Hula Valley were supposed to be mounted. Some of the master plates of this series found their way to Warsaw, where similar stamps for didactic purposes were printed, mainly stamps with animals and fruit. These were apparently the last stamps issued in Poland before the Holocaust.[34]

This category of didactic stamps should also include the series known as 'Diaspora' stamps (1943), a series of forty stamps intended to approximate the children of Eretz Yisrael to the heritage of the Diaspora and make them more aware of the fate of the Jewish world outside and its culture. This series was the antithesis of all the positions reflected on JNF stamps until then, namely negation of the Diaspora and bringing 'the Diaspora child (closer) to the far-off homeland' and to 'the landscape of Eretz Yisrael so yearned for'. During the first years of the Second World War, however, the mood changed and a decision was taken to issue the 'Diaspora' series. It was intended that 'our children and those who follow us should know what we had in the Diaspora, that this was the strength we drew from this faithful source'. An assessment of the production of these stamps and their concomitant educational activities shows the JNF's contribution to the onset of a change in attitude to the Diaspora in the Hebrew educational network in Eretz Yisrael, a change which came more fully into effect years later. Here the JNF was ahead of its time.[35]

Stamps for school certificates. As part of the JNF effort to stamp all documents in Zionist public institutions in general and in the education system in particular in Eretz Yisrael, the organisation even gained access to school certificates: of matriculation and of year-end graduation. Since every pupil in the Hebrew education network received several certificates a year, tens of thousands of stamps were needed to meet this demand. Already at the beginning of the 1920s it became customary to attach stamps to school certificates as a local initiative, albeit sporadic and haphazard. A difficulty in applying the notion of stamping certificates was due the streaming of the Hebrew educational network in Eretz Yisrael. At first the JNF national committee of Eretz Yisrael proposed 'to choose figures for the pictures from the three streams, Mizrahi, the General Zionists, and the Labour Movement, and to fix different prices for each type'.[36] Later, in 1938, the act of stamping certificates developed an almost state-like character, under the agency and responsibility of the Teachers' Council for the JNF in Eretz Yisrael.

The Teachers' Council decided to adopt the custom of pasting stamps on certificates as obligatory for schools, while distinguishing the types of certificates. For year-end graduation to a higher class they suggested attaching the Shapira stamp worth one mil, and for the matriculation certificate they recommended the Herzl stamp worth fifty mils.[37] The distinction of the stamps and their values was not fortuitous; it represented the relative importance of the certificates and the personalities depicted on them, as perceived by the Teachers' Council. Adjusting the stamps to school needs expressed itself not only in the layout but also in the text and monetary value of the stamps. After Ussishkin died, in 1941, and a commemorative stamp was issued, the Head Office asked the Eretz Yisrael JNF national committee in Tel Aviv to adopt it as a stamp for school certificates. The Committee insisted that 'the stamp also carry a special legend which will attest to its being a school stamp'. Likewise, the national committee requested that the price of the stamp be one mil (like the Shapira stamp) and not fifty mils as demanded by the Head Office (like the Herzl stamp).[38]

The Head Office tried to spread the new practice of affixing stamps to school certificates to Jewish schools in the Diaspora. In 1938, they appealed to the JNF national offices in Poland, Rumania, Czechoslovakia, and other countries in a circular, asking the operatives to try and introduce this innovation through the school principals because

There is no special need to argue the educational importance of this activity, which can raise the status of the JNF in the eyes of the pupils and parents and strengthen the ties of the children with the homeland, after they leave school as well. This practice, if adopted by Jewish- language schools in every country, might be used as a serious source of income for the redemption of Eretz Yisrael.[39]

These sentences, uttered by the Head Office in Jerusalem, unmistakably show the stamps' order of priorities. First is 'raising of the status of the JNF', second 'strengthening ties with Eretz Yisrael', and, trailing in last place, comes the economic worth of the contribution of the stamps, 'for the redemption of Eretz Yisrael'. According to the declared policy of the JNF, the stamp offered for attachment to the certificates was the 'propagator of the idea of the JNF'.

A year later, 1939, it issued the Bialik stamp for this purpose since Chaim Nahman Bialik was not only the national poet but also an enthusiastic supporter of the JNF, and his writings were included in many of its publications. In the early 1940s a special stamp for school certificates, celebrating the JNF, was again brought out, namely the Ussishkin stamp, which had to be especially designed for this specific purpose.[40]

Stamps for political protest. A small number of stamps were issued in consequence of political events or various occurrences where the JNF rendered assistance and supported political and cultural positions. The stamps acted as a means of propaganda, were easy to produce, and were a very rapid response to the events. For example, following the publication of the May 1939 White Paper, the Head Office proposed printing forthwith many exemplars of the Jerusalem stamp or the map stamp of Eretz Yisrael inscribed with the immortal verse from Psalms, 'If I forget thee, Jerusalem, may my right hand wither'.[41] The proposal was approved and the illustration chosen was a picture of the Western Wall, crowned with the above legend; this was a combination of classic elements whose symbolic importance had always been immeasurable. The political and symbolic protest behind the issuing of the stamp was salient as this was not the first time that the Western Wall had appeared on a stamp; but this time it was accompanied by the ineluctable promise 'If I forget thee, Jerusalem. . . .' Four months later, when the Second World War erupted in Europe, a message was dispatched to the national offices concerning the appearance of these stamps. It stated, 'This stamp has important propaganda value since it brings light and hope to the heart of those in Eretz Yisrael'.[42]

The map stamp can also be included in the above category. It appeared several times and became one of the most widely applied stamps on the diverse documents produced by organisations and institutions in Eretz Yisrael at that time. The map of Eretz Yisrael, with its sharply etched graphic design, made it possible for all segments of the Jewish people to identify with the stamp. The Head Office staff were aware of this, and recommended that the Eretz Yisrael national committee in Tel Aviv urge different organisations to have special rubber stamps made (imprinted

'Stamp tax paid') in the form of 'the drawing of the stamp of the map of Eretz Yisrael which is a symbol of all our work and suitable for all circles in the Yishuv irrespective of politics and ideas'.[43]

Summary

The issuing of stamps started with the aim of raising funds to purchase land in Eretz Yisrael and to finance JNF activities. But after the First World War the organisation's leadership already realised that they would not succeed in raising large sums of money through the stamps. Yet since they understood the importance of propaganda they continued with the stamp work throughout our period. The stamps served as a kind of miniature proclamations reflecting policy and ideology; through them one obtains a glimpse of the internal world of the JNF. In that period, when visual communications media were in their infancy, and even illustrated encyclopaedias and newspapers were hard to come by in the impoverished Jewish communities throughout the world, the stamps were an exciting communications innovation which presented individuals with views of the landscape of Eretz Yisrael and a range of famous people, with widespread distribution and at a relatively low cost. These small-scale posters were thus visual means of communication, of greater value than that ascribed to them today in a culture flooded with mass communications. The staff of the Propaganda Department were well aware of their worth, and exploited it to promote their organisation's interests.

The stamps represent the outlook and deeds of the JNF leadership in Eretz Yisrael at that time. The main items commemorated were projects such as the settlement in the north of Eretz Yisrael, but other motifs, on which there was broad social and cultural consensus, were not lacking: for example, Jerusalem and the fathers of Zionism. Like the stamps brought out by various national postal services at that time, the JNF stamps often presented national and cultural symbols—places and people the organisation wished to promote. From this point of view the JNF acted like a state institution and broadcast messages of national independence.

The mutual relations between the Diaspora and Eretz Yisrael found expression in the competitive and cooperative working relations between the different national committees and the Propaganda Department of the Head Office. A cooperative and complementary relationship existed from the stage of the general idea to the stage of stamp production and distribution; but on the other hand competition with the Head Office was present, mainly in the Eretz Yisrael national committee in Tel Aviv and the US national committee in New York. These committees, each in its own way, tried to take an independent approach, in opposition to the centralised monopoly of the Head Office, in the stamp work. This independence was expressed in the issuing of different stamps, in influencing decisions on the content of different stamps, or in bringing out stamps with different content.

While the didactic achievements in the development of the stamps as learning and propaganda tools regarding Eretz Yisrael for schools in Eretz Yisrael and the Diaspora were impressive, the staff of the Propaganda Department encountered great difficulties in applying their plans to raise funds through means other than the educational network. Whenever they tried to turn them into an intensively used instrument for raising funds, and to impose the stamp mitzvah on every possible piece of paper, they encountered the opposition of individuals and institutions. Considering the stamps' minor economic usefulness, the determined attitude on the obligation of stamping is not easily understood, unless one takes into account the political propaganda benefit to the organisation through the use of the stamps. Apparently, in the struggle for survival in the public Zionist consciousness the stamps acted as one of the simplest and most efficient means that the JNF used to convey its message to the people: from kindergarten children to the adult public.

Chapter 4

Successes and Failures: A Range of Propaganda Products

A Range of Products: Introduction

The instruments of collection that turned into means of propaganda, such as the stamps and the Blue Box, were only some of a whole range of activities of the Head Office's Propaganda Department. The following can be seen as the basic premises of their work.

1. The desire to innovate.
2. The need to establish a permanent tradition.
3. The desire to be a recognised presence everywhere.
4. The desire to win the approval of all Jews.

These basic premises led the Propaganda Department to spread its work over a wide range of means of propaganda. Some were elaborate and expensive, for example, the production of films or regular series of books, journals, and various newsletters; others were simpler, such as aids for schools and youth movements, circulars for donors, and more.

In the mid-1920s two personalities came into contact: Julius Berger, the head of the Propaganda Department, who was meticulous in his work, and Nathan Bistritski, the visionary writer, who was the head of the Youth and Schools Department. This partnership, together with the rise in demand for JNF material for propaganda and information, caused a quantitative and qualitative change in the institution's propaganda work. The heads of the Propaganda Department spoke of 'methodical and steady work', meaning the totality of propaganda: totality in time and target community. Good propaganda work could not be on a temporary or incidental basis, so a constant flow of propaganda materials must be available all year round, and geared for activity from young age to adulthood. The second principle is evident in their ideas about 'The Eretz Yisrael way of life' as a focus for propaganda content, a goal that guided the design of different propaganda materials—games, books, and short films. Emphasizing the way of life of Eretz Yisrael in propaganda had behavioural and educational purposes parallel to the tasks of propaganda for the institution. An additional factor that affected the patterns of propaganda was the constant feeling of the JNF personnel that their work was not adequately publicised among the nation's masses; the operative conclusions of this feeling led to the expansion, sophistication, and variation of propaganda instruments.

During the 1930s the propaganda tools and publicity reached an impressive level of activity. The Head Office's channels of communication, and those of the rest of the organisation, were adapted to the target community. These were tools of propaganda and information aimed at 'people of the inner circle', meaning the organisation's activists and operatives. Others were developed and distributed to 'the rest of the world'. An outstanding example of a publication for 'the inner circle' was the bulletin *Karnenu,* which served as a major channel of communication between the Head Office and JNF functionaries across the globe. In addition, many newsletters were brought out over the years, as were work instructions and different kinds of periodic reports aimed at the thousands of activists throughout the Zionist world.

By contrast, propaganda and information material aimed at the 'external world' was produced for the Jewish Zionist and even non-Zionist world. This included publicity material prepared by the Newspaper Department, which tried to distribute the material to general newspapers. Among the material were diverse reports and pictures that presented the JNF's achievements in Eretz Yisrael and its different projects. There were periods when bulletins were issued to newspapers every week in seven languages, and every two weeks they were accompanied by a series of original pictures from Eretz Yisrael. These pictures, mostly photographed by Josef Schweig, had explanatory captions and could be used for propaganda purposes in different ways.[1] In addition, the Newspaper Department tried to enlist well-known authors and journalists throughout the Jewish world to write articles and stories.[2]

Films and other materials made with enormous effort to draw the attention of the Jewish and non-Jewish public to the JNF and its activities belong to this category also. Still, propaganda and information material was primarily developed with a view to 'the middle circle', namely the supportive public: donors, teachers, youth movements, schoolchildren, women's organisations, and ultraorthodox groups. These include the classic devices: *means of collection* (the Blue Box, stamps, the Golden Book), in use by the organisation for decades; other means were encouraged during the period under discussion: games, short films, lectures, and series of books and pamphlets on Eretz Yisrael. At this time the JNF even became the biggest publisher of songbooks to spread the music of Eretz Yisrael, and it was the only national institution to manage this concern between 1927 and 1948.[3]

Out of all this wide range of propaganda means, in this chapter we have chosen to deal with two subjects that present different aspects of the activities of the Propaganda and Youth departments in the JNF. These are children's toys and games, and the prestigious Youth Library, within whose framework close to ninety monographs appeared that formed an important foundation for the historiography of Eretz Yisrael.

Games and Toys: Production Efforts

The desire to innovate and break into new areas of propaganda and information in order to reach additional population groups led the staffs of the Propaganda and Youth departments to support the development of notions that today may seem strange. One of them was children's games, which were produced throughout the entire period under study. The development of games accorded with the activities of schools and youth movements and clear patterns took shape towards the end of the 1920s. The intention was to reach two other groups with the JNF's propaganda: children in kindergarten and grade I, and pupils at the end of elementary school. The JNF staff tried to produce suitable games for each group, with the emphasis on the educational and ideological message intended to serve JNF goals, not just on the enjoyment of playing. The initiative to develop the games came from two sources: the organisation's own personnel, and teachers and commercial entrepreneurs from outside the organisation who were interested in obtaining the JNF's financial and organisational assistance. Several examples follow of the kinds of games, and of production and distribution problems that arose.

Like other propaganda devices, the games had already been developed in the first half of the 1920s, when at least four versions of classic games were distributed: spinning tops, dominoes, Snakes and Ladders, and paper cut-outs. The propaganda content was introduced into the basic version of the game. For example, in Snakes and Ladders, which the JNF called The Race, a Blue Box was placed at the top of the ladder and the child had to climb up in order to reach it. In dominoes the dots were replaced by pictures of life in Israel—pioneers, settlements, and buildings, which demonstrated 'how the Hebrew community was growing and establishing itself with JNF funds'.[4] The spinning top was made of olive wood from Eretz Yisrael, and in addition to the traditional letters—*nun, gimmel, he, pe,* which appeared on each of the four sides, the words *Jewish, National, Fund, Jerusalem* were imprinted. For the paper cut-outs, which were generally used to signify castles and palaces in Europe, the child had to cut out and affix a model of Kibbutz Merhavia in Jezreel valley. In the instructions for the games the office people did not neglect to point out the following:

Since the game is associated with the JNF, the losers, one or some predetermined number of times, should contribute some sort of coin to the JNF box in their home. In this way we have the opportunity both to place the box on the table and to make it a part of every game.[5]

The Propaganda Department was not satisfied with only these four games, and, in 1927, towards the twenty-fifth anniversary of the JNF, they sent out a circular proposing a four-hand card game (Quartet). 'A game of this type, with themes involving the building of Eretz Yisrael, in particular JNF activities, was thought up by one of the teachers from Jerusalem'. Among the subjects proposed were four packs of cards for the JNF's four main types of land preparation; four diagrams with the JNF revenues; four diagrams of JNF land areas at different times, and so on.[6] 'As a result of a game like this the children will naturally learn all the details and numbers connected to the JNF and will learn very important information effortlessly. The game will increase their interest and will deepen their knowledge about the redemption of Eretz Yisrael while preparing them for JNF work when they grow up'.[7] It is not clear how widely this game was distributed, but another game, which was developed at the same time, achieved distribution on commercial levels throughout the Diaspora. This game was known as My Trip around Eretz Yisrael or A Tourist Map for Eretz Yisrael.

The prestige associated with the game was evinced in the impressive production and the high quality of the map of Eretz Yisrael, drawn by the artist Nahum Gutman, who worked with the people of the Propaganda and Youth departments on various subjects during those years.[8] The game itself was based on five Jewish tourists who arrive at Haifa by ship, put money into a cash box, and embark on a tour of 101 places in Eretz Yisrael. The tourist who makes it to a 'burgeoning' site in Eretz Yisrael wins money, while the one who ends up at an abandoned, deserted place has to pay a sum into the kitty. The tourist who first reaches the top of Mount Hermon and raises the Hebrew flag wins the jackpot. A six-language booklet was attached to each game with its instructions, but also with informative material about the JNF. Games were produced directly by the Head Office several times during the 1930s and 1940s, but there was also another approach: JNF assistance offered in the advertising and distribution of games produced by private entrepreneurs. The JNF would recommend various games to the national offices around the world as soon as it determined that the game had educational facets that satisfied its propaganda and publicity goals (see Figure 4.1).

This method, whereby the JNF acted as an agent between entrepreneurs in Eretz Yisrael and the target population of youth and children, also led to the introduction of games which were innovative for those days, for example, An Electric Game for Learning about Eretz Yisrael. Bistritski wrote of this in a circular to the national offices in Eastern Europe. He informed them that the firm that had devised this game was willing to produce similar games according to designs it was given on JNF affairs, to allow children to acquire knowledge about the first settlements in Eretz Yisrael, the principles and activities of the JNF, and so on. This could be 'an excellent educational tool for spreading knowledge about Eretz Yisrael to Jewish children in the Diaspora'.[9]

During and after the Second World War the JNF did not cease its activities in the area of games and educational/propaganda tools. National offices world-wide continued their activities as best they could during war, that is, they continued to propagandise for the JNF. For example, the Education Department of the national office in Britain brought out a puzzle game (called Be a *Halutz* (pioneer) in which one had to join pieces to form a picture of the new-born Jewish landscape of Eretz Yisrael on a board showing a desolate, abandoned scene. In the game the child had to collect money for the JNF and, after she had completed the game she had a sum sufficient to buy thirty-five square yards of land in Eretz Yisrael.[10]

In the autumn of 1944, when the end of the Second World War seemed to be approaching, private entrepreneurs in Eretz Yisrael swiftly contacted the JNF so as to benefit from the post-war period by producing games to intensify propaganda among youth and children in the Diaspora. The purpose of these games was clearly to stress the role of the JNF in the building of Eretz Yisrael. A wide array of games were offered, such as paper folding (The Port of Tel Aviv) and different board games (A Trip though Israel, The Galilee, Protecting Our Land). The Head Office responded by telling them that they must await the war's end to renew the momentum of distributing the games in the Diaspora (see Figure 4.2).[11]

To sum up, games as propaganda material were never more than experiments or one-time efforts, and they never developed into a long-term tradition as did other means of propaganda. This may have been due to the target population and the technical complexity of producing these products. The cost-efficiency of the games was seen by the JNF staff as low and not worth promoting. By contrast, they saw much value in producing printed information and propaganda material for individual use, and for this they recruited the best writers in Eretz Yisrael.

The Youth Library: Achievements and Censorship

The Establishment and Purpose of the Youth Library

The JNF strove to enlist important writers and authors to increase the prestige of the institution and its propaganda. Such an opportunity arose when the Schools and Youth Department was established under the directorship of Nathan Bistritski (1926), who initiated one of the most prestigious means of JNF propaganda, the Youth Library. During the period under research the JNF had financial resources and was concerned to publish serious articles so it encouraged writing that suited its goals and philosophy. Although studies and articles by the JNF directors on subjects close to the institution and on its activities appeared over the years, the JNF wanted to expand the circle of writers and publish more printed material.[12] This explains Bistritski's decision, supported by the Teachers' Council, to create a permanent forum for the publication of popular literature; for this purpose he established the Youth Library within whose framework dozens of booklets and pamphlets appeared in the following decades.[13]

In a review of the activities of his department in 1929 Bistritski wrote about the motives for establishing the Youth Library. The aim was to serve the needs of youth in Eretz Yisrael and the Diaspora, and to provide learning aids and study material for teachers on how *aliya* (immigration to Eretz Yisrael) would educate their pupils.[14] The purpose of the library, Bistritski wrote, was 'To give youth honest and reliable information about life in the Homeland, from all parts of our communal settlements there, new and old, from all the pioneering projects from the days of the Bilu up to the days of Hehalutz; to show them who the Israeli is, at his work conquering himself and nature, on the soil of our homeland'.[15] Bistritski envisaged the library as 'a kind of modest popular encyclopaedia', whose goal was to act as an important instrument for Zionist socialisation. Bistritski formulated this more clearly three years later, writing that this should be useful, educational literature for the teacher and the students, presenting academic, popular, historical, and geographical information together with reminiscences of the original settlers.[16]

The monographs contained material intended to meet the different needs of the propaganda, not blatantly but subtly, according to Bistritski:

> Obviously, in each and every booklet of the Youth Library we will stress the importance of and the projects involved in building Eretz Yisrael, of the Zionist Organisation in general, and of the JNF in particular. This emphasis, however, will not come as a form of propaganda but as a form of pleasant literature, attractive to youth, that instructs and influences them and the evolution of their outlook.[17]

At first the initiators of the idea thought that they would publish a series at irregular intervals; later they changed their policy and decided to publish a booklet each month. For this goal the Omanut publishing house in Tel Aviv, with which the JNF had an ongoing work relationship, was approached to form a partnership. In March 1928 a contract was signed between the JNF and Omanut establishing the principle that the JNF Head Office would finance writers' payments and expenses up to the printing stage, and printing expenses and paper would be financed by Omanut. The economic expectations of the JNF staff arose from the assumption that the library would be so popular that it would enter 'every corner of the youth federations and schools'. The plan was to print 3000 copies of each booklet, and they even expected to issue reprints.[18]

Bitstriski's aspirations rose still higher when he set out on an information mission to the Eastern European Jewish communities a few months later, in August 1928. This journey convinced him that it was important to strengthen the link between the Diaspora and the project of building Eretz Yisrael. To this end, 'Eretz Yisrael has to start contributing its spiritual resources, the spiritual values it has produced, and they can serve as the basis for the creation of that national experience which has the power to fill the vacuum felt every day by our nation because of assimilation'.[19] The Youth Library, Bistritski hoped, would accomplish the important task of passing on the 'spiritual property' produced in Eretz Yisrael to the lands of the Diaspora, and of educating youth and the general public in the spirit of Eretz Yisrael.

Bistritski's basic expectations from the Youth Library were apparently not commercial but educational and informational. The JNF, however, did pay considerable sums for writing, editing, photographing, mapmaking for each booklet, so expectations of making money to cover expenses did exist. The distribution of the library literature to youth in Eretz Yisrael and the Diaspora was not a commercial success, so it was decided to reduce the number of planned booklets from twelve a year to six, and several booklets appeared twice.[20] Still, by the middle of 1932 more than thirty booklets had appeared. The first five booklets had reprints, but the rest were not in demand and of several of them only a few hundred copies were distributed.[21]

It is difficult to understand how the Youth Library continued to function considering the persistent failure in distribution. Bistritski's insistence on the continued existence of the project stemmed from its importance as propaganda and the prestige he attributed to it. His efforts enjoyed the full and active support and cooperation of the top JNF leadership, including Menahem Ussishkin, who was involved in every decision, including the work of editing and approving each booklet. Ussishkin knew the condition of the Youth Library but he allowed no one to touch it. The outbreak of the Second World War harmed the Youth Library even more, and created objective difficulties for the distribution of the booklets and receipt of raw material for the printing work. Although the editorial board continued to function, and several booklets were written and printed, their publication was sporadic. As a result the JNF directorate convened on 27 September 1943 to discuss the library. Up to that meeting eighty-four booklets had been published; the Head Office proposed to the directorate that they resolve to budget enough funds to reach one hundred titles, the concluding booklet to be about Ussishkin, recently deceased.[22]

The directorate adopted the Head Office's proposal and gave the green light to the Youth Library editorial board to continue their work. For a certain period they tried to push the project forward and continue publishing booklets, but they could not revitalise it.

Bistritski and his assistants were not greatly pleased with many of the writers. Their disappointment was for a wide range of reasons, the usual ones in this type of project: not keeping to schedule, careless writing, the use of style and language unsuited to the target population, the introduction of undesirable content, remuneration problems, and so on. Overshadowing all these, however, the major question of specific topics continually beset the Youth Library project from its inception. According to the goals set forth at the time of its establishment, the topics were supposed to emerge from four areas: settlements and regions in Eretz Yisrael; the fathers of Zionism; movements and ideological currents; and historic sites. The list of titles of monographs published over the whole period attests to a clear preference for the subject of settlements and regions in Eretz Yisrael, accounting for about half of the total (see Figure 4.3). About one tenth of their number addressed topics unrelated to the subjects listed above, and the remainder were divided among them.[23] However, the relevant documents show that the choice of monographs resulted from three considerations: commemoration, didactics, and establishing 'bonds of endearment'.

The term *commemoration* as applied to the Youth Library meant the celebration of achievements and people: illustrious, pioneering figures, leading personalities in the activities of the Zionist movement, JNF projects, and the like. Booklets on men like Herman Shapira, Ahad Ha'am, and Max Nordau belonged to this category, as did most of those on settlements in Eretz Yisrael such as Ness Ziona, Degania, Hadera, and Nahalal, which focus on descriptions of the founders. Commemorative monographs were not published for their own sake but were combined with the didactic purposes of the Youth Library. The didactic objective generated topics originally omitted from the monograph series, such as the reprinting of the classic Zionist texts *Auto-emancipation* by Y. L. Pinsker and *Rome and Jerusalem* by Moses Hess. Didactic considerations also caused the appearance of original monographs like M. Kleinman's *The Period of Hibat Zion,* E. M. Lifshitz's *Religion and Homeland,* and David Yellin's *Yehuda Halevi.* Some of the books by Yosef Weitz (one of the JNF heads) also had mainly didactic purposes: *The Forest* and *The Orange Grove and the Garden* (see Figure 4.4). Because of the didactic approach, the Youth Library included monographs on the physical geography of Eretz Yisrael that could be used as supplementary material for teachers or for high schools. Such studies were, for example, *Dew and Rain, Our Country's Air,* and *Transjordan.* Bistritski and his department succeeded in recruiting the foremost teachers and scholars in Eretz Yisrael at that time to write these books. Another consideration must be added regarding commemoration and didactics in the choice of topics, apparent already from the start of the library's existence: this was 'bonds of endearment'. The term referred to the inclusion of topics that would enlarge distribution of the monographs to populations removed from the activities of the JNF Propaganda and Youth departments. The library was primarily intended for the classic target population of the JNF, namely Zionists and secular Jews in Eretz Yisrael and the countries of Eastern Europe. But the desire to reach religious youth ('ultraorthodox' in JNF terminology) wherever they were, or even the Sephardi public, led Ussishkin to the decision to include suitable monographs for these populations. He apparently informed Bistritski of this decision at the very inauguration of the library, and recommended that a monograph on Rabbi Yehuda Alkalai be written.[24] Ussishkin was not content with the decisions on the topics deemed best suited to the goals of the Youth Library or with the choice of writers whose work was considered acceptable to the JNF. He insisted that every sentence be checked for any contradiction to the JNF outlook that might endanger its public image. Ussishkin adopted this policy following the appearance of the second monograph, by R. Sverdlov, entitled *The Dead Sea*; it resulted in the introduction of censorship and the rewriting of some of the content of the monographs, as illustrated in the next section.

Editing, Rewriting, and Censorship

After a writer of a monograph submitted his manuscript for perusal, it would be read by members of the editorial board who submitted their comments to Bistritski. Ussishkin would express his opinions separately, as would the language editor of the series, Smititsky, and all of these would be considered when the booklet was being edited for publication. During the editing it was common to suggest to the writer improvements in content and pedagogical approach, usually the addition of accounts and stories suitable for young people. As will be shown, the editors likewise worked on the ideological reframing of the books, and they applied censorship to religious and historical-political content.[25]

Relations between the JNF Head Office and directors and the religious groups, mainly Mizrahi, grew tense from 1923 against the background of public Sabbath desecration on lands owned by the JNF. They deteriorated still more from the second half of the 1920s as the *Hityashvut ovedet* (agricultural workers' settlement) grew in size, as may be seen in the JNF correspondence.[26] In this light the friction and conflicts surrounding the Youth Library at first are understandable, and this led to religious censorship of the booklets for youth.

It began when Ya'akov Berman, the religious schools' supervisor, read Sverdlov's aforementioned monograph *The Dead Sea*. He was shocked

by the heretical ideas in it and in January 1929 wrote to the JNF Youth
Department to inform it that religious people would boycott the Youth
Library since it contained 'things which do injury to matters of faith and
religion. For example, one should look in the booklet on the Dead Sea by
Sverdlov, page 12, line 5 (from the top)'.[27] The Head Office was aston-
ished by the reaction of the religious people to the booklet and at once
informed Ussishkin about it. They also replied to Berman stating that
they did not understand why religious circles were so disturbed by the
monograph, which presented scientific data of the geology of the Dead
Sea. These referred to the evolution of the southern lake after the northern, resulting in the destruction of settlement in the region; the aftermath
of these occurrences was told in the Biblical story of Sodom. Ya'akov
Berman, in his capacity as supervisor, held an important position that
could influence the distribution of the Youth Library literature, so Ussishkin
asked him to apprise him of all the passages in the booklet that he believed 'do not suit the religious views and the educational needs of the
ultraorthodox schools'.[28]

The official approach by the head of the JNF directorate to the chief
supervisor of religious schools raised the discussion to a higher level, the
political one. Berman seems to have passed the matter on to Avraham
Yitshak Hacohen Kook (1865–1935), the Chief Rabbi of Eretz Yisrael,
who sent a very sharp letter directly to Ussishkin. In it he attacked not
only the particular booklet on the Dead Sea but the very right of the JNF
to involve itself in the publication of literature at the expense of money
for the redemption of Eretz Yisrael; furthermore,

> The essence of this literature burns what it cooks up in public and spreads false
> ideas which oppose the holiness of pure belief, and in so doing it introduces
> new, additional currents of destruction, to what already exists in excess, to
> protect ourselves from, and, thus, makes the whole project odious. . . . So I
> respectfully insist that you put a stop to this painful thing . . . [and that the JNF]
> pursue its unique, sacred cause, which is to use its money to redeem the holy land
> from strangers. . . . I hereby sign in honour and admiration for your esteemed self
> and your marvellous deeds, awaiting your early and respected reply.[29]

Rabbi Kook praised the members of the JNF directorate for their work of
redeeming the land, but demanded that they utterly cease squandering
monies assigned to that purpose on heretical literature. Four days later
Ussishkin sent a long letter of reply to Rabbi Kook.[30] He began by ex-
pressing surprise at Rabbi Kook, who was known to be careful and mod-
erate, for passing judgement on such an important public matter without
a thorough investigation and on the basis of rumour alone. Most of the
letter was devoted to an explanation of the rationale of the work of the
JNF: since its income came from contributions, people had to be influ-

enced 'with much propaganda on a large scale and in different ways'. 'Our soldier-workers', wrote Ussishkin 'are youth throughout the world so we must influence them'. Here the president of the JNF expounded before the Chief Rabbi the necessary totality of the JNF's work among children and youth: 'And in the work one should begin when they are still at a tender age'. To socialise the younger generation, literature was needed concerning matters of Eretz Yisrael, telling about life in the land, about Hebrew settlements, about the great people who built them, and the like.

In effect, Ussishkin intimated to Kook that the revered Rabbi and the religious public were perhaps aware of the importance and value of the diverse charitable institutions, and how to approach the faithful, but they did not fully grasp the value of the JNF and its work methods. They did not know how to reach a public that had to be swept up by a new concept. Clearly, no one could excite the sympathy of millions of Jews to the notion of redeeming the land of Eretz Yisrael only by 'rattling the box'; the best way to capture the hearts and minds of the masses was through written material. Here Ussishkin alluded to one of the basic premises of the Propaganda and Youth Department: the importance of the written word as a major means of influencing the attitudes of the target community. The importance and continued functioning of the Youth Library had to be understood in that light.

About a week later Rabbi Kook replied to Ussishkin, pointing out in his letter that the historical and secular approaches were maladies that had to be cured, and that one must not encourage their spreading by publishing heretical material. To prove to Ussishkin that this was not an isolated case of a book about the Dead Sea but an all-embracing system, Kook wrote: 'Nor does the report that a piano was played on the Sabbath at Kibbutz Eyn Harod fill us with respect or affection, and to what purpose does the JNF literature give this prominence?'[31]

Rabbi Kook concluded his letter with a demand that Ussishkin ensure that such things did not recur. Obviously, for him it would have been preferable for the JNF to stop producing books, thereby diminishing the distribution of heretical ideas by an institution whose task it was to redeem land. Ussishkin could not accept this extreme position but was obliged to give the religious establishment some satisfaction. He therefore requested Rabbi Meir Berlin (1880–1949), a JNF director, to join the editorial board of the Youth Library and to read all the manuscripts, in order to 'make sure in practice that in future there will be no place in the Youth Library for such mistakes'.[32] A 'religious censor' was thus added to the library's editorial board under pressure from Ussishkin, 'and he read every book before the material was printed'.[33]

As noted, throughout the existence of the Youth Library religious censorship continued. From the nature of the developments just described, three factors seem to emerge that caused the JNF decision makers to accede to it: (a) A 'national state' outlook: the JNF was an institution for all the Jewish people, so it was obliged to preserve peace and harmony by not offending different sections of the nation. (b) By the same outlook (as shown in previous chapters), the JNF propaganda machine treated the religious public as a separate population, and published special propaganda material for it; the Youth Library episode may be placed in the general context of propaganda for the religious sector. (c) The commercial factor: the desire to overcome the impediment to book distribution by gaining access to the Mizrahi schools and youth.

Censorship on Historical Events

Concurrently with the problem of religious censorship, the library's editorial board had to concern itself with the approval of authors and the printing of particular content about the history of Jewish settlement in Eretz Yisrael that was controversial. Here too censorship was applied, but now it was political and historical. It has to be stressed yet again that the actual choice of subjects and writers was meticulous, so that monographs published through the Youth Library would contain subject matter acceptable to the heads of the JNF organisation. Bistritski attests that this was so right from the initial stages of the library: 'After all, we must be careful not only with the content of the booklet but also with the name of the writer'.[34]

One of the writers the JNF tried to commission for the Youth Library was Ze'ev Jabotinsky (1880–1940). He was offered several subjects, which he turned down, while others that he suggested were rejected. Jabotinsky's exclusion should be seen in the setting of the different interpretation he gave to the Tel Hai episode and the importance of Yosef Trumpeldor as an exemplary national hero.[35] As noted in chapter 3, during that period the Propaganda Department produced the first stamp to memorialise Trumpeldor. The entire issue was sensitive in terms of its social and political interpretation; accordingly, the JNF personnel were not prepared to accept Jabotinsky as the writer of a monograph on this subject.

One of the conventional methods of political censorship used at the stage of rewriting for publication was the deletion of material and informing the writer only afterwards. The booklet on Nahalal, written by a founder of the *moshav*, Shmuel Dayan (1891–1986), illustrates this. According to the JNF editors the manuscript contained 'polemical material against the kibbutz. . . . Thus we saw a need, from the standpoint of both education and of JNF prestige, to remove all the controversial material and leave only the material which positively explained the essence and value of the moshav'. Bistritski informed Shmuel Dayan of the above only after he gave instructions to Smititsky (the language editor) to remove the offending passages from the text.[36] Bistritski wrote to Dayan explaining that the Youth Library was not a forum for any kind of political body, and therefore was prohibited from publishing polemical material so as not to damage the JNF.

The JNF was extremely careful with sensitive details of the Nili underground in the First World War, a subject that arose time and again in the preparation of a booklet on the history of Jewish settlement at that time;[37] the editors had already been obliged make censorial decisions regarding previous booklets. Bistritski approached writers and explained the problematic nature of dealing with the Nili Affair. They reacted by removing the subject from their manuscripts since the JNF was forbidden 'to enter into subjects on which there was no general consensus'.[38] The Nili affair, however, appeared in other booklets, for example, the monograph on the Hashomer (Guard) organisation, written about the Zichron Ya'akov settlement.

In summarising the Youth Library, credit must be accorded to the great achievement of the Propaganda and Youth Department in the actual creation of this project, applied for the purposes of information, propaganda, and education over a long period of time. The importance is due to the creation of an important stratum in the historiography of Jewish settlement in Eretz Yisrael from the standpoint of the organisation and of course its directors. Throughout the entire existence of the Youth Library the JNF was criticised by various bodies on account of the monographs it published, despite its policy of being cautious in the printing of 'things controversial'.[39] In fact, the monographs perpetuated a certain ideology in which the heads of the organisation believed and which they spread in different ways through the Propaganda and Youth Department. Throughout their years with the JNF, Ussishkin and Bistritski saw the library as a vital project that could not be abandoned. Their held the library to be vitally important for the socialisation of the younger generation. Yet beside these achievements the distribution of the booklets was a colossal failure, caused by several factors:

a. The Head Office, which usually distributed its propaganda materials in Eretz Yisrael and the Diaspora, did not succeed in changing the custom of supplying the target population with material written about Eretz Yisrael gratis.[40] Those active in the field took the view that the institution had yet again produced its usual propaganda material; its form may have been different but its content and goals were not. Thus the expectation was that the Youth Library literature would also be distributed at no cost; when it was offered for sale the number of buyers was low.

b. It is not clear why Bistritski and his people assumed that the number of subscriptions in Eretz Yisrael and throughout the world would be several thousands. Even after it became clear that the number of subscribers was very small they continued to produce editions of 3000 copies each. Only the first five had reprints, and they were bought at full cost by the JNF and sent to the national offices to increase awareness of this medium.[41] It also appears that the editorial board did not correctly estimate the amount of organisational effort needed for the regular publication of a series of books in the numbers they had undertaken to produce annually.

    c. Although the goals of the Youth Library had been defined when it was founded, the JNF seems to have created a publishing house of uncertain constitution and laden with multiple roles. The library thus found itself in the situation of being unsuited to deal with any of the various demands. On the one hand it was supposed to be seen as an educational library—but the books were not written as textbooks. On the other hand the idea was for the library to be a form of documentation of the approach of the Jewish settlement and its leaders—but the historiography and the level of critical thinking were questionable. The material was not even edited as ordinary propaganda that had to be relatively brief and carry clear messages. Despite the use of vowel signs, the books' Hebrew language was heavy going, unsuited to the ages of those who were supposed to read them, principally in the Diaspora, a fact brought to the Head Office's attention as early as in 1928.[42]

    d. The library had been planned to deal with four areas, but it was not clear what the exact topics would be, and in practice the books that were published did not appear as the result of precise and consistent planning. This situation became even worse over the years when it was not possible to publish the number of books promised to the subscribers; this was on account of objective reasons (the anti-Jewish events and the World War) as well as JNF organisational reasons. Other problems concerned the booklets' content and their being deliberately written 'in the spirit of the JNF'—a circumstance that drew much critical fire from various circles, and this adversely affected circulation.

As with the attempts to produce games and toys, the mix of a commercial firm like the Omanut publishing house and a propaganda organisation was not successful. Ussishkin and Bistritski, who saw the literature project as an important and legitimate activity of the organisation, were unable to sever the link with the commercial publication and replace the Youth Library with something else. The material capital (money and work) they had invested for years in the Youth Library was for them profitable in terms of 'symbolical capital' (prestige and legitimisation); they did not see the Youth Library as a failure that had to be dismantled.

Chapter 5

'Trapped in Their Dream': Visual Mass Propaganda

Early Stage

One of the hidden dilemmas accompanying the development of propaganda media for all the JNF target populations over a long period was the quandary of written as against visual propaganda, 'the written word versus the picture'.[1] In the development and application of propaganda means such as books, games, and booklets of different sorts, the JNF Propaganda Department worked with conventional means, the chief innovation being in the areas of content, design, and distribution methods. The Department's belief in the written word did not falter: the staff assumed that the Jewish target population would be moved by a written text because of their religion, which indeed was manifested through the written word. The JNF staff continued to develop and distribute written forms of propaganda. In these cases they were on solid and familiar ground, as distinct from the case with other forms, such as visual propaganda, which had developed rapidly since the beginning of the twentieth century. The improvements and technological innovations in printing pictures in newspapers and books, and the different forms of projecting images, were not lost on the JNF people. From the very creation of the organisation there had been awareness of the existence of visual media and the possibilities of exploiting it for the purposes of Zionist propaganda. In the period under study we do indeed detect attempts to develop a new approach to the Jewish and Zionist world of the time through the exploitation of visual propaganda in its various forms: pictures, stamps, transparencies, filmstrips, movies, and the like.

The visual propaganda of the JNF, like that of other Zionist organisations, was intended to serve defined ideas through pictures of narrow range of subjects: the landscape of Eretz Yisrael, which represented both the Zionist dream and its realisation, and the countenances of the illustrious leaders and personages who had worked for that realisation.[2] The leaders of the Zionist movement were made aware of the use of such pictures as visual propaganda in a set of proposals published in November 1899 in the Zionist newspaper *Die Welt,* written by Avraham

Neufeld, although several other investigators had suggested it too.[3] Recall that the public screening of the first moving pictures in the world had taken place only four years before the above proposal was written, yet the possibility of using it for the purposes of Zionist propaganda was already being discussed.

The reactions to Neufeld's proposals tell us that awareness already existed among the Jews about visual media, expressed in the custom of decorating Zionist venues with pictures of the assemblies and postcards of Zionist scenes that had already won 'a place of honour in every album'.[4] Even the ultraorthodox Jewish community in Russia was exposed to the technological innovations of screening pictures with a magic lantern, as attested in another response.[5] Neufeld's proposal aroused a great deal of interest and Herzl favoured it, encouraging the preparation of a film about Eretz Yisrael. But in practice one senses that very little was done by the Zionist institutions in the first and second decades of the twentieth century to prepare propaganda films.[6] Up to the end of the First World War the Zionist institutions used various private productions for propaganda purposes. Still, in that period various connections were made concerning production and the desirable visual content for presentation as Zionist propaganda.

In this chapter I briefly review the production of the first JNF films, and then move on to another area, namely a unique JNF effort: the development of visual propaganda through the medium of projecting via the magic lantern and the filmoscope. One must reiterate that JNF functionaries such as Julius Berger and Nathan Bistritski, and their assistants, were engaged simultaneously in all propaganda forms and methods. For them these were diverse means of transmitting the desired messages of JNF propaganda. They were incapable of differentiating between the various forms of propaganda, and transferred their customary thought patterns and work premises from the field of written propaganda to the field of visual propaganda. They persisted in the practice of having lectures accompany the screening of static pictures, transparencies, and filmstrips.

The First Propaganda Films

The history of the Hebrew film in the 1920s and 1930s has been described in a number of articles, which highlight the role of the JNF in this industry.[7] The direct involvement of the organisation in 'real' films began in 1921, when it purchased the film *Shivat Zion* (Return to Zion) from Ya'akov Ben Dov (1882–1968), added a few scenes, and distributed it as its first moving picture, titled *Eretz Yisrael hamithadeshet* (The Land of Israel Renews Its Life). This film was in great demand throughout the Zionist world and was shown in many places. The JNF made a profit from ticket sales as well as from collecting contributions in the cinema theatres. The success of the first film created enormous expectations for this medium at the Jerusalem Head Office. The JNF officials tended to believe that they had the power to create 'real' films that would be profitable—both economically and still more as propaganda. Their belief prevented them from pondering some of the criticism submitted from various JNF national offices, for example, from New York in 1923:

> We cannot use the films for direct income from entrance ticket sales. Similar attempts with films from Eretz Yisrael were made many years ago and two years ago by individuals and companies wishing to make a profit, and nothing came of it. . . . [Our] hardworking [operatives] will not waste their energy and time for questionable income because, as you yourselves understand, it will be difficult for your film to compete with Charlie Chaplin and other film stars.[8]

Still in that year, 1923, the second film was already produced, this time made directly for the JNF by Ben Dov; this was *Eretz Yisrael hamitoreret* (The Land of Israel Awakens). The film documents a journey to Eretz Yisrael by a Jewish-American tourist called Blumberg as it traces his steps. The director was an American Zionist by the name of William Topkis. In both films animated sections were inserted for the direct propaganda purposes of the JNF. They show coins and banknotes making their way into the Blue Box. The JNF propaganda was present not only in the film's footage but also in accompanying texts, which were read aloud to the audience at each screening; afterwards donations were collected in Blue Boxes.

In 1923 too, in the summer, Julius Berger, who for several years had managed the office of the Zionist newspaper *Die Welt* and was close to journalistic propaganda work, took up his position as chief of the Propaganda Department in the Head Office in Jerusalem. While the Department and its work methods were still in the throes of reorganisation in the early months of 1924, filming began of a third movie called *Palestina hayeshana ve'eretz Yisrael hahadasha* (Old Palestine and the New Land of Israel). It was produced through contributions from the Danish Zionist Organisation, which dispatched the Danish director and photographer G. Zumerfeld. He apparently intended to make a film about Eretz Yisrael from a religious point of view. The film blended in animated sections about the Blue Box that showered money upon the land, redeemed it, and saved the pioneers struggling in the swamps.[9] In this script Berger used a device then common in JNF propaganda, namely anthropomorphisation of the Blue Box.

The third film proved a disaster because of its weakness technically and in content. As a result, in February 1925 a discussion took place in the Head Office about the feature films. The minutes indicate the premises for future work to be carried out by the JNF staff in the area of the content of the visual propaganda.

In reality, the collection [donation] methods of the JNF can be introduced into every film, it is nothing but a question of deft stage management. The main thing here is the principle itself: if we need to and can show the coin from both sides, in one film—both Eretz Yisrael and the Diaspora. I think the nation is yearning to see Eretz Yisrael, what is developing and being created there, to see it in the form of a live story with a strong romantic foundation. It is possible to provide every narrative with a prologue and epilogue which show the Diaspora and its work for the JNF but to leave Eretz Yisrael as the central core of the film.[10]

The Head Office staff believed that they could introduce propaganda into every visual production, and this belief influenced all the work methods for the next twenty years. They apparently relied upon the power of the camera to produce 'a true representation' of the reality, which would accord with JNF propaganda. This outlook seems to have rendered them incapable of distinguishing visual documentation from institutional propaganda. This is evident in films produced and financed by the Head Office. Here the JNF propaganda operatives by no means veered from the norm; this was not the only case where a documenting camera served the purposes of different outlooks.[11]

To those present at the meeting it was clear that the production of feature films with plots was beyond the financial capabilities of the JNF, so they recommended turning to another institution, Keren Hayesod, for the purposes of cooperation. That fund wasted no time in the race for control over Zionist propaganda, began to produce documentary films itself. This cooperation between the funds yielded several films, the most famous being *Aviv be'eretz Yisrael* (Spring in the Land of Israel) in 1928. Together with this the JNF staff continued in an additional direction, the production of short films using cheaper filming methods (a narrow film-strip). By this method several films were produced in the late 1920s and the 1930s.[12]

At a meeting of JNF and Keren Hayesod representatives on 19 May 1929, the discussion centred on policy regarding on the subject matter of films and JNF propaganda. It was decided to start negotiations with a film company to introduce current material about daily events in Eretz Yisrael into the newsreels they screened in movie houses throughout the world. A certain sum of money was budgeted for this purpose.[13] The filming of current events was quite common even before this; for example, the JNF had signed an agreement with Ben Dov (1928) to make a short film about the beginning of the planting of the Balfour Forest and the High Commissioner's visit there.[14] The Arab riots (the 1929 disturbances) hastened the recognition that there was a need to film short newsreels as well. As a result the Head Office examined the possibility of cooperation with the Paramount film company in the production of short films about current events in Eretz Yisrael.[15] During the 1930s and the 1940s the JNF and Keren Hayesod continued to support the newsreels produced in Eretz Yisrael, such as Natan Akselrod's *Yomanei Carmel* (Carmel Newsreels).[16] For all the desire and effort to develop a movie industry for the organisation's propaganda, the JNF realised that it had to vary its visual propaganda equipment, and also use simpler, cheaper, and less extravagant means.

The Magic Lantern Experience

When the JNF staff undertook the development of means such as games and books they were concerned with propaganda for the individual. But when they turned to propaganda by the projection of pictures they entered the area of mass communications, and this was new to them. An opportunity to examine and experiment with this propaganda approach was provided by the Zionist congresses, where pictures of Eretz Yisrael were projected; such was the case at the Fourth Zionist Congress in London in 1900.[17] One of the popular lecturers at the congresses who used 'light pictures' was Dr. Heinrich Levy, who first visited Eretz Yisrael in 1895 and who, after the rise of Nazism to power in 1933, emigrated there and worked for the Tel Aviv Municipality. Earlier, at the Ninth Congress in 1909, he gave a lecture using a magic lantern in which he stressed the role of the JNF in Eretz Yisrael. A year later the JNF decided to invest in this area of propaganda, and distribute Levy's lecture and the transparencies for the use of others who requested them. Dr. Levy, who became the JNF's authority in the area of propaganda using the magic lantern, gave another lecture at the Tenth Zionist Congress (1911), which was reported in detail in the British-Zionist magazine *The Zionist*.[18] The magazine notes that Dr. Levy projected pictures of houses, streets, and farmsteads in Israel and, using his powerful voice, emphasized the role of the JNF in building them. The hundreds present, according to this report, felt a pride and brotherhood that would not quickly be forgotten. As a result of this experience the participants at this Zionist congress adopted the propaganda method of using the magic lantern.[19]

The JNF began to distribute Dr. Levy's lectures for the use of lecturers and propagandists. We learn this from a report in an issue of the Zionist Organisation's newspaper *Haolam* (The World) five months after the Tenth Congress.[20] The report notes that the positive influence of these lectures was already noticeable, especially in circles that previously had evinced no sympathy for the work of the JNF work. As a successful example of an event like this the newspaper reported on the use made of these transparencies at a Hanukah party in a Köln Hebrew School where six hundred children and their parents and relatives saw the sights for the first time and listened to the lecture about the lives of fellow Jews on lands acquired by the JNF and in other settlements in Eretz Yisrael. 'This act should be seen as a shining example', the article stated, noting that what was done in Köln could be done in the hundreds of Jewish educational institutes and schools throughout the world. 'By means of the moral value that exists in presenting the pictures, they are bound to bring in considerable concrete aid to the institution of redemption. And in truth, the spirit of the light pictures has amassed considerable sums of money for the national fund in several cities'.

The goals of the visual propaganda never changed throughout the entire period, and the Head Office made many attempts to adapt the developing technology of picture projection to its needs. Even before the First World War the magic lantern was considered a modern and efficient instrument for transmitting the messages of the JNF to the wider public (see Figure 5.1). Despite fluctuations in the use of this instrument in the period under discussion it seems to have had several technical advantages such as mobility and simplicity. These made it the common propaganda instrument of the JNF operatives. With this simple machine it was possible to present pictures at schools, clubs, or private homes. Similarly one could use the same pictures for the preparation of slides and filmstrips for presenting different contents. Since this method of propaganda accompanied a written lecture, the latter could be recycled, and 'instead of not having the technical possibility of presenting the pictures one could, at a pinch, also use the interesting content of the lecture to give a speech without pictures'.[21]

The preparation of propaganda material for magic lanterns was obviously cheaper than doing so for the varied equipment for projecting movies, and this was also one of the reasons for the frequent use of the former means. Along with the economic and technical advantages in using the magic lanterns for JNF propaganda this mass communications method had the quality of bringing things to life, an effect consisting of several components.[22]

The visual experience. Today, when visual communication is an inseparable part of daily experience from infancy, it is hard to imagine life at the beginning of the twentieth century when visual communication was rare. Only a century ago viewers were greatly excited by the exposure to large pictures shone onto a wall of a far-off land. Recall that this was a time when electricity had not yet reached every city and village where Jews could be found, and the very projection of the 'light pictures' was itself an experience that left an indelible impression on the watchers. It is difficult to reproduce the feeling of those gathering at a Zionist meeting, seated in a darkened hall, when suddenly, as if by magic, on the wall appear in unnatural size the living images of the leaders of Zionism, followed by real pictures of different places: Petah Tikvah, Rishon Letzion, Jerusalem.

All for one and one for all. The JNF used the visual means of communication at propaganda meetings to foster a sense of fellowship in all present. The meeting turned into a tradition of inner contact within the community. This type of experience became manifest at meetings called for this purpose or on other occasions when adherents of Zionism convened, for example, school celebrations. People of similar outlook and shared interests came together, and during such meetings the feeling of cooperation and unity of the individual with the whole was strengthened.

At such meetings the ideological messages penetrated the hearts of those present with relative ease because of the dynamics that developed between the 'preacher' and the audience, and within the community itself. These feelings at secular Zionist meetings were akin to those at regular religious events at synagogues. The religious Jewish community was often exposed to the experience of the gathering, where the individual becomes emotionally elevated when listening to his 'guru', the rabbi. The tradition of the gathering and the role of the rabbi in delivering the message to the community probably entered the Zionist secular meeting, where propaganda messages were delivered by the 'preacher' who also used visual media.

The experience of the spoken word. In the light of the above one can understand the working premise of the propaganda staff of the JNF and of other Zionist institutions: the way to influence public opinion was through the spoken word, as stated in Neufeld's proposal. The speaker—propagandist, lecturer, emissary—was central to the event, and what he said was its most important element. The pictures, and later the films, served only to reinforce the speaker's words. The content presented in pictures seemed to have no relevance unless it was joined to spoken words. Accordingly, great efforts were invested in the writing of booklets, information sheets, or pieces to be declaimed, which played an important part in the ceremony or at Zionist meetings. These meetings may be seen as secular ceremonies at which typical traditions and rituals developed, nurtured by the JNF operatives.

The purpose of 'the meeting with the magic lantern' was to satisfy expectations for an emotional experience, but it also satisfied intellectual needs—the thirst for information about Eretz Yisrael and what was happening there. The JNF also became associated with the movement of *yediat ha'aretz* (knowledge of the country), which had become very popular from the Third Aliya period onwards. The magic lantern transparencies and the written lectures prepared by the Head Office served the different *yediat ha'aretz* lectures as well as teachers at Hebrew schools in Eretz Yisrael and the Diaspora.

The Golden Age of Filmstrips, 1925–1933:
Expansion of Production

After the JNF Head Office moved to Jerusalem, its Propaganda Department, headed by Julius Berger, began to produce series of transparencies on filmstrips, which they called 'light picture strips' or 'light picture ribbons', apparently during 1925. Their preparation was shared by two centres: the initiative to prepare the film strip and the work of editing and assembling the photographed and written material were in the hands of the Head Office in Jerusalem; technical production was done in Berlin. After copies of the filmstrips were made about a third of them were sent to the Jerusalem Head Office for distribution as promotion while the rest were distributed from Berlin as requested from the national offices and on the appropriate instructions from Jerusalem. During 1925–27 the first six filmstrips were produced in this way. These were: *The Veteran Settlements, The JNF and Keren Hayesod Settlements, The Arab Inhabitants, The Jordan Valley and the Dead Sea, The Woman in the Agricultural Settlements,* and *Twenty-Five Years of the JNF.*[23]

With this a new chapter in JNF's visual propaganda with the magic lantern began; this was not merely a change in projection technology (a sequence of transparencies on a filmstrip instead of single transparencies) but a broadening of the distribution system as well as changes in the propaganda featured. Compared with the previous period, many more copies of each series were prepared, and dozens of the last two listed (*The Woman in the Agricultural Settlements* and *Twenty-Five Years of the JNF*) were distributed within a relatively short time of each other. The circle of distribution grew, with the addition to regular subscribers (in Berlin, Vienna, Warsaw, Amsterdam, London, and Zurich) of those in Buenos Aires, Milan, Paris, New York, Salonika, and Baghdad. At that time the Propaganda Department staff considered the filmstrips, which were screened by filmoscope, more effective than single transparencies, since they could edit them and write lectures suited to their outlook and needs. The expansion of distribution and the increase in the number of filmstrips without doubt also had to do with the intensive activity of the Head Office in regard to schools and youth and to the appointment of Bistritski as the man in charge of these matters. Over the next five years (1927–32) more than a dozen filmstrips were produced, which were also adapted for use with youth. Their theme was life in Eretz Yisrael from different points of view: *Sport and Physical Culture, The Jewish Child in Eretz Yisrael, Holy Days and Festivals in Eretz Yisrael,* and *Public Life in Eretz Yisrael.* Other filmstrips described the fauna and flora in Eretz Yisrael, *The Produce of the Land,* or its regions: *The Jordan Valley* and *A Journey through the Jezreel Valley.*

To prepare the filmstrips the JNF officials approached writers and journalists throughout Eretz Yisrael, as they did for the booklets of the

Youth Library at the same time. They presented the potential writers with the idea of the filmstrip and asked them to write the lecture in a suitable literary style. The letters containing the proposal were not the only ones exchanged between the actual writers of the filmstrips and the Head Office staff; they corresponded about further clarifications regarding the appropriate content of the lecture. The instructions for the preparation of the filmstrips and for writing booklets for the Youth Library are evidently similar, meaning both were the work of the staff of the Propaganda and Youth departments. As with the Youth Library booklets, the 'correct' message and contents also guided the scripts accompanying the magic lantern.

At the end of the 1920s the JNF Education Department in New York established a special committee for the distribution of magic lantern lectures. The committee displayed great interest in the preparation of the transparency strips themselves. The Head Office in Jerusalem began to adopt the suggestions emanating from New York in the preparation process. For example, in 1930 Eliyahu Epstein instructed the committee in Berlin responsible for the technical production of the filmstrips to use the suggestion of the American Education Department to introduce the following statement at the beginning of each filmstrip: 'This lecture is one of a series of lectures prepared by the JNF Head Office in Jerusalem'. Another message would appear at the end of the filmstrip: 'The JNF redeems the land of Eretz Yisrael'. The reason for introducing these statements, Epstein wrote, was that some recipients used the pictures but did not mention the name of the JNF, which had produced them.[24]

In 1930 the chairman of the American committee, J. Lapson, sent a detailed proposal to Jerusalem suggesting the preparation of new transparency filmstrips on different subjects, for example, Yosef Trumpeldor, the geography of Eretz Yisrael, the archaeology of Eretz Yisrael, schools, products of Eretz Yisrael, relations between Jews and Arabs, and Yemenite Jews, as well as filmstrips on different regions in the country.[25] Some suggestions were adopted by the Jerusalem JNF operatives, who approached different writers with the request to prepare lectures and select pictures for the new filmstrips and directed them as to the proper content for each.[26]

The filmstrips meant for educational activities in New York were made fairly quickly, and by 1933 many had been distributed to institutes of education and Zionist youth throughout the USA; some of them were new and special but most had been previously prepared in Jerusalem. However, the Jerusalem Head Office did not keep up with the rate of producing new filmstrips as requested by the American committee, so the committee began to prepare them itself. The first were *The Hebrew University, A Day in Deganya, The Oranges of Eretz Yisrael,* and *The Feast of Tabernacles* [*Succot*]. The Head Office in Jerusalem had no alternative but to reverse matters, and inform Berlin that they could use the filmstrips made in New York for editing and distribution to the rest of the Zionist world.[27]

The lively activity of the American committee was encapsulated in the slogan 'Say it with pictures', which was distributed on special booklets to organisations such as Hadassah, Mizrahi, Jewish schools, Jewish teachers' organisations, and youth movements. These booklets presented not only the filmstrips and their contents but also simple operating instructions for the filmoscope, 'which any child can operate'.[28]

The advantages of the filmstrips as opposed to the simple transparencies were also presented: 'They do not break, do not get mixed up, they are cheap and always ready to use'. From these booklets one learns that, despite the emphasis on the importance of the lectures for explaining the content of the pictures, the intention of the American committee was to convince people that the filmstrips could be exploited for different purposes and so become available to a larger circle of users.

The Written Lectures: An Illustration

As noted, every filmstrip was made according to a certain scenario arising from the central theme of the written lecture. An illustration of the lectures prepared during the period under discussion is set out below, and it will help us discern the considerations applied in the editing and propaganda messages emerging from the Head Office in Jerusalem. The lecture was for the filmstrip entitled *Hayeled ha'Ivri* (The Hebrew Child). Among the competing productions of national scenes in the 1920s and 1930s, the photographing and filming of children and youth in kindergartens and schools was a common sight. For example, even before Yaakov Ben Dov filmed his movie *Kfar hayeladim* (The Children's Village) for Keren Hayesod (1930–31), the JNF initiated the preparation of a short film for domestic cinematograph machine in 1928.

A year before these events the Head Office made a filmstrip of fifty transparencies titled *Hayeled ha'Ivri be'eretz Yisrael* (The Hebrew child in the Land of Israel: How the Jewish settlement raise their children).[29] The transparencies were arrayed in keeping with the lecture, which was divided into twenty topics such as: the Zionist woman and her part in the building of Eretz Yisrael, clinics for pregnant women, children's houses in the village and in the kindergarten. The method was to construct the story's continuity on two motifs that contributed to each other, through the dramatic thesis and antithesis. By means of the first motif the writer made the uniqueness of the 'Hebrew child' stand out by contrasting him with two other types of children, the Diaspora child and the Arab child.[30] Through the dramatic motif a kind of tension that led to a climax at the film's ending was generated along the narrative storyline.

Some examples follow. The lecture was naturally aimed at a Jewish audience in the Diaspora, so at the very opening the writer is unstinting in his words explaining how bad things are for his audience in the Diaspora and how much they are endangering their children's lives:

> From the day of his birth the Jewish child in the Diaspora bore the suffering of double suffocation: the bad air of the poor, cramped ghetto and the poisonous air of the police around the ghetto. The field and valley, the forest and the river, which belonged to others, were his enemies, waiting to ensnare his soul. In this suffocation his body and spirit withered. Sharp-witted, skinny, pale, and nervous, the youth thus entered his life.[31]

The writer goes on to say that some Jews, indeed, did immigrate to the USA, where there seemingly was less hatred; other Jews live in Eastern Europe in little villages and there they are close to nature. But only in Eretz Yisrael can the real revolution in children's lives take place: 'Here there is the happy confluence of all the conditions needed to make future generations healthy in body and soul: *nature* [emphasis in the original], the fresh sea breeze blowing through hills and valleys; and *work*—especially work on the land, the basis for life'. The story of the Hebrew child is a deterministic story, according to the world view the JNF presented in Hebrew child as a filmstrip of social and environmental determinism.

Environmental determinism emphasizes the connection between the human's physical and spiritual development and nature: in the Diaspora, in the stifling air of the urban ghetto, children weak in body and spirit grow remote from nature. In Eretz Yisrael, by contrast, '[Hebrew] children grow under the wind-swept sunny sky, surrounded by greenery, flowers and trees, a part of all that is both animate and inanimate in their environment'. And no wonder—since such conditions produce 'exemplary human beings, like this young man projected before us in picture no. 16', which is headed 'a typical healthy and happy child'. The writer of this lecture is indeed conscious of the apparent flaw in the environmentally deterministic approach: if it is the environment that produces healthy children, why are the Arab children not as successful as the Hebrew children? In answer he furnishes his audience with socially deterministic causes: the Arabs corrupt their children and their health themselves. They do not take care of their pregnant women or of the health of their children, who grow up in conditions of 'filth, fleas, skin diseases, which often lead to blindness. The baby's tears and saliva stick to his face unwiped, and swarms of flies remain unmoved from his eyes and nose all day'. To prove his claims the lecturer presents the first transparency and says:

> In picture number one we see a group of Arab children, rolling around among bare rocks, under the scorching rays of the sun, the babies among them with unprotected heads and all with bleary, diseased eyes. And it is no wonder that the child mortality rate among the Arabs is so high.

So right at the opening of the film the thesis on the importance of the JNF endeavour is presented: in the Diaspora the hills and mountains do not belong to the Jews, so they are cut off from nature, which is so vital for raising healthy, happy children. By contrast, in Eretz Yisrael the JNF, which purchases land there, gives the Jews the opportunity to live a life of happiness in nature. It even makes sure that what happened to the Arab children (rolling around among bare rocks) will not happen to Hebrew children: the JNF is planting forests on the wastelands of Eretz Yisrael and is making the land flourish. Later in the film pictures of educational institutions and Jewish children being cared for are presented. Simultaneously the lecturer supplies data about the education and health systems of the Jewish settlement. Steadily, the lecture and the filmstrip build up to their finale: this is the festival of *Tu Bishvat* (The New Year for the Trees) and *Hag habikkurim* (The First Fruits harvest festival) in Jezreel valley:

> The girls of Beit Alfa [a kibbutz] come out dancing lithely before a crowd of children, clustered under the shade of the trees [*picture* no. 48]. And when you see these daughters of Israel growing in the air of work and culture next to *picture* no. 49—a Bedouin girl with an eye disease, also dancing her fantastic dance in the centre of the field—then you realise that, in fact, the nation's dedicated and systematic care of its younger generations has accomplished much.

The subject of The Hebrew Child was thus one of the favourite themes for the visual propaganda of national funds. It was an easy subject to photograph, but more especially it carried symbolic significance, as stated by R. Elboim-Dror: 'The children and youth who were born and educated in Eretz Yisrael served as the most concrete test of the Zionist dream to produce a new human. The youth of Eretz Yisrael, the product of the Zionist revolution, epitomised the deep cultural revolution experienced by Jewish society in the modern era'.[32]

    To sum up, the years 1925–33, in the JNF Head Office and its representative offices in New York and Europe, the preparation of transparency filmstrips for magic lanterns experienced a phase of development and diversification. The filmstrips covered many areas of life in Eretz Yisrael, and a great organisational effort was made to turn them into a familiar and useful tool for use in all Zionist institutions: community gatherings, schools, youth movement, and more. This period may perhaps be seen as the golden age of this form of propaganda. But in 1933–34 a crisis began to develop in the use and distribution of the filmstrips, as is evident from the correspondence of the Head Office during these years and later.

The Years of Disappointment and the Continuation of Production: 1934–1947

After the years of great progress, and after the lectures and magic lantern transparency filmstrips were put to practical use, a different period began, marked by budgetary problems at the Head Office and the different JNF offices abroad, and by competition from other forms of propaganda. Nevertheless, efforts continued to improve and adapt the content of the material in the filmstrips to more specific goals and to connect with other production facilities, together with attempts at new distribution methods.

The more widespread use of filmstrips in New York and Berlin in the early 1930s was not matched in Eastern European cities. Letters from Poland, Lithuania, and elsewhere described problems in obtaining and distributing the transparency filmstrips (see Figure 5.2). The main reason given was economic: the filmoscope was far more expensive than the simple transparency projector or the epidiascope that projected ordinary pictures. Most of the JNF offices in European countries, Asia, and South America could not afford to participate in financing the filmstrips, whose influence there was perhaps slight, so interest in them fell.

The production of the filmstrips and lectures by the Head Office thus entered a blind alley during the second half of the 1930s. The head of the Propaganda and Youth Department apparently did not correctly assess the department's ability to manage many propaganda instruments at one and the same time in the difficult economic circumstances of the time. The relations of the Jerusalem staff with the JNF operatives abroad were ambivalent, and although the poor economic situation of the national offices was well known, blame for it was placed on the work methods they applied. The Head Office did not seem to realise what was happening in the field and, in its opinion, this situation had come about because of the negligence and laxity of the functionaries in the different offices.

In their attempts to encourage the distribution of the lectures and filmstrips, the Head Office staff invariably took as their standard an ideal behaviour model produced by the German office. In their appeals to the national offices the Jerusalem staff frequently wrote about the success of the German lecture and filmstrip project. The cultural similarity between the Head Office people and those in the German organisation, their co-operative work relationship, and the production of the filmstrips and other aids in Berlin apparently contributed to this approach. The Head Office staff held that other countries should imitate the industriousness of the Germans, and this would finally bring success to the lectures and filmstrips. Letters from the Head Office suggested that enthusiasm for moving pictures might be damaging to the demand for the JNF's lectures and transparency filmstrips.[33] These were the days when visual culture in the world was moving from the era of silent to talking pictures (1927), and the movie was becoming a mass phenomenon with millions attending cinemas every week. Accordingly the Jerusalem JNF staff found it appropriate to praise the German Zionist public, which was also exposed to the new visual culture but nevertheless flocked to the lectures, which were accompanied by the magic lantern alone. They wished to ensure this kind of behaviour in the other countries, through the agency of the local JNF personnel.

The propaganda officials at the Head Office were also trapped by the basic conception of what the desirable content of the propaganda filmstrips should be. They saw no need to introduce changes in the aims of the lectures and filmstrips that had been set in previous decades. They continued conveying organisational messages through depictions of *Building the Land* or *The Pioneers,* in which the contribution of the JNF was emphasized. The redemption of the land in Eretz Yisrael as the supreme goal of the organisation necessarily elevated the importance of village life and agriculture in the propaganda message in general and in the filmstrips in particular. The Head Office did not conceal this fact—quite the contrary: in instructions for the writers of the lectures and filmstrips it highlighted it. So it is no wonder that from 1935 to 1939 the Head Office went on to produce several more films of classic content: *The Working Woman in the Land of Israel, The Valley of Jezreel, The Hula Valley, The Shepherds' Life, Along the Jordan, The Antiquities of Israel.* These films were aimed more at propaganda among youth and in schools and some of them were made with the help of Keren Hayesod and the Joint Committee for Educational Affairs. At the same time the turbulent political events of the period led them to try to bring out filmstrips with more political messages, and they produced two such filmstrips: *In the Campaign* in 1938 and *To the Borders of Galilee* in 1939.

For all the Head Office's organisational and financial efforts to produce a range of filmstrips on subjects at the very heart of JNF propaganda, these were not widely distributed, either in Eastern European or English-speaking countries. As a result a return to the production of single transparencies rather than filmstrips was recommended.[34] Although these recommendations had economic and methodological justification they contradicted the basic premises of JNF propaganda: the control of content through the use of the filmstrips was greater than through single transparencies. The recommendations were not carried out and the Jerusalem propaganda staff continued to explore filmstrips as the optimal solution for JNF visual propaganda.

In Eretz Yisrael the use of the magic lantern and the JNF's filmstrip transparencies was apparently greater than in the Diaspora. Although exact details of the frequency of their use are not available certain facts do suggest such a tendency. As mentioned at the beginning of the chapter, the tradition of lectures on *yediat ha'aretz* (knowledge of Eretz Yisrael) struck root in the various settlements, schools, and youth movements. Some of the JNF filmstrips were suited to this purpose and requests by schools in Eretz Yisrael for filmstrips repeatedly appear in the files. The National Committee in Tel Aviv even took part in the preparation of filmstrips, and made a special filmstrip on its own initiative. A month after the Second World War broke out in Europe the Eretz Yisrael National Committee decided that this was a suitable moment to produce a filmstrip on the JNF stamps, and it requested the help of the Head Office.[35] The filmstrip transparencies on the JNF stamps appeared at the beginning of the 1940s, and during the war the Head Office brought out a few more for use in Eretz Yisrael: *Jewish Prague, Polish Jewry,* and *German Jewry.* These filmstrips were part of the JNF project to commemorate the Diaspora in Europe, parallel to the series 'Stamps of the Diaspora', which appeared at the same time. They also produced filmstrips showing the landscapes of Eretz Yisrael and the months of the year: *The Month of Shevat, The Month of Tishrei, The Month of Tammuz, The Negev in the Past, The Jezreel Valley and Its Conquest.*[36]

At the height of the war the Eretz Yisrael National Committee again approached the Head Office in Jerusalem to resume the issuing of the filmstrips. In October 1944 a meeting of the Head Office staff was called to discuss renewing the production of 'the light picture filmstrips'. To do this they had to '. . . examine the situation regarding the strips we already have, which of them were put together in Eretz Yisrael, which of them can be renewed, how we can organise supervision of the filmstrips and the lectures' (see Figure 5.3).[37] And so about two years later a few filmstrips such as *A Day in the Life of a Kibbutz* were produced for the use of JNF offices overseas.

During the 1930s the Head Office was also active in producing another form of filmstrips, namely of monthly current events, initiated and supported by private capital. The political situation in Germany resulted in the arrival in Eretz Yisrael of two of the main JNF propaganda producers in Central Europe, Dr. Ernst Machner and Otto Walisch, who opened an advertising agency in Tel Aviv. Among other work they had done in Berlin for the organisation, they had been involved in the production and editing of filmstrips. So it was only natural for them to decide to continue in this, and in 1935 they produced a filmstrip each month reviewing events in Eretz Yisrael. Each of these filmstrips contained thirty to forty transparencies, accompanied by explanatory material. The JNF Head Office at once came to the support of this production initiative and encouraged the national offices to order these monthly current events filmstrips, hoping that they would place a regular order for them from the private firm.[38]

The monthly filmstrips produced by Machner and Walisch and distributed by the JNF can be compared to cinema newsreels that for many years were presented in movie theatres before the advent of television. Titles of these filmstrips reviewing the stormy events of the second half of the 1930s included *The Time of the Riots, The Commissions of Enquiry,* and *The Tower and Stockade Period.* Every filmstrip was divided into several parts, each on a specific subject, while the first part dealt with the most current subject.

In 1937, their first year of operations, Walisch and Machner produced about ten news filmstrips, each of them duplicated into thirty copies, the smallest number necessary to cover production costs. Despite the JNF Head Office's attempts at distribution, regular orders and the commitments by the national offices were few and far between; after about a year there were only some seventeen such undertakings. The two entrepreneurs lost a great deal of money, and they appealed to the JNF to change its policy on the filmstrips, and to provide 'not only moral, but also material support'. The Head Office, which knew well that it could not relay all the costs of the filmstrips to the national offices, subsidised the filmstrips. A full subsidy, however, was beyond the budget of the Head Office, which tried to interest other institutions in these filmstrips. Despite the financial difficulties the private entrepreneurs continued producing the monthly filmstrips until 1939, with the outbreak of the Second World War.

After the end of the war in Europe the Head Office in Jerusalem tried to reorganise its propaganda work, and the general secretary, Eliyahu Epstein, wrote to all the JNF offices overseas about the resumption of production of the monthly filmstrips by Machner and Walisch.[39] Epstein set out in details the goals and purposes of these filmstrips, pointing out that they had been very successful in several places where even entry fees were charged to view current pictures from Eretz Yisrael projected by magic lanterns. A few replies arrived during the next few years, but by the end of the period under research the monthly filmstrip project was apparently not renewed.[40]

To sum up the activity of the JNF Head Office in the domain of visual propaganda during the period under study, the differences between the beginning of this period and subsequently are notable. In the beginning, the great influence of the 'magic lantern experience event' on the community of supporters was still considerable—for some because of the actual viewing of 'real pictures from Eretz Yisrael' and for others because of the speeches of the orators. In that period the expectations by the Jerusalem staff of the use of this propaganda instrument rose. Because of the experience in Germany, and later in Eretz Yisrael, the Head Office believed that there was a future in the use of visual propaganda instruments and it sought ways to encourage their use and distribution.

The Head Office staff persisted with the device of the magic lantern, which it regarded as an important means for JNF propaganda, and so, during the period studied, they produced more than sixty filmstrips and accompanying lectures.[41] However, when this production was at its peak, in the summer of 1928, Halperin understood (from the Propaganda Department workers) that it was possible that the magic lantern had become outdated, and he wrote the following to Bistritski:

> In my opinion, in these days, when moving pictures rule, it is no longer possible to interest the public, even the children, in light pictures. A child frequently visits the cinema and, after his eyes have become sated with moving pictures of a sensational nature and complexity, he will no longer be interested in the miserable pictures of our magic lanterns, and the JNF pictures will not move him. We have to find a way to introduce moving pictures into schools and show the youth the views of Eretz Yisrael we want to as attractive, heart tugging moving pictures.[42]

Various professional and budgetary problems prevented the realisation of Halperin's plans, but the Jerusalem office staff was not sensitive enough to the changes that had taken place in the expectations in a segment of the supporting community of visual propaganda following their exposure to moving and talking pictures. During the 1930s movies with stories were part of mass culture in major cities throughout the world. For Jews exposed to this culture the magic lantern was no longer a 'stunning event'. In addition, the content conveyed by the JNF filmstrips had clearly not changed for years and the supporting public had received the same pictures and slogans for many long years in other forms of propaganda produced by the Head Office.[43]

A negative effect seems to have been sparked by the JNF propaganda, and it put the public off. This type of resistance had also arisen in regard to the stamps, when schoolchildren wearied of sticking them into contribution booklets. The Head Office personnel remained trapped in their dream and in their conceptions of what material was right for the filmstrips.

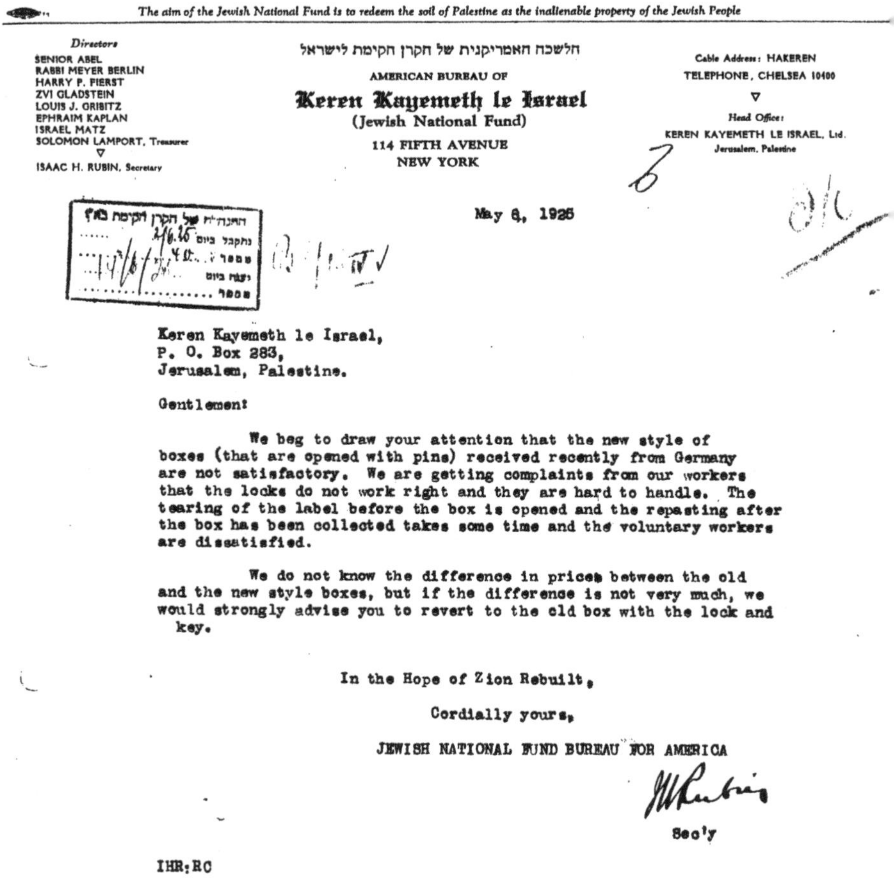

The aim of the Jewish National Fund is to redeem the soil of Palestine as the inalienable property of the Jewish People

Directors
SENIOR ABEL
RABBI MEYER BERLIN
HARRY P. FIERST
ZVI GLADSTEIN
LOUIS J. GRIBITZ
EPHRAIM KAPLAN
ISRAEL MATZ
SOLOMON LAMPORT, Treasurer
ISAAC H. RUBIN, Secretary

הלשכה האמריקנית של הקרן הקימת לישראל
AMERICAN BUREAU OF
Keren Kayemeth le Israel
(Jewish National Fund)
114 FIFTH AVENUE
NEW YORK

Cable Address: HAKEREN
TELEPHONE, CHELSEA 10400
Head Office:
KEREN KAYEMETH LE ISRAEL, Ltd.
Jerusalem, Palestine

ההנהלה של הקרן הקימת בא"י
נתקבל ביום 2/6.25
מספר
יצא ביום
מספר

May 6, 1925

Keren Kayemeth le Israel,
P. O. Box 283,
Jerusalem, Palestine.

Gentlemen:

We beg to draw your attention that the new style of boxes (that are opened with pins) received recently from Germany are not satisfactory. We are getting complaints from our workers that the locks do not work right and they are hard to handle. The tearing of the label before the box is opened and the repasting after the box has been collected takes some time and the voluntary workers are dissatisfied.

We do not know the difference in prices between the old and the new style boxes, but if the difference is not very much, we would strongly advise you to revert to the old box with the lock and key.

In the Hope of Zion Rebuilt,

Cordially yours,

JEWISH NATIONAL FUND BUREAU FOR AMERICA

Sec'y

IHR:RC

Figure 2.4. Letter of complaint from the American Bureau of the JNF about the quality of the boxes made in Germany, 1925 (Source: Central Zioniost Archive, KKL 5, file 232)

𝕾outh African Zionist Federation. ·ה הפררציה הציונית דנגב אפריקא.

JEWISH NATIONAL FUND
(KEREN KAYEMETH LEISRAEL LTD.)
קרן קימת לישראל.

PHONE 3106.
P.O. BOX 18

TEL. ADDRESS
"ZIONFED."

All cheques must be made payable to
" Jewish National Fund."
A printed and numbered official receipt
is sent for all remittances.
All communications must be addressed to
THE ORGANISER,
JEWISH NATIONAL FUND.

CENTRAL OFFICE FOR SOUTH AFRICA:

PROGRESS BUILDINGS.

COMMISSIONER STREET,

JOHANNESBURG.

BY AIR MAIL.

19th October-1934

The Head Office,
Jewish National Fund,
JERUSALEM.

Dear Sirs,

      I have to acknowledge receipt of the specimen Box of the new type by last mail.

      I must say that I do not like this Box very much, nor do the few members of my Committee, and other individuals to whom I have shewn it. While the innovation of a map of Palestine on the one face is an advantage, the attempt at modernistic design on the back face is, in my opinion, undiginified, nor is the blue and white effect impressive.

      On the other hand the look of this box seems to be considerably superior to that of the old type. It is firmer and more difficult to wrench or prize open.

      I notice, however, that none of the keys of the old box fit this specimen. I take it, however, that a new type of key also will have to be distributed. This would cause obvious confusion between the old box and the new. I strongly doubt whether my Committee would agree to supplementing the old box by the new; nor do I think they would agree to introducing this new box at all.

      Should it be possible to combine the Map on the new

Box with the simple and dignified appearance of the old Box, and with, of course, the better lock, I think this would be a valuable means of developing "Box Work" in this country, which is languishing, partly, I have no doubt, owing to the poor quality of the old boxes.

With Zion's Greetings,
Yours faithfully,

ORGANIZER.

Figure 2.5. Letter of protest from South Africa about the new design for the Blue Box with the map of Eretz Yisrael, 1934 (Source: Central Zionist Archive, KKL 5, file 6247)

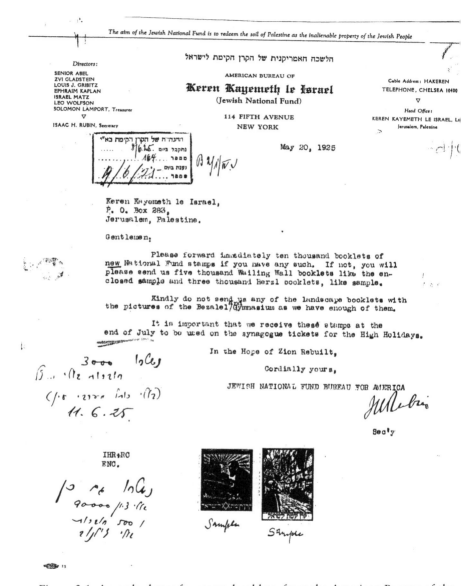

Figure 3.1. An order letter for stamp booklets, from the American Bureau of the JNF, 1925 (Central Zionist Archive, KKL 5, file 232)

Figure 3.2. Leopold Schen, the head of the British JNF Office, addressing a new settlement in Palestine, 1943 (Photographer: Dinar. Source: Photo Archive JNF-KKL, Jerusalem)

Figure 3.3. The disassembled stamp-map of Jerusalem drawn by Sapoznikov, 1930 (Central Zionist Archive, KKL 11, Godkowski stamp collection)

Figure 3.4. Sketch for the Yosef Trumpeldor memorial stamp, 1937 (Photographer: A. Melavski. Source: Photo Archive JNF-KKL, Jerusalem)

Figure 3.5. Sketch for the Degania stamp, 1930 (Photographer: A. Melavski. Source: Photo Archive JNF-KKL, Jerusalem)

Figure 3.6. Sketch for the Hanita stamp, 1938 (Photographer: W. Christaler. Source: Photo Archive JNF-KKL, Jerusalem)

L/R/241/97   AIR MAIL   2nd Nov.,1936

Rabbi J.Schwartz,
Montreal,

Dear Rabbi Schwartz,
                    Children's Games
            Some years ago inquiries were made from us by certain
countries as to whether a Palestinian game of lotto for children were
available or whether such could be prepared. With the co-operation of
the Palestine Teachers' Council for the J.N.F. a game of this kind is now
being prepared, based on the devices of the general game of lotto, with a
Palestinian motif. There will be 12 coloured illustrated cards each
containing different Palestinian scenes. The artist preparing the
drawings is Mr.Nahum Guttman. The object of the game will be to tell
the history of the immigration to Palestine of a Jewish family of
two adults and two children, and of their adventures in Palestine from
the moment they land.

            The size of each card will be about 8" x 11". The work
of the Keren Kayemeth in Erez Israel will, of course, be adequately
represented.

            Apart from this information and the additional fact that
the Palestinian Teachers' Council for the J.N.F. considers the game a
fascinating and useful one, we are unable at the moment to give you
further information. Before embarking on the final issue of this
material, however, we should like to learn from you whether you believe
that such a game could be popularised in your country. Until you see
a specimen and are advised of the price you cannot, we appreciate, place
a definite order. But you will no doubt be able to intimate in
principle whether such a game could be disposed of in Canada. Please
let us have your reply by Air Mail as soon as possible.

                        Thanking you,
                        Yours sincerely

                                    Secretary, English Dept.

Figure 4.1. Letter from Jerusalem to the Canadian JNF office about children's games, 1936 (Central Zionist Archive, KKL 5, file 7482)

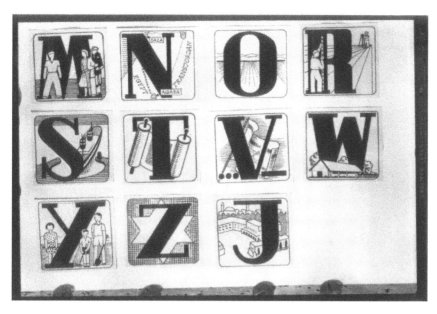

Figure 4.2. Draft for an *aleph-beth* card game, 1945 (Photographer: A. Melavski. Source: Photo Archive JNF-KKL, Jerusalem)

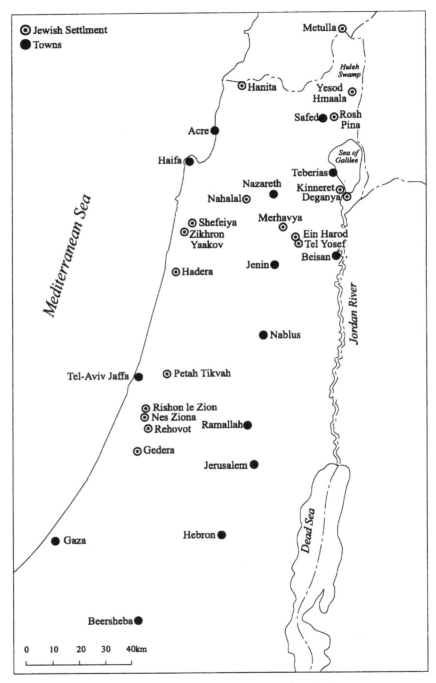

Figure 4.3. A map of northern Eretz Yisrael, 1940 (selected place-names)

Figure 4.4. Yosef Weitz, one of the Head Office staff in Jerusalem and author of many books of the JNF library, 1948 (Photographer: Dr. Rosner. Source: Photo Archive JNF-KKL, Jerusalem)

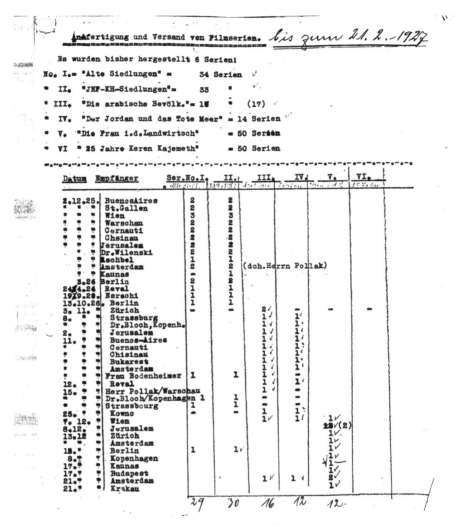

Figure 5.1. A world-wide distribution list of film strips, 1927 (Central Zionist Archive, KKL 5, file 965/1)

PALESTINE FILMSLIDES

A Jewish Educational Project
for the
Hebrew School,Sunday School, Club Meeting and the Home

Produced by the Head Office,, Jewish National Fund,Jerusalem

What Are Palestine Filmslides?

They are strips of film containing series of beautiful pictures taken in Palestine.

How Are Palestine Filmslides Shown?

1) On a screen or ordinary white wall.

2) By using any filmslide projector made for a standard width(35mm)film.

What Preparations Are Necessary?

1) None - but **familiarity** with the subject as described in the lectures.

2) Teacher,club leader or lecturer should read the lecture before each showing and,if possible,project the filmslides privately in order to be fully familiar with the subject matter.

3) Lecturer may add personal observations or experiences based on reading or visits to Palestine. This always helps to make a lecture more successful.

The Palestine Filmslides have been endorsed by leading Jewish educators and institutions.

Subjects: The Woman Pioneer; Child Life in Palestine;Religious Life in Palestine; Communal Life in Palestine; 15th Shevat; Redeeming the Soil; Fauna of Palestine; Theodor Herzl; Recreation and Sports; A Trip through the Emek; Festivals and Important Events in Palestine.

In the U.S.A.apply to:PALESTINE EDUCATIONAL COMMITTEE
Chairman:Judah Lapson   Secretary:Joseph Shaffer
71 West 47th Street,New York

Figure 5.2. A flier about the Palestine Filmslide. Issued by the Palestine Educational Committee, New York, mid-1930s (Central Zionist Archive, KKL 5, file 6195)

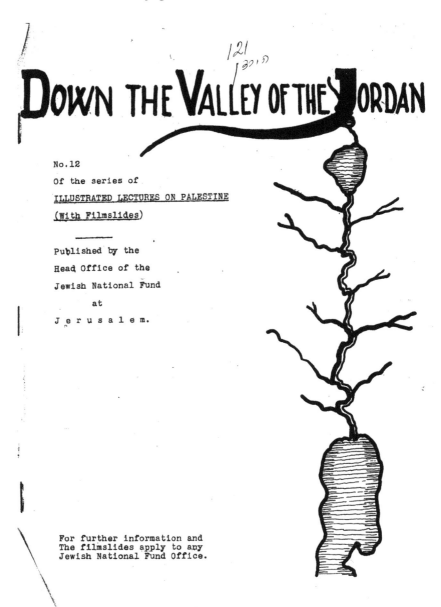

DOWN THE VALLEY OF THE JORDAN

No.12

Of the series of

ILLUSTRATED LECTURES ON PALESTINE

(With Filmslides)

Published by the

Head Office of the

Jewish National Fund

at

J e r u s a l e m.

For further information and
The filmslides apply to any
Jewish National Fund Office.

Figure 5.3. Front page of the illustrated lecture booklet on the Jordan Valley, 1936(?) (Central Zionist Archive, KKL 5, file 4810)

Figure 6.1. The 'Holy Trio': Sabbath candles, the Blue Box, and the slogan 'Redeem the Land of Eretz Yisrael' (in Hebrew). From a pamphlet issued in Jerusalem, 1937 (Central Zionist Archive, KKL 5, file 7501)

Chapter 6

The JNF Culture: Blue Box
Ceremonies and Rituals

The JNF Culture

A very important and integral part of the JNF's propaganda work was aimed at altering the behaviour of adults, children, and young people. This can be seen as a process of socialisation, the changing of attitudes and approaches in the general spirit of Zionist ideology and outlook as formulated by the JNF and its various agents in particular. These processes were introduced into the daily activities of the adult public in formal and informal education in Eretz Yisrael and the Diaspora, producing what we shall term the 'JNF culture', which had behavioural components, social codes, and special ceremonies. The JNF culture, centred on Eretz Yisrael and the organisation's symbols, was part of an entire system of social change that developed during the period under study. In this respect the JNF was arguably one of the important agents of the creation and internalisation of the new Hebrew culture, its symbols, and its products. It was part of the 'cultural opposition' that contributed to the crystallisation of Hebrew culture in Eretz Yisrael.[1] Specific ceremonies, behavioural norms, and a range of texts distributed by the JNF became the cornerstone of the official (even canonical) culture of the Yishuv in those years. Evident examples are school festivities, money collection campaigns in the streets, and the popularisation of the songs of Eretz Yisrael.[2]

The JNF culture presumably contributed to forming the character of Israeli *civil religion*.[3] Those who use this term refer to the similarity of features between religions and their ceremonies and the development of national rituals. 'The God that the believers in civil religion worship is the nation, the state, the homeland. . . . The fact that Zionism was a national revolution, which drew upon symbols, myths, and folklore from ancient Jewish history and the Bible, only strengthened the religious character'.[4] Accordingly, in the case of a sort of *civil religion,* defined goals are also sanctified and a social order is legitimised. In this way the concepts associated with it are sanctified, ceremonies are created, traditions of doing what is proper are established, and a diversity of myths are created.

On the premise that the JNF culture displayed civil religion (or *civil culture*), it clearly created rituals also. In every religion the object of the ritual is charged with great symbolic value, to the point of sanctification and becoming sublime. This sanctification gives rise to rules of behaviour and deeds that are to be done by the members of the community who are committed to the ritual. The object of the ritual blends into the social-cultural fabric and gives special importance to the totality of the ceremonial activities connected to it.[5]

Clearly, one of the important components of the JNF culture's ceremonies was the Blue Box ritual, which became an almost metaphysical, sublime symbol, not only of the organisation but of the whole Zionist national revival. The aim of the Blue Box, as a symbol and object of the JNF ritual, was to link the individual to Zionist values such as nationhood, land, sacrifice, contributing to the community, and so on. This ritual, in which a money box became a kind of cultural icon, was not a random process but arose out of the belief of the Head Office personnel that it was the spearhead, the true symbol of their organisation, by means of which they would conquer the hearts and pockets of their admiring public.

Apart from the box they employed other methods to maintain their presence everywhere at all times. They aspired to establish an intimate relationship between themselves as a Zionist institution and the wider public, an ambition that yielded a vast array of communication means: newspaper advertisements, bazaars, participation in events and exhibitions, lectures, excursions, and so on. In the creation of the JNF culture a feeling of national patronage was apparently communicated: 'You have someone to rely on'. The patronage was not only broadcast on the political level but was even produced by the intimacy that developed between the JNF and the public through simple elements such as the birthday greeting cards that children received from the JNF, or the decorative tree planting certificates, which were sent to mark a joyous celebration such as Mothers' Day and which were displayed in the living room at home.

Out of the enormous range of cultural elements mentioned we have chosen to present several forms of the box ritual. In this chapter the discussion will focus on the different ceremonies that were developed through their inspiration and definition as a national mitzvah (duty), the donation of money to the JNF. We shall examine how JNF propaganda was blended into the ceremonies and how decorations were devised according to the domain, whether of the individual (a person's home) or of the public (classroom, school, and community institutions). In fact, the different practices arose from the same motives: raising funds to carry out missions, to insure the organisation's survival, and to nurture the prestige of the institution, its heads, and its activists.

The Box Ritual in the Individual Domain

Ritual service is usually conducted at specific places and times by a given religion or culture. The ritual is characterised by several elements: the object of the ritual and its presentation, decor and setting, ceremonies, performance of actions and duties, a community of believers, and 'priests'. Under these defined conditions of time and place ceremonies (the rituals) take place and commemorate the beliefs, values, and philosophy they represent. One of the important characteristics of every ritual is its separateness in time and place from everyday life in order to emphasize the unique sanctity of the ritual object. In contrast to classical ritual objects, in the case of the Blue Box the separateness in time and place was not so clear. On the one hand, elements of sanctity and separateness are evident in it. Just as the Torah scroll is taken out of the holy Ark in the synagogue only during worship, and is placed upon the prayer pulpit, so in schools the Blue Box was only taken out during ceremonies of greeting the Sabbath and was placed upon the table next to the lit candles. On the other hand, the JNF functionaries wanted the Box Work to be everywhere all the time, and they aspired to turn the ritual object into a Zionist icon, something that would be the hallmark of every Jewish home. This is illustrated in the following tale.

Little Joel was used to looking for a Blue Box in every Jewish home, believing that there always was one. Once he went with his mother to visit an acquaintance. As was his habit he looked for the Blue Box and couldn't find it. Joel went up to his mother and whispered into her ear: 'Look, Mummy, we are in the house of Gentiles here, but they have a *mezuzah* on every door!'

'Why do you think that this is a house of Gentiles? The people who live here are Jews', his mother replied.

'If they were Jews they would have a JNF box in their house!' Joel said.

The next day the acquaintance who had overheard this conversation telephoned the JNF and asked them to send a box to her home immediately.[6]

The Head Office distributed the story of Little Joel, which described a situation of conceptual conflict. The story made it clear that having a *mezuzah* on every door was not enough to signify the residents' being Children of the Covenant. Only the Blue Box indicated real Hebrew/Jewish completeness. The Head Office believed that the desirable public norm was a Blue Box in every Jewish home, just like the *mezuzah*. The story of Little Joel exemplifies one of the common techniques of sanctifying the Blue Box: likening it to conventional, widespread Jewish religious-cultural items. The paralleling of the Zionist Blue Box to ubiquitous Jewish cultural items helped to elevate its aura and make it a cultural symbol with historic depth and a lofty ethical and ideological status.

JNF propaganda produced the images for the desirable forms of behaviour among children and young people, as well as earmarking those who belonged to the friendly camp as opposed to the others, unbelievers, strangers. As a result their image of the right decor for a Jewish house always included the Blue Box. A sixth-grade child in a Tarbut school in Poland in 1939 attests:

> Sometimes I go into a Jewish house; the room is adorned with the pictures of our national leaders: Dr. Herzl, Dr. Weizmann, Sokolov, Ussishkin, and others. Under the wall clock there hangs a calendar. But I feel that there is something missing here: the Blue Box is missing, and without the Blue Box, there is no point to these pictures. One *pruta* [a small coin] a day and Eretz Yisrael will be redeemed.[7]

The publication of this letter, like the story of Little Joel, had a didactic purpose. This kind of preaching about designing private living space was typical of the JNF culture and did not end with young people and children. A similar concept of relating to the designing of private living space with the right decor for the JNF culture can also be found in the propaganda booklets distributed by the Head Office to the adult public in a range of languages. In 1936, for example, the opening pages of these booklets presents a black background against which is a table with two large candlesticks with lit Sabbath candles on it, and beside them the Blue Box; behind this array appear the words *Redemption of the Land*. Further on in the booklet the combination of symbols recurs in textual form:

> Like Sabbath candles,
> which have a place of honour in every Jewish home.
> It is both right and fitting that we place
> the Jewish National Fund box
> in a place of honour and importance.
> To honour means: not to put it in a cupboard,
> and not to store it away like a useless object
> in an out-of-the-way corner.
> For if it is visible to all the household
> it will take its rightful place,
> and be a symbol, a reminder of our
> duty to call for deeds every day.[8]

The JNF officials constantly stressed that the conspicuous place of the box in the individual domain was to remind one of one's daily obligation to contribute, just as the Sabbath candlesticks signified the weekly commandment. At the end of the booklet the daily national duty was presented: 'The contribution of five *prutot* will bring redemption' (see Figure 6.1).

According to the Head Office plan, the act of emptying the home Blue Box was intended to assume the character of a brief ceremony. Exact instructions on how to turn the visits into a special event, a small celebration, another meeting of the Jewish public with the organisation and its activities, were given in the sheets distributed to volunteers assigned to the collection of the coins.[9] The volunteer had to be in 'personal and spiritual contact with the box owners', and when he got to their houses he not only had to empty the boxes, but also had to tell the householders all the latest news about the JNF's activities in Eretz Yisrael. Each volunteer had to encourage the householder to make another donation in the future, and had to note the personal attitude of the homeowner to the box by observing its location in the house. If the box stood in a place where it could not be seen, the homeowner was to be advised of the necessity of *'placing the box in a place of honour'*, and this was done immediately 'with their permission' (emphasis in the original) To complete the decor of the 'JNF Home Corner' the volunteer had to ask the homeowner's permission to hang a JNF map next to the box.

The designing of the individual domain, and the box work carried out at home and at school, reinforced the cultural experience for children, turning it into a way of life with clear-cut norms.[10] Procedures like this for the box work even helped bring about unity in the living space of the Zionist home; the organisation's symbols clustered together reminded the householders of their daily duty and informed all visitors that this was a Jewish home, in the words of Little Joel. They were a source of identification with the Zionist idea in general and with the JNF's work in particular. The Blue Box, the pictures of the leaders, and the JNF map of Eretz Yisrael were thus domestic marks of distinction whose presence became a part of the 'natural' landscape of childhood for many people from the 1920s onwards. For them, the box work, the weekly contribution on the Sabbath eve was a normative ceremonial event. These ceremonies, to which young people were exposed, were held not only in the private living space but more especially in the public domain: kindergartens, and schools. In the public domain the act of contributing acquired dramatic amplification, which made it a major ceremony in the Blue Box ritual, which became engraved into the Zionist collective consciousness.

The Public Blue Box Ritual: In the Street and in School

The JNF culture, with its ceremonies, decor, and symbols, seems to have attained greater sophistication in the public domain than in the private. This came about because of the greater ability of public JNF adherents, such as teachers, to exercise control over the design of time and space in schools according to their views and philosophy.[11] The hierarchical structure of the education system aided the percolation of the JNF culture into every corner of the schools: a JNF Corner in the classrooms, special corners in the corridors, mass ceremonies in the schoolyard or hall, and finally going out into the public domain: the street.

The JNF influenced not only the design of the decor in these public spaces but also the design of time in schools, especially the annual organisation of festivals and events. The deep involvement of the JNF in the Hebrew schools in Eretz Yisrael and the Diaspora even transcended this, reaching into the planning of curricula, choice of textbooks, and teaching materials for many subjects such as Geography, Bible, Hebrew, Arithmetic, Nature, and Drawing. To a certain degree the total philosophy of the JNF was realised in the schools with the assistance of representatives and emissaries such as the Teachers' Council of Eretz Yisrael. An analysis of direct JNF involvement and the indirect influence of its various agents on the Hebrew and Israeli school systems is beyond the goals of this work, and many of its aspects have been discussed in previous studies.[12] Instead, we shall concentrate on a number of concrete examples of the Blue Box ritual and the JNF culture from two aspects: the design of the decor in public space and the design of the ceremonies in the education system.

The Design of the Decor: The JNF Corner

At the conference of the Association of Kindergarten Teachers in Tel Aviv in 1944, Mrs. Weissman-Dizengoff spoke about incorporating the JNF into the kindergarten. It was important to create a JNF presence in kindergartens so that this institution would not be an empty concept. The way to accomplish this was through the JNF Corner, which must contain the following:

> *Pictures* of Herzl and Bialik, set permanently at the centre of the Corner; these are our cherished people, like the nation's ministers, who have to be constantly made part of the kindergarten's life. Likewise the picture of Ussishkin, as head of the Jewish National Fund, as the children knew him when he was alive. . . . In the JNF Corner the *box* is hung. This is the object closest to the child's understanding and it plays a real role in the fulfilment of the child's practical obligations. On festivals and Sabbath Eve the box receives a place of honour and it is beautifully decorated. In the Corner one should place plants, saplings, budding plants—in villages but especially in town, as a hint of the connection between the JNF, the land, and the workers of the land. On festival days the flag should be hung flag in the Corner. . . . Before festivals and other important events connected with the JNF all should assemble at the Corner.[13]

The pictures of the leaders, the Blue Box, the flag and articles connected to nature in Eretz Yisrael and the annual calendar were the basic elements of the JNF Corner (see Figure 6.2). The traditional design of these corners evolved over a number of years. At first there was a little corner, in which stood a Blue Box decorated with various slogans. Over time the other elements were added: the leaders, pictures of the Eretz Yisrael landscape, and the rest. The JNF Corner was presented unchanged in this particular form for the whole year, and it soon became clear that the children were ignoring it. The teachers then began to vary it and adapt it to different age levels, having the children participate in its preparation. As a result special elements were added to the corners, such as compositions, drawings, and sketches from the lives of the children and the school, all combined with the materials sent by the JNF.[14] At this stage the JNF Corner was still permanent and its design did not change for the whole year. Its continued failure to retain the children's attention caused the Eretz Yisrael Teachers' Council to recommend a number of changes, the main ones being:

1. To replace the content of the Corner and alter its design frequently, preferably every month.
2. To incorporate the subject matter of the Corner into the curriculum.
3. To move the Blue Box from the centre of the Corner to the side and to present current events about Eretz Yisrael in the centre.

Thus the JNF corners began to emphasize study subjects such as History, Bible, and Geography. The items on display in the corners changed according to the Hebrew calendar, current events in Eretz Yisrael, as well as the yearly JNF calendar of activities. A major change was the transfer of the Blue Box from the Corner's centre to the periphery. This change signified not a devaluation of the JNF by the educators but a change in their approach, to indirect, camouflaged propaganda. Still, JNF propaganda continued to maintain a presence in the Corner, through other exhibits such as maps of settlement, forestation projects in Eretz Yisrael, and miscellaneous drawings.[15]

The idea and design of the JNF Corner were distributed during the 1930s by the Eretz Yisrael Teachers' movement, who deemed the expansion of the Corner sufficiently important to devote a special room in the school to the idea; this was *hadar hamoledet* (the Homeland Room). To achieve wide propagation of the Corner and its design the JNF and the Teachers' Council issued various booklets giving examples and suggestions on how to build them in schools. The recommendations did not only addressed content but also gave practical advice such as the kind of materials needed to establish the Corner. The propagation the Corner idea reached its peak in 1938 when a national exhibition was arranged in Tel Aviv, where 'model corners' were displayed and *hadar hayizkor* (the Remembrance Room) made a great impression. The success of the exhibition and the public interest it aroused led to its being shown in Jerusalem and Haifa; this exhibition is considered a turning point in the distribution of the idea of JNF corners in schools and their form.[16]

The Corner thus became a place for assembling national symbols, a sort of little temple of the Zionist movement. The change of the Corner's decor added a dynamic to the school's decoration and played a part in the passage from the secular daily activities to the 'holy' work. The Corner was located so as to be exposed to the view of most pupils and visitors, not tucked out of the way. In some schools it was placed near the entrance or next to the teachers' room and the school office. In many ways the Corner acted as the school's showcase, and symbolised the level of the school's and the teachers' loyalty to the Zionist idea and the philosophy of the Jewish National Fund. From the JNF's point of view the Corner was everywhere a sort of local monument to the organisation that constantly displayed its projects to hundreds of thousands of Jewish schoolchildren. It was not a one-time static monument (such as an exhibition), but a dynamic one exemplifying the momentum, activity, and strength of the organisation and its ideas.

The Planning of Ceremonies and Festivals

In addition to the decorations in the school space, the JNF Propaganda Department influenced the planning of ceremonies and festivals, at which the 'box ritual' reached its mighty climax in the process of Jewish socialisation. These ceremonies were institutionalised behavioural frameworks conveying diverse values and messages, utilising the drama of the event.[17] Since the ceremonies were a conventional means of demonstrating unity, solidarity, and commitment to the basic values of the collective, they were adopted by the Teachers' Council for their activities in the school system.

The content and form of the festivals were not devised in one fell swoop. As early as 1928 the Head Office began to produce and distribute booklets for the festivals and holy days, and likewise commissioned texts, plays, and songs from a range of writers. The members of the Teachers' Council collaborated with the Head Office staff in collecting and processing material. In the second stage the first festivals were celebrated in the form suggested to different schools; lessons were drawn from this experience, so that the set formula for the festival crystallised over time. The suggestions for ceremonies appeared in many publications issued by the Head Office or the Teachers' Council, and these contained the texts, commentaries, directions, instructions, and plan of the ceremony, as well as guidance on the appropriate decorations.[18]

By the 1940s, standard, agreed ceremonies were held throughout the Jewish educational network, centred on the JNF and its symbols; the JNF's presence was felt in discussions and songs, but particularly in the duty of dropping a contribution into the box. Shoshana Sitton states that although the celebrations and festivals were customary in Hebrew schools in Eretz Yisrael at the time of the first *moshavot* (private landholding settlements), their consolidation as an inclusive educational unit was the product of the late 1920s and 1930s, and it was inspired by the Teachers' Council.[19] For their curriculum in ceremonial experiences the members of the Teachers' Council adopted the methods practised in Jewish religious education, discarding the usual religious significance of those methods. They saw religious education as a fully realised totality, based on the inculcation of certain daily activities that would become inseparable parts of a person's personality.

The approach of those involved in Jewish education was to reverse the 'direction of flow' of cultural practices. They wanted it to flow from the school to the home and the parents. Such a reversal could come about by the creation of a cultural bridge, and it was achieved by means of the system of celebrations that had begun to develop in the schools. The Teachers' Council understood that a central element in traditional education was the festival, with the preparations for the actual ceremonies serving as climactic experiences in the life of the child and helping her to internalise Jewish values. They saw the festivals as a kind of mechanism for strengthening social feeling and identification with the ideas of the collective. They believed that the festivals broke down the barriers within the school and created feeling of camaraderie among teachers, schoolchildren, and parents; such an atmosphere was conducive to the absorption of messages and values. They knew that the special aura of the festival, so different from the mundane, radiated holiness and reverence, endowing the messages and values with awe and a halo of sanctity. In the course of formation of the cultural tradition of Jewish education on festivals and manner of their celebration in schools, several criteria arose that influenced the planning of the ceremonies. They were to be celebrated according to the Jewish festival calendar; the uniqueness of each festival was to be highlighted; the unique spirit of each festival was to be emphasized; and the atmosphere created was to affect school's daily routine. The planners likewise stipulated that the pupils had to be active in performing the various tasks connected with the festivals.[20] The pupils' activity concerned their chief duty, which they had to carry out as part of the various ceremonies: making a contribution to the Blue Box. Despite the decision to highlight the uniqueness of each festival and to avoid the repetition of elements, the contribution to the Blue Box was ever present, becoming an integral part of the ceremonies of the different festivals, a part of the educational ideology (see Figure 6.3).[21]

     For every festival in the Hebrew calendar a ceremonial pattern developed, interweaving topics about Eretz Yisrael, the JNF, and the redemption of the land. Some of the festival's ceremonies took place in the class-room or school, while some were events for an entire settlement with many participants, which demanded a high level of organisation. For these complex festivals, manuals were written containing detailed instructions on proper conduct, dress, and songs, as well as the performance of the tasks connected with the JNF. Examples are tree planting on *Tu Bishvat* (15th of the month Shevat) and the purchasing of the first fruits on *Shavuot* (The Feast of Weeks: Pentecost), all of which have been described else-where.[22] For our purposes we have chosen to demonstrate the use of the Blue Box as an example of how the JNF left its impress on the more frequent lower-key festivals in schools, namely the celebration weekly of *Kabbalat shabbat* (Sabbath Eve) and monthly of *Rosh hodesh* (New Month).

Kabbalat shabbat and *Rosh hodesh*

The ceremony of greeting the Sabbath in Jewish tradition is one of the major rituals that characterise the calendar and determine the rules of personal and public behaviour. It is a deeply meaningful ceremony mark-ing the separation of the sacred from the profane, and its observance is one of the most important religious duties. The designers of secular He-brew education adopted the practice of greeting the Sabbath and blended it into the life of school using traditional elements and adding innova-tions that suited their educational stance. The ceremony was intended to mark the end of weekday activities and separate schooldays from the day of rest. The ceremony was repeated every week and became a regular tradition that left its mark on the experience of childhood; from kinder-garten age onwards the children took an active part in it time after time throughout the year.

During the 1930s, at the Midreshet Tarbut (Cultural Academy) in Grodno, Poland, the ceremony took place before the whole school. A. Lifshitz docu-ments it thus:

> Every Friday during the third hour lessons are suspended in all departments for a few minutes. The school choir takes its place in the corridor and sings the school anthem and *Hatikvah*. The doors of the departments open up to the sound of the melody. The children stand there and listen. The department's [JNF] representative makes his way past the desks with the Blue Box in his hand. Every pupil puts in his contribution. The lesson ends . . . the representa-tives hurry away with the boxes to the school office to empty them.[23]

Lifshitz continues that after the boxes were emptied in the school office, the sums that each class had contributed were written in red ink in a table. The chief JNF representative at the school would leave the office, go to the pupils who were waiting expectantly in the corridor, and hang up the table; and the sound of cheering from the best class 'would burst out along the corridor'. In Eretz Yisrael the practice in schools was to hold the ceremony of *Kabbalat shabbat* during the last lesson on Friday, after which the children would go home.[24]

The ceremony developed a regular form in which variations could be introduced according to the spirit of the times. The ceremony, which was celebrated by each class separately or by the whole school together, would open with Sabbath songs such as *Lecha dodi* and *Shalom aleichem malachei hashabbat*. Later the candles would be lit and the contribution to the Blue Box would take place. The second part of the ceremony would be a discussion on current events in Eretz Yisrael or on the week's Torah portion or the special nature of that particular Sabbath. To maintain a uniform and traditional framework, the ceremony would end with the reading of some psalms or sections from *Pirkei Avot* (Ethics of the Fathers) and the singing of '*Shalom aleichem*', '*Tseitchem leshalom*', and '*Hatikvah*'. In the framework of the *Kabbalat shabbat* five special Sabbaths were marked, as was the practice in the Hebrew calendar. These were *Shabbat bereishit, Shabbat shira, Shabbat shekalim, Shabbat zechor,* and *Shabbat shuva,* and specific content concerning them was added to the ceremonies.[25]

The Eretz Yisrael Teachers' Council assigned an occasion to the act of emptying the boxes, namely the monthly *Rosh hodesh* ceremony. In this they adopted a practice already current in schools in the 1920s, itself based on original directions given by the JNF Head Office in 1921. According to those, boxes were supposed to be emptied done four times a year in line with the Hebrew calendar.[26] To promote the idea of emptying the boxes monthly in schools a Box Anthem was composed in 1930. The members of the Eretz Yisrael national committee applied to the Head Office for permission to distribute the anthem to kindergartens and schools. The song became part of the monthly and weekly ceremonies, as the words themselves attest:

> The new month has come
> The new month has come
> This is our holy day
> When we will rejoice and be happy
> Today we will open the Box
> The Box, our Box
> Which redeems our land.
> You increase the fields in the country
> The trees in the hills and valleys.[27]

The association of the box-emptying ceremony in schools with *Rosh hodesh* was no coincidence. According to Biblical tradition special sacrifices were offered on *Rosh hodesh,* trumpets were blown, and beacons were carried aloft to signify the beginning of the month; in synagogues special prayers are added to mark this day. To substantiate the special character of the calendar in the Hebrew schools and to include the tradition of Jewish festivals in it, the planners sought to re-introduce the practice of celebrating *Rosh hodesh* into the school framework.

The day before the ceremony the pupil representatives of the JNF would visit all the classrooms in the school and announce: 'Tomorrow is a month'. For the teachers this was a sign that on that day no homework was to be given, and for the children it was a sign that the next day they would have to make sure that they and their clothes were especially neat and their shoes polished.[28] On the appointed day the ceremony was the same. The children would line up in the schoolyard or hall, sometimes after a short parade at the head of which strode the flag bearer accompanied by two children holding the symbols of the outgoing month and new month. The bearers of the flag and the symbols ascended the stage, upon which the proclamation of the month was made. The proclamation itself was accompanied by the reading of a literary passage; or the children of the class that had excelled in collecting contributions for the JNF during the previous month would perform a song or dance. The ceremony included readings from the Bible, traditional blessings, the blowing of trumpets, and also the presentation of events connected to the season of the year or to an important occurrence that marked the month.

The second part of the *Rosh hodesh* celebration was the box-emptying ceremony. In the centre of the stage, in full view of the children, a table especially decorated for the ceremony was placed, and on it the school's principal Blue Box. Next to the table stood the school's JNF representative. The goal of this part of the ceremony was to announce the class contribution collected during the *Kabbalat shabbat* ceremonies during the previous month and to declare the winner of the class shield for excellence in JNF activities for that month. This part of the *Rosh hodesh* ceremony had a variety of forms, but they all served the same purpose: the public announcement of the size of the collective contribution to the JNF. Then the school's JNF representative would declare from the stage: 'And the land will never be sold, for the land is mine, and you have held all the land and you will redeem the land'. The pupils rose to their feet and repeated those words after him. After reading out the sum contributed by each class, the month's announcer would raise his emblem and say: 'This month the school contributed the sum of . . . to the Jewish National Fund. Blessed be the Lord whose army moves, whose hands are willing'. Then followed the 'Changing of Astrological Sign' event, after which the announcer would leave the stage holding the outgoing month's shield and the announcer of the incoming month would take his place next to the table with the Blue Box. The ceremony closed with the singing of *Hatikvah* after which the new month's sign was hung in the school's JNF Corner.[29]

The Box Ritual: Competitions and Street Campaigns

The Hebrew schools and the formal educational frameworks were a favourable milieu in which the JNF could function in a vigorous manner and establish the characteristic cultural patterns of Hebrew education. In addition, it operated in the non-formal educational frameworks of the Zionist youth movements, where propaganda and commitment to the organisation were more heavily emphasized. Opposition to JNF activity was less in the youth movements than in the schools. In the youth movements the JNF operatives could, in their free time, effect the formation of a committed generation, loyal to the organisation and ready to carry out its missions. In both educational frameworks (schools and youth movements) the JNF strengthened its attraction by introducing competitions and prizes for those who excelled in work with the Blue Box.

As early as the 1920s the staff of the JNF Propaganda Department announced prizes for the holders of boxes containing the largest sums. The various JNF bulletins and circulars announced many competitions and prizes, for example, 'An automobile trip to the new settlement sites which have been established on the land redeemed by the Jewish National Fund (free and including food and accommodation)'.[30]

As we have seen, competitions as a motivating factor for the Box ritual in the educational system was common on the most local levels, namely in the classrooms and schools, and was expressed in the box-emptying ceremonies where the winners received prizes. The competition motive was also translated to the widest level, the national level, with the introduction of the Jerusalem Flag competition in Eretz Yisrael and the Redemption Flag competition in Poland.[31]

With the establishment in 1933 in Eretz Yisrael of the Teachers' Council for the JNF, the Jerusalem Flag competition became a special occasion for the teachers, to be referred to throughout the year in educational work.[32] It was a cyclic ceremony that was deliberately linked to religious events on the festivals of *Succot* (Tabernacles) and *Simhat torah* (Rejoicing of the Law): pilgrimage to the Holy City and marking the end of annual cycle of Torah reading and the beginning of the new cycle. In this competition the schools' activities were tested for their devout adherence to the ideas of the JNF; this was in order to 'consider their failings and call for their correction', as well as to 'provide moral rewards to those groups of pupils who faithfully and constantly preserve Zionist education'. Ussishkin himself in 1933 donated an embroidered flag he had received from the Jerusalem Community Committee, and initiated the idea of the competition: the flag was to be given to the school with the most successful activities each year. From 1933 awards clear criteria were laid down, as well as an intricate set of rules for judging the success of each school's activities in various areas: its contribution to the JNF, the study of Zionism, social life, JNF Corners, the birthday project, links with the Diaspora, and more. The schools were supposed to demonstrate ongoing activities and be among the 'First Seven' for two continuous years in order to win the flag.

The Jerusalem Flag ceremony, held annually in the courtyard of the National Institutes building in Jerusalem was designed as a state ceremony in which elements were introduced that made it into 'a special day of assembly for all the schools in Eretz Yisrael' (see Figure 6.4). Representatives from all the schools in the country and various delegations would make the pilgrimage to Jerusalem and gather in the Institutes' courtyard with their flags. On a raised platform in the centre of the courtyard the 'public fathers' sat: the heads of the Jewish Agency, the JNF, the National Committee, Keren Hayesod, and so on. The ceremony opened with a flag parade, followed by a reading of the Orders of the Day and the judges' decisions. The keynote speech was made by the president of the JNF, a member of the executive of the Jewish Agency, or the director of the Education Department. The best school, the winner of the flag for that year, received a certificate of merit and exchanged greetings and gifts with the outgoing winner of the flag.

The criticism levelled at these ceremonies it was regarded as political, made by the Revisionists who were opposed to the JNF's approach in the Zionist movement. This criticism did not obstruct the ongoing JNF activity in schools, but it seems to have afforded a certain degree of support to teachers and parents who opposed the various methods of JNF money collection, particularly the Box ritual. They saw this as fund-raising and the crossing of the fine line between propaganda and education. Other teachers claimed that children were recruited for the general donation campaigns that took place in all the settlements, and in this way were fulfilling their national duty; they should not be coerced into putting contributions into the box at school.

Together with the national competition for the Jerusalem Flag, young people were recruited in the national level to perform their national duty in the contribution campaigns that took place in the city streets ('ribbon days'). In exchange for the *prutot* (small coins) the man in the street would drop into the box held by a child, he would have a paper ribbon pinned to his lapel upon which was written that he had made a contribution to the JNF. Ribbon days were held at various times, usually on festivals or on anniversaries such as the death of Herzl on 20 Tammuz. Recruitment of children and young people to collect contributions on ribbon days was common already in the early 1920s, and increased as the activities of the JNF Department for Youth and Schools grew. Ribbon days were seen as a positive educational activity in which the children helped the wider public to fulfil their national duty, to contribute to the JNF. As the circle of contributors expanded—from the home to the classroom, and from there to the school—it became perfectly natural to leave the schoolyard for the streets to involve the public in the Box ritual. This activism of the pupils even won a prize from the Head Office: money collecting on ribbon days was made one of the criteria for determining points to win the Jerusalem Flag. In other words, inter-school rivalry as motivation for excellence and achievement and as part of the system of norms propagated by the JNF and the Teachers' Council encouraged schools to send children to collect money in the city streets, sometimes even at the expense of regular studies.

The Box Ritual: Implications

The Sanctification of the Box in Time and Space

Objects or signs that become social symbols are imbued by the society that produces them with meanings that transcend the concrete dimensions of the objects or signs. As social symbols, these objects or signs can function as bridges between worlds, between reality and vision, or as representatives of art, ideas, or values.[33] The Blue Box, with the aid of the Hebrew education system, underwent a certain process of symbolisation: from a useful object to the representation of a national idea.

In evaluating the Box ritual in terms its acquisition of symbolic meaning, we may refer to several features noted in the school rituals described above, namely *Kabbalat shabbat* and *Rosh hodesh*. In both of them there was a conscious attempt to blend traditional patterns into the Hebrew school culture in order to form bridges and connect the children with Jewish tradition. Certain parts of the ceremonies were familiar to the children from their homes and therefore nothing new, while other parts needed to be recreated. The use of well-known, familiar elements in the ceremonies seems to have given them legitimacy, so the parents and children accepted them as a natural, inseparable part of the Hebrew educational system (see Figure 6.5). Yet note that there was some opposition to the activity of contributing money to the Jewish National Fund in school, although it was not 'sharp' enough: this will be discussed further on.

Both these ceremonies had a shared characteristic that arose out of their similar function: to separate specific periods of time that were qualitatively distinct from each other: the Sabbath from weekdays or one month from the next.[34] Every ceremonial separation of this kind has to be accompanied by some action that clearly marks the transition from one unit of time to another. For the Sabbath, the transition is determined by the lighting of candles, while for the New Month Ceremony it is the announcement of the month. So these two events, accompanied by the declamation of texts or by singing, served as the opening stage that proclaimed the transition from the everyday to the holy (with the *Kabbalat shabbat* ceremony) and from past to future (with the *Rosh hodesh* ceremony). These proclamations were in some respects the climax of the ceremonies and produced in the children the exciting feeling of the transition of time. In this state of heightened spirituality, when the feeling of another time was present, the second part of the ceremonies began, the Blue Box ritual: a contribution in one ceremony and the emptying in the other.

During these ceremonies several interesting dialogues developed. First the completion dialogue between the two ceremonies, which were mutually interdependent, and which together produced the unity of time: the filling and emptying of the box as a cultural rhythm that arose out of JNF philosophy. Symbolically, in the monthly emptying ceremony the JNF representative would drop a few coins into the box in front of the audience, to show that 'it should never be left empty'. Another dialogue was that between the events of ancient times, the heritage of the Hebrew Patriarchs, and the present: the Blue Box, set before the children in these ceremonies, acted as bridge across the aeons, for it was perceived as something that brought the great redemption closer through the 'redemption of the land'. This was the most concrete symbol, as their personal actions, the carrying out of the weekly duty by each one of them, could well bring the End of Days closer and realise the national hopes for a homeland.

As previously noted, drama was blended into both ceremonies, connected to national duty: the personal contribution during the *Kabbalat shabbat* and the comparison of the class's collective effort of with that of others in the *Rosh hodesh* ceremony. This was not a form of collecting money that was anonymous, a typical characteristic of some of the Jewish charity funds. Quite the contrary: even schools accepted the JNF's working premise about the importance of making contributions publicly—something practised by the JNF from the very beginning. Accordingly, the public nature of the contribution played a major role in the *Rosh hodesh* ceremony, a factor that subjected to public scrutiny the attitude of the individual pupil and his group to the collective national goals.

As mentioned, the exaltation of the Blue Box in the ceremonies described above was linked to the notion that it was connected with, was a part of, a different dimension of *time* (sacred or cosmic time). This feeling was strengthened by the special organisation of the *space* in which the ceremonies took place—where the box was presented as something distinct in defined space with a different, sublime quality. During the *Kabbalat shabbat* ceremony the Blue Box was placed on an adorned table that was given the aura of a holy space through the lit Sabbath candles.[35] The box gained extra brilliance through the light and fire motifs of the candles, charged with emotional force. The light and fire are common motifs in religious and national ceremonies and ritual: the lighting of beacons, torch parades, or fire and fireworks displays. The light and fire of the Sabbath candles helped imbue the Blue Box with the dimensions of a place that was different (see Figure 6.6).

In the *Rosh hodesh* ceremony too the organisation of the space in which the box was placed helped to elevate it and transport it to other spaces. It was placed upon a table in the middle of the stage, raised and removed from the pupils. This table was usually covered with a cloth, and beside it stood flags and the school's excellent students and selected representatives, who projected their radiance onto the space of the table and the Blue Box upon it. In the *Rosh hodesh* ceremonies the Blue Box on the stage was endowed with a spatial advantage characteristic of sculptures and monuments set atop high mountains, which arouse feelings of adoration and respect in the congregation of the faithful standing below and at a distance from them. The Blue Box as the object of a cultural ritual taking place in the framework of the school was loaded with unique, sacred attributes by its being made distinct in time and space in such ceremonies.

The Personification of the Box

In the course of the construction of the Blue Box ritual, 'the tin receptacle' went through a process of sanctification and personification. Sanctification, as noted earlier, was achieve attaching it to the routine religious-national calendar of events. These produced an aura of sanctity in time and space around the box, while creating ritual manifestations of such concepts as purification, theatricality, and a special liturgy. Parallel to this sanctification, the image of the box was also constructed by endowing it with certain human characteristics that greatly aroused the emotions and suggested the most powerful of positive images. This was achieved by way of literary allegory and it became a central ingredient for the box in the ceremonies and other presentations produced or inspired by the Head Office.

Early in the twentieth century a trend had already developed towards personifying the metal object and turning it into an anthropomorphic creature: one that had feelings and influenced events, as well as having a clear aim that could be imposed upon others. Obviously, the characteristics attributed to the box were only positive, and were transmitted to its human surroundings—even the power to change the natural environment. The box expressed its feelings: it laughed, got angry, felt sad—all according to the various local and national events taking place. Personification of the box was designed not for the level of school propaganda alone but was also probed for use as propaganda for adults. In 1924, for example, when the third film was produced by the Head Office, animated sections were inserted in which the Blue Box was presented as human and appeared as the film's real hero: it spoke, asked for contributions, kissed children, and cried. It acted to save dying pioneers, planted forests for them, and brought redemption to Israel.[36]

Personification of the Blue Box was chiefly accomplished in written texts and in songs and plays written for schools. One of the important texts in the process of personification was written by Dov Kimhi (1889–1961). Entitled *The Tale of the Agurah That Fell into the Slot of the Blue Box, the Box of Redemption,* it was published in a fine edition by the Head Office in 1926.[37] Although the main personification is of the coins, not the box itself, the tale opened up a new genre of texts for children in which the personification of the Blue Box, coins, or trees was common. In this tale the anthropomorphic coins placed in the Box in different countries each related their own story. They told of their survival in the East European pogroms, or of good children who saved their candy money. Some coins there came from America and Africa, but they were all together in the same box, one of the Boxes of Redemption hung on the wall at school.

After the coins' adventures in school are described in great detail, it at last transpires that they will 'roll on and turn into' land, which makes them inexpressibly happy. The tale ends with an account of the final transformation of the coins, their achievement of the ultimate realisation of every Zionist coin: 'Behold we are a dunam of land—in the Valley (of Jezreel) on the way to Ein Harod and Kfar Yehezkel'.

Other pieces and versions of this tale appeared in diverse publications, including anthologies for learning reading and writing at Hebrew schools. In these the personification process was even more explicit:

> The children are playing:
> First child: 'Blue Box, Blue Box standing there sad'.
> Second child: 'Blue Box, why are you standing there sad?'
> The Box: 'The little children have forgotten me. They do not bring a *pruta* every day for me'.
> The children rush off quickly to ask their fathers for a *pruta* for the Box.
> The Box laughs, the Box laughs, the Box dances and dances for joy.
> The Box: 'To Eretz Yisrael, to the beautiful land, I will soon go'.
> The children: 'To Eretz Yisrael, to the beautiful land, we will all go'.
> Children from Eretz Yisrael: 'In Eretz Yisrael the children are happy.
> Thank you.
> 'Thank you to the Box'. They sing.[38]

This text can be considered a classic example of the personification of the Blue Box. On closer examination this is not merely personification but endowment of the box with the image of a woman and a mother (presumably, the fact that Hebrew word for 'box' is feminine assisted in this personification). Of the human images attached to the box, that of the woman, is the most powerfully significant since the woman symbolises fertility, renewal, and blessing; hence in the text above the box (Mother) stands there sadly because the children have not done their duty. They run to Father to ask for a *pruta* to satisfy her, and their guilt feelings fade when they see her (the Mother) dancing with joy. The box is no longer just another 'tin container', an empty volume, a place for storing *prutot*, but a woman who takes the coins into her womb and transmutes them into 'land'. If this is so, the box, as a symbol of fertility, fulfils its function, the enlargement of national land, and so links up with another object that has an ancient, powerful feminine image, namely 'Mother Earth'. To enhance the symbolic significance of the ritualistic ceremonies of the Blue Box in the schools, the two 'mothers' (land and the box) have been augmented by yet another female symbol that possesses sacred dimensions: *Shabbat hamalkah* (Sabbath the Queen).[39]

Thus, the Hebrew educational system helped to propagate the ritual of the Blue Box, which assumed the image of a 'personal rite' (or rather a 'feminine rite'). The Head Office, its emissaries, and the Teachers' Council succeeded in recruiting writers and artists who glorified and exalted its name; and in passing did the same for the organisation itself and its particular and national goals.

Summary

As indicated at the beginning of the chapter, the JNF culture and the Box ritual, which developed over the years, took different forms and were motivated by a certain concept maintained by the organisation: total commitment, loyalty, and unconditional support, which they endeavoured to achieve by creating a Zionist public outlook (see Figure 6.7). Bistritski and the Head Office Staff carried their demands to extremes through their intervention in and influence over the socialisation process, especially in the youth and children's divisions. These youngsters were perceived as clay in a potter's hands, which could be moulded according to the organisation's goals. In their search for a total design they produced various instruments to aggrandise their presence in the public and personal domains, on festivals and every day of the week.

The distribution of the annual calendar to children and young people at events and the range of instruments described and analysed here are only the tip of the iceberg concerning the JNF's activities. Every day they touched the lives of hundreds of thousands of children who studied in thousands of educational institutions in Eretz Yisrael and the Diaspora during the period under review. Their activity encroached on other spheres not deeply probed in the present study. Among these are following: planning of elaborate ceremonies such as the Tu Bishvat celebrations, the Harvest Remembrance, and Hanukkah; collective birthday celebrations for children in kindergartens and school classes, and the distribution of JNF mementos; projects for contributions and remembrance in JNF forests, accompanied by the distribution of artistic certificates; collection of money and inscription in The Golden Book or The Children's Book; supply of decorative materials for studying, placards, pictures, song books, plays, films, wall charts, and diaries; outings and work camps; collection of bottles or paper for recycling; local and national conferences; sending flowers to children in the Diaspora; publication of books, journals, and pedagogic circulars for teachers; and much more.

To reinforce the organisation's positive image and its contribution to the redemption of the nation and its land, the JNF developed the Blue Box ritual. During the period being studied it established its form and characteristics by means of secondary agents of the organisation such as the Teachers' Council and the youth movements. In the planning of the Blue Box ritual the JNF linked the project to well-known, positive elements (religious and national) while making use of visual, audio, and written media, which it consolidated into one network through a collective dynamic. JNF propaganda elevated the Box ritual to the level of a holy national ceremony, which found its way into the public and the private sector, creating new traditions in the design of sites and behaviours in these domains. The propaganda thus brought about identification of the Box ritual with the official and openly declared goals of the institution: 'Redemption of land' and 'The future of the youth'. The importance of these processes exceeded the JNF organisation itself, and they exerted considerable influence on formulation of content, patterns of behaviour, ceremonies, and festivals in the Hebrew educational network and its successor, the Israeli educational system.

Alongside the openly stated level of motives for this activity, there was a hidden level of motives that brought about the creation of the cultural patterns discussed here. I am referring here to the motive of maintaining the prestige of the organisation and its leaders, as well as the motive of organisational survival within the Zionist political system. These motives drove an approach that ensured the presence of the JNF everywhere and at all times; this engendered variety in JNF activities and stimulated much creativity in its publicity and marketing. This hidden level was also responsible for the transition to a different monetary approach, one that became the principal method of raising money for the organisation in Eretz Yisrael; this was the imposition of a 'tax' on the public. It was clear to the leaders of the JNF that the contribution would not be a financial solution to their needs, and to make possible the organisation's continued existence and the execution of its goals, they had to impose several such 'taxes'. This form of income-gathering might have been seen as improper, so the propaganda and information network strove to conceal it, packaging it in an ideological wrapper emblazoned 'The fulfilment of national duty'. If someone did not perform this duty the JNF, in subtle ways or through coercion, would explain to him that it would be better for him not to place himself outside the camp, but to respect the organisation and its 'taxes'.[40]

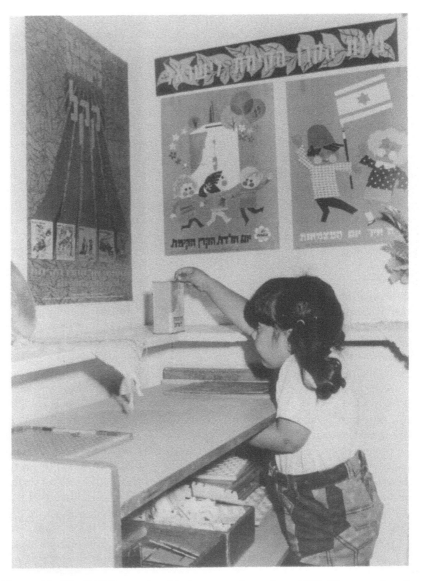

Figure 6.2. The JNF Corner in a kindergarten, Jerusalem, 1973 (Photographer: D. Shefner. Source: Photo Archive JNF-KKL, Jerusalem)

Figure 6.3. Children's donations at the Pentecost festival in Jezreel valley, 1938 (Photographer: Weisenstein. Source: Photo Archive JNF-KKL, Jerusalem)

Figure 6.4. The Jerusalem Flag Ceremony, 1935 (Photographer: A. Melavski. Source: Photo Archive JNF-KKL, Jerusalem)

Figure 6.5. Donation to the Blue Box in a kindergarten, Jerusalem, 1945 (Photographer: Rozner. Source: Photo Archive JNF-KKL, Jerusalem)

Figure 6.6. Birthday card, sent by the JNF to children at the Hebrew school in Eretz Yisrael, 1944: typical JNF propaganda illustrations (private collection)

Figure 6.7. Propaganda poster, with typical JNF slogans, 1945 (Photographer: A. Melavski. Source: Photo Archive JNF-KKL, Jerusalem)

Figure 7.1. The pictorial stamps-map of Eretz Yisrael drawn by Sapoznikov, 1930 (Central Zionist Archive, KKL 11, Gotkovski stamp collection)

Figure 7.2. A typical index of the JNF propaganda maps: distinctions between 'Jewish lands' (broken underline) and 'JNF lands' (solid underline), 1938 (Central Zionist Archive, KKL 5, file 6212)

Figure 7.3. A typical propaganda map emphasising JNF land and the 'no-man's-land' of Eretz Yisrael, on both sides of the Jordan river, 1937 (Photographer: A. Melavski. Source: Photo Archive JNF-KKL, Jerusalem)

Figure 7.4. A modern Blue Box bearing the old map messages (Photographer: D. Shafner. Source: Photo Archive JNF-KKL, Jerusalem)

Figure 8.1. The JNF Executive on a visit to the northern Negev desert, planning to convert the land into a 'blooming garden', 1942. From left: A. Granowski, Y. Weitz, A. Kaplan, M. Berlin (Photographer: Y. Schweig. Source: Photo Archive JNF-KKL, Jerusalem)

Figure 8.2. Symbolizing the wilderness: The Hula valley swamps stamp, 1939 (Photographer: Walter Christaler. Source: Photo Archive JNF-KKL, Jerusalem)

Figure 8.3. Planning to drain the Hula valley swamps, 1950. A. Granowski indicating on the map. Y. Weitz standing to the right of the map (Photographer: Braenhaim. Source: Photo Archive JNF-KKL, Jerusalem)

Figure 8.4. Jezreel valley landscapes on a JNF stamp, 1946 (Photographer: A. Melavski. Source: Photo Archive JNF-KKL, Jerusalem)

Figure 8.5. Otto Walische's 'The five tasks of the JNF', 1937 (private collection)

Figure 8.6. Dancers at Pentecost (*Shavu'ot*) festival in Jezreel valley, symbolizing the richness of the land, 1945 (Photographer: Dr. Rosner. Source: Photo Archive JNF-KKL, Jerusalem)

Chapter 7

Political and Organisational Propaganda on JNF Maps

Propaganda on Maps

The Blue Box was not only a container for collecting coins and foremost an object in ceremonies developed under the inspiration of the JNF, it was also an important instrument for broadcasting a political-geographic message, the declaration 'This is our land'. The message was transmitted by means of a map depicted on the box that was (and still is) captioned *The Map of Eretz Yisrael*—clearly a propagandistic map. As we shall see in this chapter, this map was not just an innocent, ingenuous chart drawn on the contribution box, but a definite political statement, seen every day by hundreds of thousands of children who took part in the above ceremonies. It was a version of what may be called the JNF propaganda map, which appeared in different ways and forms in a multitude of advertisements: on stamps, in booklets, and in learning materials such as wall maps, in JNF films, in series of slides, and more.

Propaganda on maps is nothing new, nor is it unique to the JNF; states, institutions, and organisations frequently use this form of presentation to convey political propaganda or commercial advertisement. These bodies deliberately use the techniques of producing maps in order to transmit their particular messages, or to produce their particular truth.[1] The intentional use of cartography for the purposes of propaganda was discussed in professional literature during the Second World War following the massive use the Germans made of map-assisted propaganda.[2] The Germans discussed the power of maps to present reality in a new light; for them the most important goal for the production of maps was their efficiency in creating communication between the authorities and the populace. They devised means for the transmission of political messages through agreed signs, colours, projections, design of page or text, and so on.

A map is not a divine truth, it is not reality itself, it is not objective: rather it is a representation of the reality that the mapmaker wishes to present. People who peruse maps tend to be uncritical, and they usually become still firmer in their opinions by looking at them. Some give the name *cartographical hypnosis* to this universal phenomenon of blind trust in map representations.[3]

The average person cannot discern and is not even aware of all the manipulations used when maps are prepared, either by the deliberate choice of the information that appears on the map or by the way it is presented. For example, the scale of colours chosen for a map and the level of contrasts applied can serve to emphasize certain details and to eliminate others. An element coloured in a dark, prominent shade on the map will be better perceived by its reader, so it will leave a greater impression than elements in pale, light shades. Likewise in the map's wording, the name of a settlement printed in large letters will indicate its importance and centrality for the mapmaker and will be perceive by the map reader as a more important place.

Daily exposure to maps is extensive and it is dependent on culture and ideology. Maps appear in travel books and atlases; there are road maps, settlement maps, weather maps on television and in newspapers. All of them convey ideological messages, even inadvertently.[4] Daily exposure to the same form of cartographical presentation produces the tendency in the viewer to see it as objective reality. Even if the mapmaker has no ulterior motives and performs no conscious manipulations, by virtue of its being a culturally dependent graphic representation, the map transmits ideological messages like a story, a film, a drawing, or a song. So the map teaches us not only about the reality that it is supposed to present but also about its creator, the presenter. This is true of all types of maps regardless of the techniques of preparation or scale, be they detailed topographic maps, urban maps, or political and settlement maps in an atlas.

Even though a Hebrew map of Eretz Yisrael appeared in that country as early as in 1885, prior to the First World War the Hebrew maps in use there were generally based on a small number of foreign language maps from turn of the twentieth century. These maps were mainly for teaching, and most appeared as addenda to books written about Eretz Yisrael, although there was one wall map.[5] The establishment of the British Mandate, the increase in Zionist political activity, the Balfour declaration, and above all the development of the Hebrew educational network in Eretz Yisrael and the Diaspora created a demand for Hebrew maps. The number of prepared maps of Eretz Yisrael grew during the first half of the 1920s and were even assembled in a Hebrew atlas, the *Jabotinsky Atlas*.[6] For these reasons, in 1922 the Zionist Organisation in London had a map of Eretz Yisrael made in which the text was in English and German; two years later the JNF began to print general maps of Eretz Yisrael.

The Background to Publication of the Maps

The financial investment in the publication of maps by an institution like the JNF was presumably intended to serve the organisation's goals in the transmission of its ideas and ideology and/or as part of its 'war for survival' in the political environment in which it operated. One may conjecture that in its maps the JNF was obliged had to meet a number of political and organisational challenges. Let us briefly consider two of them: (a) the justification of its approach, namely 'the purchase and nationalisation of land', and (b) the borders of Eretz Yisrael.

a) During our period of study the Jewish National Fund found itself in an intra-Zionist political situation that obliged it to justify its ideological path. At the 1920 conference in London the JNF approach clashed with that of the American Zionists, principally the followers of Louis Brandeis. They believed that the right way was not the one followed by the JNF. They believed in free enterprise and privatisation as regards land: the encouragement of private settlement and the private purchasing of land, not the collection of money for a fund that would nationalise the land. The crisis with the Brandeis group culminating with the latter's resignation from the leadership of the Zionist movement in the United States in 1921 was the result of the decision to establish yet another fund, Keren Hayesod. But despite the accords between the funds and the transfer of monies from Keren Hayesod to the Jewish National Fund, their survival was felt to be in danger. This feeling was exacerbated through of the purchase of land in Eretz Yisrael by private individuals and various companies.

Despite its great efforts and the purchase of land in the valleys (Jezreel and Jordan), by the late 1920s and early 1930s the JNF owned only twenty percent of all the Jewish land in Eretz Yisrael.[7] Thirty years after its establishment the Fund had not fulfilled the hopes placed in it, and an alternative to its agrarian approach existed. Only at the end of the 1930s, when the political tension in Eretz Yisrael intensified and the flow of private capital weakened, did the purchases of the JNF increase. But even then it held less land than the private sector. In these circumstances JNF propaganda was obliged to provide a decisive response. It had to transform the organisation's image completely, to convince all that it was a dynamic body, the only one assiduously expanding the land of the Jewish people, one that had a right to exist and whose approach was unquestionably correct. The JNF functionaries set about this mission, among other ways, using maps.

b) At the Versailles Peace conference after the First World War the Zionist movement had to specify the size of the area required for the Jewish homeland.[8] A memorandum presented in February 1919 by the Zionist delegation, headed by Chaim Weizmann, expressed the wish that the area should cover both sides of the Jordan and should also include (in addition to the land west of the Jordan) areas located today in southern Lebanon (Sidon), the Golan Heights, and the kingdom of Jordan. Since the British had promised Transjordan to the Hussein family, the emir Abdallah was appointed ruler of the land east of the Jordan in 1923. The borders of the British Mandate in Palestine (Eretz Yisrael) were ratified in 1922 by the League of Nations. The outbreak of the Arab Revolt in 1936 and the establishment of a commission of enquiry revived the question of what the territory of Eretz Yisrael was, where its borders would be demarcated, and what the division between the Jews and Arabs should be. In 1936 a British Royal Commission, headed by Lord Peel, arrived in Eretz Yisrael, and the positions of the Zionist Organisation and of others were presented to it. Following this enquiry a debate arose in the Zionist movement over the territory of Eretz Yisrael and over the partition plan proposed by the Peel Commission, which was adopted by the British government in 1937.

Even before being appointed head of the JNF Ussishkin expressed his opposition to the British Mandate's plans to 'amputate Eastern Trans-Jordan' from the area that had been designated part of the Jewish homeland.[9] Thereafter, at any and every Zionist forum he opposed such moves, and was one of the greatest opponents of the partition plan. No wonder that in 1938, fifteen years after the original decisions regarding the borders of the British Mandate, Ussishkin declared that: 'To this very day we have not accepted, and will not accept, the closure of Transjordan, which represents more than half our historic homeland—to Jewish settlement'.[10] He expressed the necessity to reject absolutely any proposal to partition Eretz Yisrael, and admonished those who wished to present the Zionist movement with a fait accompli. He opposed Weizmann's ideas and set forth historical, religious, and practical arguments for the whole territory, even taking the extreme position of negating the establishment of the Jewish state under the conditions proposed by the Peel Commission. Hence one can understand Ussishkin's remark: 'The future of Eretz Yisrael is to spread throughout the whole of Palestine'. By 'Eretz Yisrael' he meant Zionist territory, and 'Palestine' in his view was the area of the British Mandate on both sides of the Jordan.

Ussishkin's views were set out in his speeches, but were also made plain on the maps that appeared in the different propaganda materials produced by the JNF, in the first place the Blue Box, through the use of various cartographic techniques as we shall see in the following section.

The JNF Maps of Eretz Yisrael

The maps produced by the JNF in those years belonged to two categories: scientific maps and symbolic maps. The former term refers to maps prepared by cartographers who were strict in using exact standards of measurement, as accepted in this profession. Symbolic maps were those that appeared in various publications and were prepared by graphic artists, who were less strictly accurate, emphasizing instead certain details in the maps; an example is the map on the Blue Box. Note that despite the difference in these two types of maps, various propaganda elements appeared in both.

Considering the time that elapses between deciding to publish a map and its actual publication, the decision to publish maps of Eretz Yisrael was made very soon after the JNF Head Office moved to Jerusalem (when Ussishkin headed the organisation and Berger was in charge of the Propaganda Department).

In 1924 and 1925 the JNF brought out three maps whose physical sizes were relatively small (about 60 cm high) and whose standard scale was 1:500,000. Two of these maps were photocopies of a relief map prepared by the Society for Research into Eretz Yisrael and they were printed in Germany:

> . . . it gives a faithful rendering of the physical structure of Eretz Yisrael, especially its higher areas and forms. The hills, the plains, the valleys are depicted in it in a highly visible manner, and the lands which belong to Jews according to the situation in 5635 (1925) are marked out in red, and of course the railway lines and important roads. . . . We are certain that this map is outstandingly suited to propaganda purposes and many from all circles will want it. We especially suggest distributing it to schools, clubs, and the halls of various associations.[11]

This document indicates that the purpose of publishing the maps was propaganda, with the assumption that they would be used in schools and youth clubs, and among the wider public of all circles. From this period onwards the map of Eretz Yisrael became a common item in the propaganda material published by the JNF before the establishment of the state of Israel. A number of scientific maps appeared between 1931 and 1938, and they served as a basis for reduced-size propaganda maps that appeared during this period. From 1926, symbolic maps of Eretz Yisrael appeared on stamps and were reproduced in various forms, mainly as rubber stamps on stationery (see Figure 7.1).[12] Graphic decorations of the maps appeared as ribbons to be pinned on lapels, as pictorial (drawn) maps of Eretz Yisrael, in games ('I will travel through Eretz Yisrael'), and on the detachable stamps issued for didactic purposes in the 1930s. A thin sheet of metal with the map of Eretz Yisrael stamped on it also appeared on the binding of the fourth Golden Book (1928) and formed the background on a stamp marking the organisation's fortieth anniversary (1942). At the beginning of the 1930s the map appeared as a new symbolic illustration on the Blue Box and became one of the best-known graphic symbols published by the organisation. The last symbolic map during the period under study appeared on the State for Jews stamp in 1947, showing the borders of the partition plan. These maps were designed in accordance with the organisation's propaganda policy. Next we discuss several of the cartographic propaganda characteristics of the JNF maps that were brought out according to different standards over a period of about 20 years.[13]

The Distinction between 'Land and Land'

As stated, the purpose of these general maps was propaganda: to present not only Eretz Yisrael and its landscape but also to show where the 'Jewish land' was located. The map showed only the northern half of Eretz Yisrael, from the Beer Sheva line northwards to the Litani river. In the east the map ended at the western slopes of the Transjordan mountains. In those years a similar map appeared in London, published by Keren Hayesod, covering the same territorial region. There too 'Jewish land' was marked in red ink. From a cartographic point of view these maps issued by the two funds were fairly simple, and the different elements do not stand out. Both highlighted the element called 'Jewish land', a term interpreted differently by each fund. By this time the JNF had formulated its approach, namely that maps (for the organisation's propaganda purposes) had to distinguish land purchased by the JNF from land purchased by individual Jews and different companies. Accordingly, from this year onwards the JNF differentiated 'JNF land' from 'Jewish land' in its maps (see Figure 7.2).

The first element that characterised the JNF propaganda map concerned JNF land, which was highlighted in a very bold, emphatic colour—much more striking than the hues marking other 'Jewish land'. This method of accentuating JNF land causes the eye to perceive the prominent element faster, thus increasing its relative importance. Recalling that at that time the area of land owned by the JNF was small, its colourful highlighting compared to the other land enhances the impression of its relative size and tends to reduce the perceived size of the rest. Emphasizing the JNF land at the expense of other 'Jewish land' was aided by another fact. The JNF land was concentrated in several large, contiguous blocks, mainly in the Jezreel and Zevulun valleys. In contrast, the 'Jewish land' was scattered, and on the maps this factor lessened the effectiveness of the colour as perceived by the eye. This cartographic trick with colours diminished the salience of extensive terrain not owned by the JNF, such as privately-owned areas stretching from Hadera to Bat Shlomo. Areas belonging to the *moshavot* (villages) in eastern Galilee and in the centre of the country also paled in comparison on the JNF maps.

Obviously, the technical possibility of distinguishing the colours of areas that are small and scattered becomes more difficult as the scale of the map is smaller. Yet apparently it was not only the size of the map that determined the prominence of the JNF land, but propaganda considerations as well. Evidence of this can be found in letters exchanged by the Head Office and Leopold Schen, the head of the British JNF national office at the end of 1931. That year the Head Office issued a propaganda map in which all land owned by the Jewish people nationally and by private Jewish interests were signified by a single colour. Leopold Schen was critical of the map, stating that in contrast to earlier maps it was not suitable for propaganda purposes as it contained no cartographic differentiation of types of land. He added that one could barely identify land that had been purchased in Eretz Yisrael.[14] In reply, Epstein, the secretary of the Head Office, wrote that this map was primarily intended for general purposes, and in the design of the map teachers and pupils had not been taken into consideration. Since the scale of the map was small those little areas could not be marked off from others by means of different colours, especially since this map also included areas of eastern Eretz Yisrael. This had an advantage, he added: since the total amount of land depicted on the maps was very small it might encourage donors who would see that most of Eretz Yisrael had not yet been redeemed.[15]

But Leopold Schen's criticism found a sympathetic ear at the Head Office, and Epstein's response notwithstanding the JNF continued publishing maps that distinguished the types of land, regardless of the scale or kind of map. Not surprisingly, then, a JNF publication for teachers issued in 1946 contained a small map with the legend 'The black areas in the map: JNF land; the grey areas: other Jewish land'.[16] Certain JNF maps give textual support to these cartographic messages. For example, several slogans appear on a 1934 map of scale 1:500,000 (which continued to appear in additional editions and different languages).[17] The first slogan on the map states: 'Your eyes are viewing the areas of land of the Homeland which have been redeemed by the Jewish National Fund and settled by the Keren Hayesod', a statement that confirms what has been written above. Other 'Jewish land', while marked on the map (with its cartographic power reduced), is not accompanied by any text indicating that any other factor has 'redeemed' land of the Homeland; credit for redeeming the Homeland that appears on the map refers to the JNF alone. The text thus reinforces what is shown on the map (see Figure 7.3).

The JNF's marking and accentuating its land separately did not escape the notice of people who were sensitive to cartography, such as Yosef Azaryahu who was Supervisor of Education in the Department of Education of the Zionist Executive and one of the planners of the geography curriculum for Hebrew education as early as the Second Aliya.[18] He used his professional critical judgement when the JNF sought the authorisation of the Education Department for the use of its maps as teaching aids in the schools. Azaryahu gave the JNF Head Office a detailed list of carto graphic directions that would make the maps suitable for the Hebrew education system. Among other things he pointed out that the JNF land should not be separately marked, and that 'the areas belonging to Jews should be marked in a stronger colour so that the impression made of the topographical structure of Eretz Yisrael not be blurred'.[19] These comments were taken into account only for the copies of the maps prepared for the education system at that time. In other editions of the map published during the 1930s and the 1940s the JNF continued to highlight on its maps its own lands, separately from lands bought by private Jewish individuals. In sum, as a result of the JNF's problems, stemming from its struggle for survival in the Zionist movement, and in response to the challenge of private ownership of land as well as criticism of its working methods, the JNF set forth its achievements in the 'Redemption of the Land' on its maps, while minimising the part of those who opposed this activity. This form of cartographic propaganda was intended to help make the others disappear by diminishing their value by cartographic means. In this respect the JNF maps created a sort of delegitimization of the private sector and a belittling of its importance in the redemption of the land.

The Area of Eretz Yisrael and the Borders of Palestine

In Azaryahu's directions to the Head Office noted above, he stressed among other things that the demarcation of the political borders of the Mandate on the maps must be precise. There was a real purpose for this, as one of the characteristics of JNF maps during the period under study concerned the drawing of the borders of Eretz Yisrael. The map to which Azaryahu referred specifically was the scientific map prepared for the JNF by A. Y. Brawer, which initiated negotiations with the Head Office at the end of 1928.[20] A year and a half later, in April 1930, Brawer decided on his plan for the map, informed the JNF of his views concerning its design, and gave details on the subject of the borders:

> I have undertaken to prepare a map of Eretz Yisrael according to your request and I hereby inform you about my plan for this work. The boundaries of the map: the map will contain our country within the borders of those who came from Egypt up to the Egyptian River in the Southwest and the *Sela Edom* (the Rock of Redness) in the Southeast. From the Desert in the east to Sidon in the west.[21]

These geographical areas of the map of Eretz Yisrael were acceptable to Ussishkin and the JNF officials. The boundaries of the country would be defined by 36.5° or 37° longitude in the east and by the Mediterranean coastline in the west. The Jordan river ran down the middle of the map, meaning that the Jordan system, especially the three lakes, which were coloured bright blue on the map, lay in the centre of the country. The southern boundary of the detailed map passed south of Beer Sheva and the northern boundary passed north of Sidon. This way of presenting Eretz Yisrael in its Biblical borders was typical of maps that appeared before the establishment of the British Mandate and the division of the Middle East, for example, those in the early Hebrew school textbooks.[22] The separation of Transjordan from the area of the Jewish national home and the determination of the borders of the British Mandate resulted in the drawing of different maps, in which the Jordan system formed the right (eastern) margin of the map, and not its centre; an example is the map issued by Keren Hayesod in 1925.

This way of presenting the country on maps did not suit Ussishkin's political outlook, so to distance itself from the division of Eretz Yisrael and the Mandate's borders, the JNF continued to issue maps in which the Jordan river lay in the centre of the map. This was a political statement made by means of cartography, a way to delegitimize Mandatory rule and a criticism against the supporters of a division of the country. Consequently, in a large number of the scientific maps produced by the JNF in those years not only was the area shown bigger than the area of western Eretz Yisrael, but several of the British Mandate's borders were not marked at all. Azaryahu's comment that the adaptation of the JNF maps for the Hebrew School system would have to include the marking of the political boundaries is therefore not surprising.

This manner of presenting the area and borders of Eretz Yisrael was not a technical, cartographic matter, but arose out of a distinct policy, as one can see from a response by the Head Office. On 2 November 1938 the daily *Haboker* published a letter to the editor written by S. Yardeni of Jerusalem headed 'Why is there no map of our entire country?'

> For the purposes of a well-known work I needed a map of the entire area of Eretz Yisrael, which is on both sides of the Jordan. I decided to go to JNF offices: 'Surely there something like this could be found', I assumed. So how astonished was I to receive this answer from the Head Office: 'We do not have such a map'. At the JNF centre, an institution which is redeeming the land and at whose head stands one of the more vigorous opponents to the truncation of the country—in this institution which has all the maps in the world—with one exception, the map of the complete Eretz Yisrael.
> Why do they not have such a map? [. . .]
> You published a map with the slogan: 'This is the land which will be given to you to settle', and this map only contains half of Eretz Yisrael. Can this be so? The Germans always included areas to which they had no right, and which did not belong to them, on their maps of the boundaries of Germany, and in the end they obtained some of these places because the nation knew: 'This is our land—and strangers tore it away from us'. And we, shall we not include our areas upon which is written 'Eretz Yisrael' within our borders?

The JNF Head Office sent a short response to *Haboker*:

> If Mr. S. Yardeni examined the map of Eretz Yisrael which was issued by the Jewish National Fund and published in thousands of copies he would learn that this map does include all of Eretz Yisrael, from the Litani in the north to Aqaba in the south and Arabia in the east, according to the stipulations of the letter writer—even the parts of Lebanon and Syria which border Eretz Yisrael. . . . Incidentally, how does the letter writer know that 'at this institution they have all the maps in the world—with one exception, the map of the complete Eretz Yisrael?'[23]

In this sarcastically written, slightly contemptuous response, the Head Office reveals its cartographic policy on the presentation of the areas of Eretz Yisrael, as evident in the different maps produced at that time.

Additional support for the argument that from the outset the clear intention of the JNF maps was to present an extensive land, exceeding the borders of the Mandate, can be found in correspondence about the map shown on the Blue Box at the beginning of the 1930s. At the end of the 1920s the illustration on the front of the Blue Box included a Star of David in the centre, under which was written 'The Jewish National Fund'; at the top was the emblem of the organisation.[24] This version of the box recurred in various advertisements during the 1920s and early the 1930s, especially in *Karnenu,* the JNF official journal. At that time there was a tendency to decorate the cover of the journal with maps and to use photomontages. Accordingly, in November 1928 the cover of *Karnenu* included for the first time the map on the Blue Box. The journal's graphic artist made an illustration whose background has the classic Blue Box on which appears a map of Eretz Yisrael: from the Litani River to Beer Sheva and from the sea to the desert. Jewish Land is highlighted.

At the beginning of the 1930s, when a new design was being made for the classic Blue Box, the above idea that appeared in *Karnenu* was adopted, and the new design was publicised thus in 1934:

> . . .On the new box, drawn in blue on a white background on one side is a map of Eretz Yisrael, with the areas of land redeemed by the nation's contribution marked and with the legend 'Jewish National Fund' above the Star of David. On the other side is drawn the monogram of the JNF with the Star of David on a blue-white background.[25]

On this map, on a white background, with no borders marked, and encompassing an area reaching north into Lebanon and east into the desert, the Jordan system and the three lakes appear highlighted in a bold blue colour. The white colour does not end at the edges of the front of the box but spills over onto its right side. The map on the box presents a space coloured white, without borders, whose force is amplified by the blue background colour of the Mediterranean Sea (see Figure 7.4).

Not everybody was content with the design of the map of Eretz Yisrael on the Blue Box. When distributed In Austria it sparked a negative reaction, and the JNF national office in Vienna wrote to Jerusalem:[26] 'The Revisionist wing has found a fault [in Hebrew handwriting is written: 'The map of Eretz Yisrael on the box']—the other side of the Jordan cannot be seen on the boxes. Do we have to conclude from this that the Jewish National Fund has relinquished its claim to Transjordan?' The reply from the Head Office is fascinating:

> We see the complaint of the Revisionist Zionists, which has been passed on in your letter, as one of the baseless pretexts against our Fund that we often hear about. However, who in their right mind and who is responsible can take seriously the claim that the Jewish National Fund relinquishes its claim to the other side of the Jordan? On the map on the box as well, anybody who is not looking for faults can see the other side of the Jordan in all the land which also continues up to the side of the box. Incidentally, on the boxes prepared in Eretz Yisrael this area is even greater on the front side of the box as well.[27]

The Head Office's reply to the Vienna national office certainly confirms the theory that the design of the map on the Blue Box was not accidental—a borderless map that also extends into the areas of Transjordan in the east (up to 'the side of the box'). Thus, this is a graphical presentation of a political statement made by the organisation and its leadership. Just as political propaganda found its way into scientific maps, it was transmitted by the most important icon of the JNF. The contrasting colours (a bold blue contrasted with white), and the highlighted line of the Jordan in the centre of the white area, were thus a simple and convenient cartographic device to catch the eye and transmit the political message. Not only adults were exposed to it, but also millions of children in the Hebrew education system who contributed their coins in the special ceremonies.

Hebrew and Non-Hebrew Space

The third prominent characteristic of JNF cartographic propaganda was the creation of a selective presentation of the mapping of the settled space. This was accomplished by having places vanish or their importance reduced by cartographic means, if they were not Hebrew locations. An extreme expression of this appeared in the symbolic map of Eretz Yisrael drawn on the Blue Box. During the period under discussion the country appears as an area coloured white—an empty space, with no settlements and no inhabitants. The large cities—Jerusalem, Tel Aviv, and Haifa—are marked on it, but in small, low-profile print against the background of the great void of the white space. Arguably, in a small symbolic illustration on the Blue Box it is in any case impossible to show all the settlements, and its purpose was only to display JNF lands, making them salient in contrast to the still unredeemed areas. Such an argument is logical and reasonable. However, as we will be able to see from other maps, the policy of cartographic selectivity in the presentation of places was characteristic of JNF maps. This selectivity stemmed from the Zionist context of the perception of the space of Eretz Yisrael in general, and that of the JNF in particular. Accordingly the following statement appears, written by the Head Office in a release publicising a map drawn by Brawer and printed by Omanut in 1931.

> On the basis of a physical map, all the roads and all the locations of important settlements will be given; and apart from this, every place which is important in our history, whether it is settled or a ruin. The guardians of the priesthood in Galilee and the visible ruins of synagogues will be denoted by special markings.[28]

Since this was a scientific Hebrew map issued for propaganda, educational, and general practical purposes by the Hebrew community and the Zionist movement, the details it contained clearly had to suit the target community. Hence, *all the Hebrew settlements* were marked on the map as well as *all the important historical places*. This view of Zionist-focused cartographic selection was set forth by Brawer, the editor of the map, and he informed the Head Office of it when he presented the map project. Being aware that the selection of places and settlements marked on the maps was a wholly subjective choice by the editor of the maps, he wrote to the Head Office:

> . . . the evaluation of the importance [of the places] is, of course, a matter for my choice and understanding, and it will be easy for any superficial critic, unfamiliar with the technical difficulties, to say something about this or that place which as not been included. I hereby accept full responsibility for the names I include and have no desire to discuss this matter with anybody, because it is a matter for interminable meetings.[29]

When this scientific map project was brought before the Education Department of the Zionist Executive for authorisation, Azaryahu was also quick to respond, in an entirely professional way, to the subject of how the selection of settled areas was to be suited to the needs of the schools.[30] He wrote, '*only* [emphasis in the original] the most important villages, from the point of view of population or economic worth, should be marked'; but he added that small villages located on main roads should also be marked. He recommended that only historical sites associated with well-known historical events should be marked, 'but not all the places mentioned in the Bible, the Talmud, or other historical sources'. Furthermore, one should not exaggerate in the agreed upon marking of Jewish settlements and that the Star of David 'which is too big in proportion to the size of the place' should not be added to them. Azaryahu does not advocate ignoring Arab settled areas, and he specifically writes to the Head Office that the names of all Arab cities in Eretz Yisrael should be marked on the map, not only Jerusalem and Hebron. The Arabic names of hills, rivers, and other items should be printed (in smaller type) on the maps as well. There is no reason to suspect that Azaryahu's approach did not emanate from a Zionist viewpoint concerning the spaces, but he asked for a moderation of the Hebrew cartographic selection on the JNF maps and their adaptation to the needs of Hebrew schools.

In contrast to Azaryahu, the adaptation of the scientific map prepared by Brawer to the requirements of the Head Office called for different choices, as is seen from the correspondence about the propaganda maps in other languages, which appeared in the following years. E. Epstein, who dealt with these maps, wrote to Brawer:

> The map we are preparing now is solely for the propaganda purposes of the JNF activists and the donors. Because of this there is no need for a great number of details, which may have some scientific interest, but which certainly are not likely to attract the attention of the activist or any average donor . . . from this point of view it is therefore clear that we have to give all the details of all the Jewish settlements in Eretz Yisrael, but there is no need to mark, for example, in the map of the Negev, all the (Arab) villages and hills the location of which no normal donor even knows about.[31]

Epstein thus notes that the reduction of cartographic information applies to aspects of Arab culture (place-names) and to their settlements in the land, as these details are of no interest to the potential map readership. Consequently, in the JNF propaganda maps the number of Arab settlements is relatively small, a fact that creates the impression of a sparsely populated space. This feature is chiefly apparent in the areas of Galilee and the hills of Judea and Samaria, areas with a dense Arab population in the 1930s. The presentation of these seemingly sparsely populated hilly regions is conspicuous against the background of the detail and prominence of the Jewish settlements in the valleys, and it creates the impression of heavily populated Jewish areas.

The cartographic distinction between the Zionist region and the Arab region in the JNF maps is heightened by the differences between various Arab settlements, despite the conventional homogeneous marking applied to the Arab settlements. For example, in the 1934 propaganda map, which was published in additional editions, a cartographic distinction is made between Arab settlements marked with a solid black circle, which signifies the importance of the place, and Arab villages marked with a hollow circle on a pale background.[32] The Hebrew settlements are prominently distinguished by diverse underlining of their names, according to the level of assistance they received from Keren Hayesod. Those 'established by Keren Hayesod' are highlighted by a continuous black line, in contrast to those only supported by it, which are highlighted by a broken line. These emphases enhance the effect of marking places on the map; they amplify the impression of the importance of national settlements on JNF lands. The *moshavot* (private Jewish settlements) such as Zichron Ya'akov and Ness Ziona, did not receive any extra emphasis on the map, so their cartographic fate was to be not more than one rank above the marking used for Arab villages on these maps.

The cartographic or graphical selectivity in the maps of Eretz Yisrael is expressed very aesthetically on the maps drawn for the JNF's detachable stamps, these being pictorial maps reminiscent of certain present-day tourist maps. In these maps illustrations depicting sites and places are superimposed on the map background; since the map page is limited in size, the addition of the drawings highlights certain places at the expense of others. At the end of the 1930s the Head Office decided to issue a series of didactic stamps in the form of puzzles made from pictorial maps. The work of preparing the maps was assigned to A. Sapoznikov who early in 1930 presented the draft of the drawings to the Head Office. In a discussion on the illustrations for the map, the participants commented on the fine details but there was no argument over the fact that only Hebrew sites appeared in the illustration. Of course, neither the area encompassed by the map nor the absence of marking of the country's borders was discussed.[33]

No wonder then that in the above stamp map, the farmer ploughing the fields Jezreel valley and the great orange trees in the Sharon area stood out. In the hills of Judea and Samaria there are no settlements at all, only enormous olive trees; and the monumental buildings in Jerusalem (David's Tower), Bethlehem (Rachel's Tomb) and Hebron (The Tomb of the Patriarchs) are evident. The desolate areas (i.e., a place with no Hebrew settlements, therefore no settlement at all) are not only the hilly parts in the middle of the country but also Galilee, the southern regions, and Transjordan: the land of nomads, shepherds, sheep, and camels. In these wildernesses Sapoznikov drew a few ancient ruins and gave the Hebrew names of the Transjordanian mountains (Moab, Amnon, Gilead, Golan, and Bashan), evidence of their ancient Hebrew character.[34]

Summary

The influence of these maps drawn on the didactic stamps was presumably not considerable, and was mainly limited to the schoolchildren exposed to them. Yet these stamps did strengthen the message broadcast by the Head Office in different materials prepared for propaganda purposes. The messages emanated from an organisation with a political and social outlook, which used cartography as it used other means, films, books, and games, to create together a complex propaganda network. The JNF officials believed that the various maps would strengthen the positive image of the organisation, and would make its projects seems more substantial as maps were perceived as objective presentations of reality. Important supporting evidence for the theory that the drawings on the various maps were not accidental can be found in a report in 1947 in *Karnenu* on the appearance of a new model of the Blue Box with the drawing of a new map:

> The map of Eretz Yisrael drawn on it already introduces the *more crowded* [emphasis in the original] sites of JNF and Jewish lands in Eretz Yisrael, and it makes clear and concrete both the progress made and the empty, desolate areas that we still have the duty to redeem, to provide ourselves with land under our feet.[35]

This brief report illustrates that the new drawing of the map of Eretz Yisrael (which now included the Negev) did, in fact, serve the following purpose. It elevated the organisation's reputation and work ('the more crowded sites. . . and makes clear and concrete the progress made'), as well as delegitimizing non-Jewish landowners in Eretz Yisrael ('the empty, desolate areas'). We can conclude that through this glorifying of the JNF it was possible, by cartographic means, to reduce the importance of the Other (namely British rule; the Arabs; the Jewish private sector). This would contribute to their delegitimization in the political and social battles then raging, in which, so it seemed, the JNF was not actively involved.

Chapter 8

The Propaganda Image of Eretz Yisrael

Site and Place

Studies have shown that different 'geographical sites' (mountains, rivers, houses, fields . . .) are culturally loaded with a system of significant, symbolic weight which transforms them into 'places'.[1] Furthermore, people living within certain cultural contexts acquire their feelings about a space through social systems of socialisation; that is, place identification. Thus, in formal and non-formal educational systems, emphasis is placed on younger ages, when personal identification develops, for the teaching of subjects such as Geography and Homeland studies. These involve ideological messages regarding space.[2]

Charging geographical sites with cultural significance is one of the well-known processes of establishing a collective memory, in which historical events important for the narrative of national restoration are linked to specific sites. Such sites may be of different sizes, beginning with those as small as a room (e.g., the study of Herzl, the visionary of the Jewish state), and proceeding to monuments such as statues, trees, gardens or cemeteries and even entire territories of a country.[3] The transformation of a geographical site into a place of cultural significance follows diverse paths, influenced by events and the role of such a space in the national consciousness. At times these processes of constructing place identification are prolonged and stychic (unplanned) from a historical point of view; in other cases they are relatively rapid, and they planned by interested elements exercising social control. These elements are capable of utilising the building of places for practical or symbolic purposes which are important for their survival as organisations and for the continuation of their hegemony over the socio-cultural system.

Apart from the these cases, which are characteristically ideological, social and cultural processes, another system exists that transforms 'sites' into 'places'; this is the economic system. In a consumer society space has economic significance, expressed in the prices of land and real estate. Organisations that profit from the sale of the space, such as settlement or building companies, apply mechanisms to influence the demand for sites: the higher the demand, the larger their gains. In these economic systems the accepted terminology is the 'marketing' or 'selling' of the sites, aided by high-powered advertising to create the desired demand.

The transformation of 'geographical sites' into 'places' for cultural or economic reasons is linked to the creation of an image of the place and its wide distribution. 'Place', then, is a spatial element, loaded with significance and images and perceived as having a separate identity from other places. Places are different not only in their locations but also in the functions they fulfil within the economic, social and cultural whole. The identity of places constructed by society with the support of a variety of cultural representations: poetry, stories, texts, films and newspapers. The ongoing dialogue between a certain social group and the space produces the diverse representations that assist in the transformation of a 'neutral space' into a network of places for which people are even prepared to sacrifice their lives. Hence, three different components converge in each 'place': the geographical site, the cultural representations related to it and the personal perception of the place (see Figure 8.1).

In the process of its crystallisation from a social movement to a political entity, Zionism changed 'sites in Palestine' into 'places in Eretz Yisrael' through processes of symbolic transformation around which political and economic claims developed.[4] This process was undoubtedly based on Jewish tradition, which had endowed the landscape of Eretz Yisrael with symbolism for millennia, by means of representations from the Bible and cultural and historical contextual interpretations. The Jewish National Fund played a central role in the continuum of this Zionist identity-building by virtue of its creation and distribution of myths about places. This was a pivotal strategy in its propaganda, and it utilised a vast range of means and opportunities: speeches of emissaries and leaders, publicity in writing or through visual representation, texts in schools and kindergartens, and so on.[5] For the JNF, Eretz Yisrael was not a space with equal values, and the organisation immortalised it by creating an evident network of ideal, central space as opposed to the marginal landscape.

The JNF Landscape

The Ideal Landscape

The ideal symbolic landscape of Eretz Yisrael in the JNF's representations was formed along general lines even before the First World War, as we learn from the sale of the second JNF Golden Book, which was designed in 1913 by the artists of the Bezalel school of art.[6] Its metal-beaten cover shows illustrations of vineyard workers and farmers, shepherds, seed-sowers and ploughmen encircling a symbolic figure of a Hebrew farmer ploughing the fields, which stretch out to the horizon. This landscape represents an idyllic Biblical rural scene in the Judean Hills. The regional preference for the Judean Hills and Jerusalem was even reflected on JNF stamps and was typical of the period lasting until the early 1920s. From then until the mid-1940s the north of the country in general, its valleys in particular, received preferential treatment in the JNF's propaganda and publications.

The ideal image of the country as *a land of farmers and villages* was a cornerstone of the JNF, reinforced still more in the latter period, under Ussishkin's leadership. Just as his political opinions were given expression on the JNF maps, the prominent images of the Eretz Yisrael landscape were designed according to his agrarian outlook. This outlook was expressed by the saying: 'The internal strength of the state is the village, the external lustre is the town'. This outlook had brought Ussishkin from Russia on his first visit to Eretz Yisrael in 1891. Travelling from Haifa to Nazareth he traversed the Jezreel valley, of which he wrote: '. . . You see all this richness, granted by nature in this place and you remember how happy within was the wandering nation when it returned to this land. Sadness attacks one's soul today. And suddenly one of our party started to sing a farmer's song: Our hope has not been lost, our ancient hope. . . .'[7] Ussishkin's idealistic, romantic approach is reminiscent of the ideas of Tolstoy and Dostoyevsky, to which he was exposed as a student in Russia, about the evils of the city and the nobility of village life. This outlook linked the nation's happiness to 'its return to its land', a combination which translates into agricultural village settlement. No wonder that the members of the mission broke out into 'a farmer's song' whose words were those of *Hatikva*.

Together with Ussishkin's idealistic approach to the nature of the country's future society, which influenced the presentation of the landscape of Eretz Yisrael in JNF publications, this was also affected by the organisation's strategy for its own survival. The *land*, as the chief object of JNF work in Eretz Yisrael, had to be made prominent in the propaganda to prove the vital importance of this organisation and its adherence to the goals for which it was established. The working assumption of the organisation was that armed with a slogan about the need for land they would be able to open up the hearts of Jews for contributions, particularly when the subject of the 'land' was romantically supported by the return to the countryside as in the golden age of the Bible.

The JNF functionaries found support for these ideas in the writings of Hebrew authors and poets; many of them wrote works in which the land and villagers were the central feature of the narrative. Throughout the whole period under review the ideal space depicted by JNF propaganda was a romantic, rustic domain, while the urban spaces being constructed in the country were belittled.[8] In the urban spaces private enterprise was active and the properties purchased were not the 'the nation's possessions' so JNF propaganda saw no need to publicise them as ideal Hebrew spaces. The prominence given to rural spaces in the propaganda and education material indicates the real and proper direction to be followed to reach the desired Zionist goals. JNF propaganda thus conformed with the social and ideological messages of the socialist current in the Zionist movement, which developed during the Second Aliya and which ascribed to the countryside and working the land with the greatest symbolic and practical advantages.[9]

The plough was the chief tool used to bring people close to the ideal landscape, so it gained renown and permanence especially in visual representations such as JNF posters, stamps and films. Together with the plough, and the preparation of land for village settlement, the tree and the forest were used as direct instruments of the transformation brought by the JNF to the landscape of Eretz Yisrael. While the JNF shared the work of creating the rural landscape with Keren Hayesod (at first), afforestation belonged to the JNF exclusively. Naturally, *forest and tree* became one of the most common motifs in its publications and propaganda. This was because the open landscape that the JNF leaders saw as ideal of Eretz Yisrael was the landscape clothed in planted trees planted by humans; that was the living testimony to the dimensions of the project to make the desert bloom and to the change of the orientation of the country.[10] Accordingly, the tree and forest are shown in JNF representations as positive symbols, and in their eventual widespread form they are the child and the tree. These two motifs symbolised the hope of the individual and collective for a better future, and their representation took a variety of forms: a poster of a child planting a tree, footage from a film of children running through Herzl Forest, or children and trees in stories, poems and plays distributed to schools and youth movements.[11]

From the outset the JNF learnt how to use the tree and forest not only for programmatic motifs such as land but also for symbolic, cultural motifs. From a practical point of view the need always existed to raise funds for the organisation so that it could carry out its afforestation work. One of the ways of meeting it was to turn tree-planting into a symbolic act by linking the forest to a personal or collective commemoration. Because of the circumstances the JNF forests became spaces in which many symbolic elements joined together and were commemorated. How the down-to-earth matter of afforestation was raised to the level of symbolism can be seen in the commemoration of the students of the Hebrew University in Jerusalem who fell in the riots of 1936. A document prepared by the JNF for the establishment of a commemorative project and as an appeal to Jewish students in Eretz Yisrael and throughout the world stated the following:

Jewish students throughout the world will undertake one regular project for
Eretz Yisrael and its sons. In my opinion there is no project more suitable than
the afforestation project; this project can be a symbol, a living symbol, of the
link between Jewish students who enter the world of the intellect and the work
of creating and reviving the Jewish Nation.[12]

The above proposal wishes to link the collective commitment of Jewish
students to the work of reviving the Jewish people (i.e., donating money)
and afforestation, which expresses this revival, against the background of
memorialising the fallen. Note in this regard that the human-planted forests of the JNF became part of the personal experience, of the collective
memory, which the officials of the JNF Department of Propaganda and
Education created. This memory was formed in different ways: from special ceremonies for planting trees on Tu Bishvat (the festival on the 15th of
the month of Shevat, the 'New Year for the Trees') to the naming of forests and woods after personages and communities. Moreover, on the personal level, symbolic consciousness about trees was aroused through the
widespread project of 'tree donation' in which JNF commemorative certificates were printed for different personal occasions.

The activities of the JNF's Department for Propaganda and Education helped to transfer the tree motif from the practical level of an
organisation engaged in afforestation to the field of symbolism. The human-planted forests became monuments to JNF deeds with the country's
landscape and were loaded with weighty political messages about the
national struggle in Eretz Yisrael. The forest became a foremost symbol
of the JNF in the 'conquest of the wilderness' and in the construction of
the images of the landscape of Eretz Yisrael.

The Landscape of the Wilderness

In contrast to the ideal landscape (the countryside and the forest), JNF
propaganda presented its antithesis, the wilderness in its dark, gloomy
colours. The term *wilderness,* which recurs in a variety of forms, contains
a complex world of nature and humanity. In the art of Eretz Yisrael in the
1920s the motif of the wilderness was the same as the motif of the desert—
a part of the orientalist outlook of Europeans. During the 1930s and
1940s this image disappeared from the art but remained in Zionist consciousness and was presented in the propaganda and graphics of the time.[13]
Wilderness embraces all those spaces of potential conquest in which there
was no Zionist or Jewish presence, and its symbols were drawn from the
physical world of Eretz Yisrael. Descriptions of the wilderness spaces were
generally replete with such phrases as 'steep hills', 'exposed slopes', 'rocky
boulders', 'swamps and fever', 'heat and aridity' and 'shifting sands'. These
marginal spaces were perceived as potentially conquerable by Zionist

action in general and by the JNF in particular; the 'conquest of the wilderness' was not merely a symbol but a value and an operative goal, whose achievement proved the rightness of the ideological and practical path.

Four types of spaces in the Eretz Yisrael acquired the status of 'wilderness': the hills, the valleys, the desert and every place where Arabs lived. The wilderness was presented as a hostile space, both because of the hand of God (heat, drought and fever) and because of the hand of man (the Arabs). A fairly regular pattern seems to have evolved in the description of the wilderness, in accord with the propaganda line, the publicity and the various presentations of the JNF. This pattern included concepts, nouns and adjectives intended to signify the opposite of the 'ideal space'. Ussishkin's words, uttered in 1929, exemplify the point:

> The desolation of generations was everywhere, and throughout this great, broad hardly a soul could be seen. Only here and there did we come across a cluster of nomadic Bedouin tents. All around there were swamps and sand, desert scrub, thorns and thistles. One could only see one thing: the desolate, exposed Mt. Carmel in the distance, with no greenery, no trees or grass, no sign of settlement; and the town of Haifa itself, small and undeveloped, languishing in slime and filth. Only one neighbourhood in the surrounding area captured our attention with its beauty, the German Colony which had just begun to develop.[14]

This speech was delivered on the festive occasion of the 'Redemption of Haifa Bay': Ussishkin was sharing his recollections of his visit to Eretz Yisrael in 1891, when he passed through Akko (Acre) valley accompanied by Ahad Ha'am and others. This was a group of young intellectuals who had grown up on the landscape of Russia and Lithuania, and had been exposed to the scenery of Eretz Yisrael and the culture of the Orient; Palestine was a great shock to them. Several of the common images used in describing the wilderness are present here: 'swamps', 'desert scrub', 'thorns and thistles' and in the distance the mountain 'with no greenery' (see Figure 8.2). This was nature's wilderness, made more extreme by man's wilderness: 'nomadic Bedouin' and a small, oriental town 'languishing in slime and filth'. A suggestion that the space they had seen could have a different future they saw in the Germany Colony in Haifa, a little piece of Europe in the Orient, which offered them lodgings for the night in a hotel. Even if it is argued that Ussishkin's testimony is tardy, forty years after the events, these recollections still assemble all the motifs which the JNF used for the wilderness space at the end of the 1920s.

The presence of the wilderness in description of the JNF sites was used as a preface to the narrative of events: the wilderness was the backdrop to the formation of the Zionist space. In visual presentations such as films or transparencies the opening pictures present the wilderness as photographs of a desert landscape or bare hillsides. At times the pictures presented were detached from the geographical context, and used the wilderness stereotypes. For example, in the 1928 film *Aviv be'eretz yisrael* (Spring in the Land of Israel), which could be used to show the desolate landscape before the construction of Tel Aviv, pictures of the stony desert landscape are presented.[15] The pattern of presenting the wilderness as a background to the practical work in Eretz Yisrael was also introduced into the propaganda aimed at younger ages. In the instructions for the preparation of the Lotto game, distributed by the JNF to kindergartens and the lower grades of elementary schools, the following was written:

> Table no. 1. Content: wilderness. The pioneers, none, the JNF has not yet redeemed the land. The landscape: hills, valley, sand dunes, stretches of sea; on one of the hills a poor Arab village, cactus plants; on the hills solitary trees, typical animals; below on the right Bedouin tents, an Arab woman with an urn from the Well; in the middle a ruined well. On the left a green swamp, frogs, daffodils, swarming mosquitoes; on the sea shore, a camel, a strip of sea, a boat.[16]

These directions for the preparation of the Lotto game demonstrate the wilderness stereotypes as they took shape during the 1920s and 1930s; this was the pre-Zionist landscape of Eretz Yisrael, publicised by the JNF's propaganda and education system. In other words 'the desolation of Eretz Yisrael' was not only due to the hand of God but also to the deeds of man; the wilderness covered up the glory of the past, the 'land of milk and honey'. The presentation of the wilderness as a temporary and transient state imposed on the country because of historical circumstances gave hope for the success of the Zionist project. Accordingly, messages about hope for the future were transmitted together with the wilderness stereotypes by the interpretation of the situation as temporary and reversible. The motif of the temporary nature of the wilderness was reinforced by the rhetoric of the Zionist leaders. Not surprisingly, the JNF published what David Ben-Gurion said about the conquest of the wilderness in the press: '. . .we have ended the shame of the wilderness, we have proven our ability and the latent power of the country, we have discovered that it is not the laws of nature and divine will but the neglect and abandonment by foreign conquerors and illegitimate offspring that have ruined this cherished and blessed land..'.[17] Ben-Gurion's words buttressed what Ussishkin had said years earlier when he had seen the valleys during his first visit. 'We understand that a shining future awaits it in the coming period: here is the centre of the country and here is the most suitable place to build a large, modern port on the shores of the Mediterranean Sea. . . A great, shining future. . .and what is distressing and terrible was the present of those days'.[18]

The presence of the wilderness in the propaganda of the JNF was apparently necessary for the narrative of the organisation—the larger its presence, the greater the impression made by the work of the organisation in conquering and controlling it. Throughout the years under review the motif of the wilderness was therefore constantly emphasized as the baseline against which the success of the JNF's work in redeeming the land was to be measured (see Figure 8.3). These messages were transmitted through various propaganda and socialisation methods, which repeatedly presented the ethos of redeeming and conquering the wilderness and recycled the same stories and texts over the years. An example is the play *Kinus hakufsaot* (A Gathering of the Boxes) by Edna Amir (Finklerfeld), in which the wilderness is presented through the images of mosquitoes which appear on the stage and complain about what the JNF is doing:

> *Mosquitoes* (burst in on left, buzzing noisily): Ssh, please make those who are threatening our lives stop because we mosquitoes are withering because of them. Thanks to your appearance, you Blue Boxes, you are making us extinct, the more you succeed, the greater our catastrophe is. Please—we will leave if you continue to dry up the swamps which are the joy of our lives.[19]

In this play the tale of the draining of the swamps in Hadera, which is part of the ethos of the First Aliya (1882), is linked to the activities of the JNF as the organisation, which is battling the wilderness. The eucalyptus trees, 'the heroes of Hadera' muster on the stage with the pine trees of the forests of Ginegar and Mishmar Ha'emek which were planted by the JNF, and together they drive out the country's wilderness. By this simple literary technique of contracting time and space in the play, events are transposed and the images of landscapes important to the narrative of the building of the Zionist landscape are linked to them. The JNF Education Department distributed such plays throughout Eretz Yisrael and abroad. These conveyed the vastness of the wilderness, and on the other hand the power of the project that was vanquishing it.

JNF propaganda, which contributed to the building of the image of the transformation of the country's landscape, reached its peak with the spreading of the ethos of the Emek (Jezreel valley), the territory at the centre of the organisation's activities during the 1920s and eventually the symbol of its success. Three points characterised the JNF Emek propaganda. (a) This region was given more attention in the propaganda than any other part of the country; (b) the struggle of the wilderness-conquering *halutzim* (pioneers) was immortalised in it; (c) its 'human-made' landscape became one of the most frequent representations of the JNF throughout Eretz Yisrael and the Jewish world. Below we demonstrate the special nature of the story of the Jezreel valley in JNF propaganda, and discuss the means by which it was disseminated. The purpose of this section is not to analyse the history of the settlement and redemption of the land in the Emek but the role played by the JNF in the creation of the image of its landscape and its distribution through various means of propaganda. In passing we shall touch on historical events that JNF propaganda wished to elevate and immortalise.[20]

'The Emek Is a Dream': The Unfolding of a Story

In 1932, on the thirtieth anniversary of the JNF, its Propaganda Department prepared a filmstrip for the occasion and wrote the lecture to be distributed with the transparencies. Between the first picture ('Wilderness: swamps and death') and the third ('Diaspora—snow, gloom and the wandering Jews') a second transparency was shown, 'The panorama of the Emek', which was photographed from the slopes of the Nazareth hills. The accompanying text contained the following:

> If you wish to see Eretz Yisrael in all its glory, take a trip on one of those bright, sun-filled spring days along the road which leads from Haifa to Nazareth which is covered in green . . . and when you reach that point [on that road] you have to look down at the view. [The Emek] a chessboard. Here and there a wood. Ornamental trees shading, or trying to shade the surroundings, and within this widespread area, point after point begin to appear, orderly white rows of little houses surrounded by green. Don't try to count these little points, for there are too many. And don't ask what this show is, you will find out anyway: The hand of the JNF has touched this place: The JNF . . . an institution which has become part of Jewish Experience, which has educated a generation, tied it to Eretz Yisrael, which has cast its net over a hundred and twenty seven countries in order to conquer the heart of every Jew and turn it to here, to these same wild areas in the close but distant Eretz Yisrael.[21]

This text, and its context within the filmstrip, demonstrate the essence of the story of the redemption of Jezreel valley and its settlements, which was regularly circulated by the Jewish National Fund. The view of the Emek represents Eretz Yisrael in all its glory, and this glory obviously came about because the hand of the JNF has touched this place'. The JNF does so much work to turn Jewish hearts towards 'the wild areas' of Eretz Yisrael. Later in the lecture the establishment and the work of the organisation till after the First World War is presented; by 1920, it is written, twenty years after its establishment, a total of 20,000 dunams throughout the country was under JNF control. And then the great moment arrived: Jezreel valley was redeemed, and within a year (1921) the area of land under JNF control tripled. From then on the redemption of the Emek was presented by the JNF as the most important event, which not only changed the landscape of the region's wilderness (as presented in the first picture) but even affected the fate of the Jewish people of the snow-bound, gloomy Diaspora (third picture). To grasp why the account of 'the redemption of Jezreel valley' was more compelling in the historiography of the JNF than any other story, the historical and political circumstances must be described briefly (see Figure 8.4).

Apart from the fact that the area of land under JNF control tripled and even quintupled later, the organisation's historiography presented the purchase of the Emek lands as the end of a process which had gone on for about thirty years, starting in 1891 when Y. Hankin concluded an agreement in principle for the sale of land with the owners of the Emek estates.[22] Although the Emek lands were offered for sale to other Zionist bodies over the years, only the JNF was capable of accomplishing the purchase after the historical turning point marked by the Balfour Declaration. This piece of evidence in the history of the settlement of the Emek is supported by Arthur Ruppin, who said that the purchase of Jezreel, for the first time gave Zionism the opportunity to begin settlement on a large scale and on large tracts of land which had never before been available. According to him, settlement in the Emek would also create a continuous link between the veteran Zionist settlement areas in the north of the country and those in the centre.[23]

The decision to buy the land in the Emek was not taken without disagreement in the Zionist movement, and there were repercussions in the JNF directorate itself. The question of whether to buy then (1921) became the central issue. The JNF president Nehemiah De Limah resigned his post in opposition to the purchase and was succeeded by Ussishkin.[24] Obtaining authorisation from the Twelfth Zionist Congress in Karlsbad (1921) to purchase land in the Emek was a personal victory for Ussishkin and his practical approach. This was also the closing of a circle begun in 1891 when he joined the *Hovevei Zion* mission to Eretz Yisrael and saw these lands for the first time. Then he had likened their worth to the revival of the nation in its own land. During that same period (1920–23) the JNF was involved in a struggle with the Brandeis group which led to the establishment of Keren Hayesod. This diminished the status of the JNF, leaving it only with the task of purchasing land; the other task of the JNF, preparing the land, was authorised by the Thirteenth Zionist Congress in 1923.[25]

In the period between the Twelfth and Thirteenth Congresses a battle for the survival of the JNF as an institution and a personal feud between Ussishkin and Weizmann raged. The tension greatly increased towards the convening of the Thirteenth Congress, and the JNF intensified its propaganda accordingly. For example, the JNF sought to justify its existence by publishing a series of photographs of Jezreel valley in the magazine *Ha'olam,* which usually only published texts. In the accompanying article Adolph Pollak, a leader of the JNF in Germany, wrote:

... Nahalal and Noris [Ein Harod] have, today, already become mottos for Zionist work throughout the entire world ... because of a total awareness of the goal the Jewish National Fund continues to improve these supporting settlements by purchasing new land and, if the Hebrew nation does not abandon its finest and most admirable institution, then the day is not distant when from Haifa to the Kinneret Lake a whole series of flowering settlements will arise, and all the Valley of Jezreel will be packed with Hebrew settlements.[26]

So it transpires that a few months before the opening of the Thirteenth Congress the JNF leaders harboured a suspicion that that the 'Hebrew nation' was about to 'abandon its finest ... institution'. This feeling waxed during the Congress itself. At the very opening of the Congress Weizmann and other speakers heaped great praise on the work done by Keren Hayesod, especially regarding the money it had succeeded in raising in the USA. At the second session of the Congress Ussishkin delivered a speech describing the situation in Eretz Yisrael. He exapanded on the epic draining of the swamps in the Emek, 'a glorious chapter in our struggle and victory over this country'.[27] The minutes indicate that at the Congress it was generally believed that at that time only one 'Zionist instrument' had gained success and fame, namely Keren Hayesod, founded only three years before. The minutes attest that the image of the JNF was then lower than that of Keren Hayesod; with good reason the JNF delegate managed to push through a resolution confirming that the JNF was the body that would take charge of realising the Zionist Organisation's land policy.

At the end of the Congress's deliberations the JNF was left with two main tasks, purchasing and preparing land, together termed *land redemption*. In practice this divided the areas of responsibility between the JNF and Keren Hayesod. This was an important gain in the JNF's battle for survival in the framework of the institutions of the Zionist movement. Ussishkin, however, suffered a disastrous defeat: Weizmann succeeded in removing him from the Zionist Executive.

The political tension that accompanied the allocation of authority in the Zionist Organisation and the poor image of the JNF may well be seen as the prime motivation for the building of the ethos of the Emek and its conquest. This is demonstrable in the visual propaganda created by the JNF. As previously noted, even before the Thirteenth Congress the JNF published pictures of the project of conquering the Emek in the magazine *Ha'olam* and at precisely that time prepared an information 'blitz'. To shore up Ussishkin's position in the political battle, and to prove his words, at the Thirteenth Congress the JNF showed its film *Eretz yisrael hamitoreret* (The Land of Israel awakening), which later it screened elsewhere as well.[28] The first script for the film was written by William Topkis and the photography was by Ya'akov Ben Dov. It was shot in May in 1923, when these men travelled throughout Eretz Yisrael on a filming mission which was recorded by Topkis in his diary.[29] But his film did not suit JNF propaganda purposes, so Akiva Ettinger, with the help of the young photographer Yosef Schweig, re-edited the scenes and prepared the version screened at the Thirteenth Congress.[30] The film is based on a dialogue between an American tourist (Mr. Bloomberg) and a tourist guide (Penualli) who are travelling around the country. Bloomberg, who disembarks at Jaffa, is visiting the country and the first Hebrew pioneers (*halutzim*) and farmers whom he meets are in the settlements (*moshavot*) of Judea, a region where for the first time he sees the JNF's afforestation projects. According to the second script (the version presented to the Congress, apparently about three quarters of an hour long) the film contains 220 scenes and about 70 of them (one-third) are devoted to Jezreel valley. There are typical rural scenes from Nahalal, Ein Harod, Tel Yosef, and Beit Alpha: work in the fields, women and children, pioneering figures, tent encampments, and so on.

According to Topkis's diary, which described the shooting of the film, they did not spend notably more time in Jezreel Valley than in other places such as Gan Shemuel, Ramla, or Sebastia, of which only brief scenes remained in the film. Thus, being a JNF propaganda film it was edited such that Jezreel valley would be central, the place where the important things in the 'awakening' of Eretz Yisrael were happening. Note too that the wilderness and its symbols, the swamps and malaria, are hardly referred to in the film, which conveys exclusively a feeling of the good life, a life of work and creativity for the *halutzim* in the Emek. Wilderness and swamp, as the antithesis to the Zionist landscape produced in the Emek, are hardly sensed in this film.[31]

Also in 1923, as noted earlier, Julius Berger was appointed director of the JNF Propaganda Department. With his encouragement the third JNF film was prepared in 1924: *Palestina hayeshana ve'eretz yisrael hahadasha* (The old Palestine and the new Land of Israel). As noted in an earlier chapter, animated sections were inserted into the film, by means of which Berger presented the apparent wonders created by the Blue Box in the Emek. One scene portrays the *halutzim* who had come to Eretz Yisrael and had no land to settle upon; the box comes to their rescue and collects money for them. In the next scene the *halutzim*, who had been given land by the JNF, are attacked by Anopheles mosquitoes. They succumb to malaria and collapse. At this dramatic moment the Blue Box re-appears and pours out its contributions over the swamps. They disappear, and the *halutzim* are restored to health resume their work of building the country.[32]

The story of the trials and tribulations of the *halutzim* during the redemption of the Emek seems to have began to appear as a motif of the propaganda in the setting of a battle waged by the JNF over the definition of tasks at the Twelfth and Thirteenth Zionist congresses. Through the dissemination of these motifs of land redemption not only did the JNF justify its positions in the disputes, it also proved that the contributions were being used for the noble goal of redeeming Eretz Yisrael. Later in the 1920s the war of the *halutzim* against the swamps as a necessary stage in the creation of the ideal Zionist landscape became a central theme in the narrative of settlement disseminated by the JNF. A popular way of doing so was through songs and community singing.

Many sources exist in support of the claim that there were orders from the top about the story of the Emek, and we have chosen some correspondence concerning the creation of the Youth Library to demonstrate this. In negotiations with the writers of the monographs, detailed instructions were given about the desired messages to be presented in the written history. An example is the case of *Merhavia*. A letter from the Head Office to the author commissioned to write the monograph contained the following:

> In your writing you must, of course, accentuate Merhavia's being the first Hebrew location in the Valley of Jezreel, the desolation and waste which existed in this place before the arrival of the Jewish pioneer, and the cultural and construction work done by us in such a short time. Mention the war against the wilderness and the wild Bedouin that the Jewish settlers had to fight at the beginning, the sacrifice of property and the victims we sacrificed on the altar of redeeming the Emek. . . . Especially stress the general human side of our work, the drainage of swamps, the rehabilitation of the place and construction after the waste of generations. And, above all, you must, of course, mention and stress, in brief, pithy statements, the goal of the JNF's work as the redeemer of the Emek and the one conducting the homeland to progress not only in the Jewish national sense but also in the general, human sense.[33]

These instructions evince the clear-cut messages that the JNF sought for the immortalisation of its narrative, through emphasizing its activities. These can be found by tracing the use of powerful expressions taken from struggles for survival and religious rituals that penetrated into the Zionist ethos: '*War* against the wilderness', 'victims . . . *sacrificed* on the *altar* of redeeming the Emek'.

The most striking example of the construction of textual images of the Emek as a landscape and the immortalisation of deeds done there by the JNF's Department of Propaganda and Schools concerns the moshav (cooperative settlement) Nahalal. Many factors explain its becoming the symbol of new settlement in the Emek: its being the first moshav, its special, social method of organisation, its perfect (circular) design, its location, and more. So already in 1923, two years after groundbreaking, Nahalal became the leading subject of JNF propaganda films, which were screened throughout the Jewish world with the assistance of JNF supporters. This visual propaganda was mainly for adult and youth populations and was accompanied by additional propaganda activities. For example, in 1925 the JNF organised a delegation of Emek settlers who visited Eastern Europe to tell the story of their personal experience Among the members of this party was Shmuel Dayan, a well-known public figure, who had come to play a major part in 'The Story of the Nahalal'.[34]

Parallel to that story, which was disseminated by word of mouth by various lecturers, propagandists and activities, it began to be immortalised in writing; one of the first to do this was Shmuel Dayan. Immediately after the return of the delegation from Eastern Europe he wrote a booklet describing the beginnings of the settlement. It appeared in 1930 in the Youth Library series, and was reprinted several times during the period under study.

The most impressive and moving part of Dayan's text about the early days of Nahalal, according to his contemporaries, was that in which he describes what he saw:

> . . . For the first time we saw that the land was good. We saw the site and its inhabitants. We studied the swamps, their origins and sources and their size. One's heart filled with hope and fear alternatively. We were afraid of failing, of a great failure which would begin with fever, followed by black urine and then. . . . Not speaking we walked, downhearted. We talked about draining the swamps. And we consoled ourselves: Yes, the whole country is full of swamps, and are we supposed to indulge ourselves? . . . [We climbed a hill. . . .] For a moment we stood there, still. We shifted our eyes to the hill and behold, there was a large cemetery, hundreds of crowded graves, big and small. We were amazed. We were amazed. We were speechless. Before us to the west a fertile, broad valley was spread out and our feet were treading on graves, on forgotten graves . . . and when we descended from that hill we knew that here we would build a settlement'.[35]

In short sentences of three or four words Shmuel Dayan conveys his emotions, his fears, his feelings and his hopes when he looked down and saw the place upon which he and his friends were supposed to build a new settlement and save the land from the suffering of generations. He links the swamps, the malaria and death—the symbols of the past—with the hopes of the *halutzim,* because they had the power to change this place, as had their predecessors throughout the country. The account left an enormous impression, and the JNF published it in different versions for special events such as anniversaries of the organisation or festivals celebrating breaking new ground for a settlement in the Emek.[36]

Together with the intentional dissemination of the story of the Emek by the JNF's Department of Propaganda and Schools, the above events entered the people's collective memory through a constant and continuous system of educational propaganda which was the creation of the people of the Third Aliya. Ben Avraham and Nir have estimated that the influence of this system was especially great in the pioneering youth movements, and as a result few in these movements knew about other sectors in the Jewish community in Eretz Yisrael or could correctly evaluate their significance. The symbols and historical memories of these movements played up the role of the Third Aliya people, who were central to the creation of the ethos of Jezreel valley; the authors argue that the JNF played an important part in promulgating the ethos of this Aliya and its deeds.[37]

The propagandistic educational system that Ben Avraham and Nir refer to was grounded in the agents of acculturation then developing: book publishing, newspapers and journals, stories and poetry from the life of the *halutzim* and the Emek. Their propagation expanded during the 1930s, a time, as Gratz has noted, of interdependence between the political world and the literary world. The approbation given by the literary world to the Zionist myths approximated the ideological approach of the labour movement, thereby also sanctifying the pioneering settlement projects such as those in the Emek.[38] She goes on to state that the political world exerted strong pressure on authors to write cheerfully and supportively of the experiences and beliefs of the *halutzim*.[39] JNF propaganda and the unfolding of the story of the Emek proved to blend very well into the general atmosphere which swathed literary activity in those years and belonged to the cultural consensus that upheld the Zionist and pioneering ethos. Indeed, many writers and poets express feelings of identification with the settlement project in the Emek in their work. This was writing which became more raw material for the JNF to use as propaganda for the immortalisation of the organisation and its work.[40]

Together with verbal texts, the JNF created a tradition of using visual texts to describe the epos of the Emek: pictures, transparencies and films. These were cut and reassembled into one technical medium, the photograph. Parallel to this a tradition of using drawn sketches for distributing and building the images of the Emek also developed. Over time stereotypic drawings depicting this landscape appeared and were used for other areas in the country also. These drawings became very popular and recurred constantly in JNF publications: stamps, posters, placards, certificates, calendars, greetings telegrams, postcards, booklets, and more.[41]

The stereotypic sketch of the Emek would generally be a vista of a plain or low hills stretching across most of the picture, and drawn from a very low viewing point, ground level. From this point of observation most of the area of the picture would be covered in bold lines depicting furrows, ploughed fields, or fields of grain. These portrayed a future of plenty and happiness; the change in the landscape and the *halutzim*; the realisation of Zionism; and of course the part played by the JNF in redeeming and preparing the land. In the background, hills appear blurred, signifying the other place that encircles the Emek and that represent the past, the wilderness, the area not subdued by the JNF. Between the hills on the horizon and the furrows in the foreground, other elements of the new landscape appear: the houses of the settlement, a water tower, a tractor and plough, children picking flowers, or people working. A fine example of the stereotypic sketch of the Emek is the Emek stamp issued in 1946 in honour of twenty-five years of settlement in Jezreel.[42]

The landscape of the Emek is framed by ears of corn and sheaths of wheat, and in the foreground a tractor ploughs the earth. Another drawing, widely published by the JNF, is Otto Walisch's 'The five tasks of the JNF'. In the centre of five aligned rectangles, which together form one picture of the Emek scene, with hills in the background, the symbols of the JNF's tasks are presented: redeeming the land (a tractor), draining the swamps (reeds), supplying water (a water tower with a Hanukkah candelabra), planting forests (cypress trees) and leasing land (ears of corn) (see Figure 8.5).[43]

The creation of the story of the Emek and its dissemination by the JNF was a central component in the construction of the image and the immortalisation of this terrain in the collective memory. This immortalisation did not end in the distant past; it still continues today in a new form, as Tamar Katrieli shows us. She observes that today the Emek, the glorious domain of the creation of Socialist-Zionist ethos, serves for pilgrimage to 'settlement museums in which the story is recycled and acts as a continuing component in the Israeli discourse'.[44]

Summary

All the patterns of the JNF propaganda refer to 'the ideal space' and 'the wilderness space'; together they become the narrative's archetype, which was adopted for the other areas of the country. For example, from the mid-1930s, the JNF conducted an additional 'onward' campaign, named *Hagalila* (to Galilee) and likewise in the 1940s: *Negba* (to the Negev). In both campaigns motifs and symbols that crystallised in the story of the Emek were used. It seems that the structuring and metamorphosis of this story were fostered by several factors:

Political and organisational elements. The redemption of the Emek took place during a critical period in the JNF's battle for survival at the time of a re-organisation of the Zionist movement. For its president, Ussishkin, this was a personal test of his ideas, his independence, his freedom to work in Eretz Yisrael and his status within the Zionist leadership. Furthermore, he saw the Emek as a place where the redemption of the human being and the land merged.

Ideological elements. Settling the Emek conformed with the utopian agrarian approach of the JNF. This was a pastoral landscape, with no cities. It was a territory on which hardly any private enterprise in building Eretz Yisrael existed, so whatever contributed to the formation of its landscape was ascribed to the collective socialist ideology. The landscapers, the people of the Third Aliya, became part of the settlement elite, and their personal and the collective story was accepted as a model by the mainstream of the Zionist movement of Eretz Yisrael.

Deterministic elements. The Emek as a microcosm is an entire landscape unit, clearly distinguished from its surroundings by a range of hills; it is a broad, continuous area of land, which can be seen in a single sweep from an observation point. It had been a terrain untouched by human hand and environment, and became the creation of the *halutz*.

From the JNF standpoint, as expressed by Ussishkin, 'Here [in the Emek] will be the centre of the country'—a vision disseminated by the organisation's propaganda. It was the 'centre of the country' in the map drawn on the Blue Box that appeared at the early 1930s. The front of the box showed Jezreel valley in the centre of Eretz Yisrael, and all of it shaded brown: JNF soil (this map extended down to the Beer Sheva area). Today the present symbol of the JNF may perhaps be seen as a graphically re-called echo, one that focuses our attention on the furrows in the fields of the Emek (see Figure 8.6).

Conclusions

About a century after the Jewish National Fund was established as one of the institutions charged with carrying out Zionist policy, it still continues its activities in Israel and throughout the Jewish world. The historical episode we have tried to illuminate in this book thrown into relief the uniqueness of its activities and the changes they underwent within only one generation (1924–48). Our intention was not to realise a de-mystification of the organisation or any of its activities, nor to effect any historical revision of its symbols; quite the contrary: we sought to re-locate its role in the Zionist ethos. In concluding, we shall try to indicate the reasons for a general operational institution becoming one of the most important agents of Jewish culture.

The Organisational Theory Aspect

Researchers who have attempted to analyse the activities of the organisations adopt approaches and concepts from the field of ecology. They treat the as an organism trying to exist and survive in its environment. This environment is no isolated concept but is very concrete: it consists of other organisations, they too battling for survival and success. They wish to acquire as many resources as they need to survive and realise their goals over time. In all organisations different strategies develop for adaptation to the conditions of a changing environment. These strategies are determined by the decision makers, who interpret the information flowing from the environment into their organisation. Organisations may choose to influence their environments through propaganda or lobbying, and in this way they improve their chances in the battle for survival.[1]

In this respect the Zionist Organisation itself was one of the main components of the environment in which the JNF endeavoured to gain advantages in order to survive. As early as the first decade of the twentieth century the JNF, as an operating institution, began to collect money and carry out activities in Eretz Yisrael. At that time few Jewish national institutions existed that worked actively in the country, so JNF involvement in 'building Eretz Yisrael' outreached its initial goal. At this stage it seems to have functioned within the friendly environment of the Zionist Organisation, and the heads of the JNF could create fruitful relations with its leaders and win the rewards of status and appreciation. Political events in the aftermath of the First World War changed the environmental conditions from the JNF standpoint. Now it was obliged to operate in unfriendly and uncertain conditions. Political and personal tensions arose between the heads of the two bodies (Chaim Weizmann and Menahem

Ussishkin) and furthermore a rival institution, Keren Hayesod, was established that was liable to seize its share of the pool of resources.

Organisational theory maintains that organisations will modify their activities in order to survive, not only in order to produce the goods for which they came into being. To endure, over time organisations develop what the theory terms an 'organisational culture': a system of behavioural patterns, verbal expressions, or symbols. This culture is for the organisation's internal needs, and it imparts to its members significance and purpose; it provides them with belief, anchored in social values. The stronger the belief in the justice of the organisation's existence, the greater the effective support for it. Organisational culture even defines a unique image for itself out of the desire to convince others that the organisation is positive and innovative.

By means of these hypotheses it is possible to understand the massive entry of the JNF into cultural activities during the period under discussion. It had to develop some unique, institutional speciality that would blend into the Zionist environment and be part of its value system. JNF cultural activity aimed to serve internal and external purposes alike. For internal purposes it encouraged activists in the field and strengthened their solidarity; it boosted their motivation to undertake voluntary work and it rewarded them in diverse ways (such as publicising the sums of money raised or giving prizes and certificates). For external purposes JNF cultural activity served to 'capture hearts' on the public and the institutional levels of the Zionist movement. The JNF was obliged to change its image and continue to be the 'baby' of the Zionist movement. Wishing to emphasize its indispensability and to sharpen its competitive edge, the JNF adopted the tenet expressed by Ussishkin: it had been assigned the duty to redeem not only *Eretz Yisrael,* the Land of Israel, but also *Am Yisrael,* the People of Israel. This basic premise of JNF activity during this period became a major strategy for survival, from which emanated the institutional activity and cultural patterns it developed.

The Organisational Culture Aspect

The JNF propaganda work had begun in its very first years, but the real turning point was only after the First World War when the Head Office moved to Jerusalem and its work was re-organised. The decade of the 1920s was marked by enormous creativity, expressed in the great wealth and variety of materials produced by the Department of Propaganda. During this period the many forms of propaganda were enlarged and improved, and the technological innovations in the sphere of propaganda, in printing, graphics and photography, which had developed throughout the world were quickly integrated. But from the mid-1930s creativity succumbed to conservatism, and most of the means that had been developed by then became sacrosanct and the Propaganda Department was mainly occupied in recycling them in its different publications. Yet this conservatism was not a drawback as it helped in the assimilation and distribution of the language and images that the organisation developed (slogans, graphic symbols, songs, plays, texts) throughout the Zionist world and Eretz Yisrael.

The greatest achievement of that period was the penetration of JNF propaganda into the social niche of the Hebrew school system in Eretz Yisrael and the Diaspora. The outcome was a powerful alliance, from which both sides—the schools and the JNF—benefited. This alliance encouraged the JNF functionaries to continue innovating and distributing propaganda tools, which would cause not only the 'redemption of the land' but the redemption of the people too.

As noted earlier, for the heads of the JNF, and for the staff of the Propaganda Department in particular, the terms *education, propaganda* and *public relations* were not distinctly defined, and this was a function of the social philosophies of those times, the era of grand ideologies. No essential distinction existed between the products of the Department of Propaganda and those of the Department of Schools, and the materials devised and published became intermixed. Education and propaganda were perceived as two sides of the same coin, separated largely owing to the structural necessities of the organisation's budget. The materials and work accomplished by JNF operatives in education, publicity and public relations were indistinguishable. *Education* and *propaganda* served the same goals: justifying the existence and assuring the organisational survival of the JNF in the social and political environment in which it functioned.

Between the organisation (the JNF) and the different environments (such as the Zionist movement and the wider public) a symbiosis existed. The environment supplied the system with the resources it needed to survive, influenced the values of its leadership, and endowed it with a lexicon of concepts and images. The organisation, for its part, digested them in its own way, recycled them and re-distributed them to the environment in its language and symbols. For example, symbols such as *halutz* (pioneer) or *avoda ivrit* (Jewish labour) were not the JNF's invention but it made them more vivid in its publications. The organisation also contributed symbols to the environment, as well as new and original images and verbal expressions. These were the work of the Propaganda Department, as we have seen in the examples of the JNF map or in the images of the Emek as a Hebrew regional model. Nevertheless, in the relations that developed between the JNF (the organisation) and the Zionist public (the environment) the former attempted to impose behavioural norms. This was to be accomplished by reward and punishment in response to people's adherence to or deviation from the JNF path. The evidence is the prizes and personal and group benefits that the JNF developed to signify the different contributions (the Outstanding Box) but also the devices of social pressure and coercion to raise contributions (such as the stamp mitzvah duty).

Organisational theory asserts that every organisation has both overt and covert mechanisms for preserving its organisational culture, yet it is also open to changes in its culture in certain ways, and these are assimilated through educational processes, ceremonies, or rituals. The ceremonies are a mechanism for enhancing identification with the social or institutional framework and for internalising values and beliefs. The JNF used this mechanism mainly in events called *ceremonies of strength* occasions connected with religious and national holidays and festivals that were important for the entire society. The ceremonies created by the JNF, such as *Tu Bishvat* or *Shavuot* (Pentecost), stressed the values and tasks of the organisation and linked them to the religious essence of the festival. The organisation exploited these festivals to consolidate the identification of the wider public with its goals and deeds. Moreover, the JNF instilled its culture by means of special ceremonies associated with the annual calendar of work and historic events (such as the Anniversary of the JNF). In these celebrations praise was lavished on the organisation's achievements and its uniqueness; feelings of pride were stimulated in the activists; the founders and leaders were mentioned; and a variety of prizes and rewards (such as the Jerusalem Flag) were handed out. To the same category belong the rituals, which were important means of institutionalising and strengthening the cultural components in the participants. As we have seen, the most important ritual created by the JNF in the educational system was the Friday contribution. It contained all the elements of an event empowered by religious fundamentals: the chief symbol of the organisation (the Blue Box) and the religious symbol (the Sabbath candles) united in a special ceremony. The Friday box ritual continued to exist for many years after the establishment of the state of Israel when the purposes and goals of the organisation were different from those during the period under study.

Organisational Structure and Leadership

The JNF, as an organisation, was unique in the complexity of its structure and the geographic dispersal of its activities. It was an organisation based on the amalgamation of a relatively small number of paid managers and thousands of widely scattered volunteer activists. On the one hand, it was an organisation with the clear hierarchy of a directorate, president and executive board, which controlled its activities, while on the other hand it was a widespread network with national branches whose emissaries reached every village and neighbourhood in the Zionist world. These branches, which acted as the peripheral space of the organisation and the backbone to the Head Office in Jerusalem, sometimes enjoyed great autonomy. In terms of power, several JNF branches stood out during this period. One was the Berlin branch, from which were drawn technological innovations in the field of propaganda, advertising and communications, and which was a centre for accomplishing much work for the Head Office. Others were the national branches in Warsaw and Tel Aviv, where ideas in the field of culture, education and propaganda were developed; these branches were central targets for receiving the finished products of the JNF. During the 1930s the position of the national centres in the English-speaking world, especially in New York, grew in strength not only as targets for propaganda material but also as sites for JNF activities as a whole and for the fundraising.

Relations between the centre in Jerusalem and the periphery fluctuated. At the top level of the organisational structure, collected contributions flowed in, while at the bottom, the different propaganda materials flowed out, as did instructions, budgets and rewards. Examples exist of where the JNF's organisational structure worked as planned and decision making and operations were carried out within the accepted hierarchy. Other examples, however, attest to equality in relations, and even competition, between the centre and the periphery; in some cases the standing of the Head Office declined while that of the branches rose, the latter striving to form lateral links among themselves and to reinforce their autonomy.

According to the theory, the organisation's leaders and managers are the key figures in the creation of an organisation's culture. These people are seen as the leaders, so they are expected to determine the essential nature of the organisation. They act as role models. The leaders nourish the organisation's culture with ideological messages, which penetrate deep into the organisation with the assistance of declarations, slogans and expressions attributed to themselves. Another method leaders apply to create the organisational culture is that of decision making and actions. The leader's image greatly influences the organisation so leaders invest heavily in their images, with whose help they hope to transmit their messages. One of the important concepts here is transformational leadership, where formative leaders act as mentors and behavioural models for their followers; they fashion the organisation's culture based on vision, goals, values and self-fulfilment.

Research has indicated that Menahem Ussishkin, the president of the JNF during the period under study, was such a leader, who was closely involved in the formation of the organisation's culture. He influenced the operations level of the Department of Propaganda, especially in topics of a politically controversial nature that might have damaged the status of the JNF or his own personal status (for example, the censorship imposed on the Youth Library). Other figures who influenced the formation of the

JNF culture were on the senior executive level: Berger, Bistritski, Epstein, Ettinger, Granot and the staff of the Department of Propaganda who worked together on propaganda and educational topics. They made use of Ussishkin's image, speeches and writings to spread the ideas of the JNF among the wider public. They ensured that Ussishkin's comments, his particular expressions, and especially the slogans he invented were heard at the different ceremonies they established and were visible everywhere: on school posters, in Zionist magazines, and so on. The image of Ussishkin the leader was magnified in every filmstrip, slide projection, or film produced by the JNF during that period. He could be seen giving speeches from podia, ever-present at important public events, as befitted the leader of a major national organisation. In this respect the person of Ussishkin was the formative figure of JNF culture, and one of the tasks of the staff of the Department of Propaganda and schools was to disseminate this figure and present him as a great leader. The bearded figure of the JNF president harmonised well with the other eminent figures, the leaders and heroes of the Zionist movement, whom the JNF had helped glorify: Herzl, Bialik, Trumpeldor, Shapira, and others.

Practical Aspects

Organisational researchers tend to measure the success of an organisation according to two standards: efficiency and purposefulness. The first concept expresses the relationship between the output and the input of the organisation; the second denotes the gap between the goals and their achievement. A partial examination of JNF activity in the period under discussion using the concepts of input/output, in comparison with other Zionist institutions, was conducted by Ulizur. By this means, the economic achievements of the organisation can be traced.[2] By the same approach one can estimate how capable this organisation was of continuously acquiring resources from its environment. This is based on the assumption that an organisation exists as a result of reciprocal relations between itself and the environment, and it can continue to exist only when the intake of resources exceeds what is required for the organisation to function. For the period under study it is difficult to isolate the JNF's independent capability of acquiring resources as various agreements were concluded with Keren Hayesod. These agreements apparently restricted the JNF's ability to collect funds but they brought to it many resources collected by its rivals. Capital from other bodies flowed into the organisation, which helped it in its activities and the attainment of its goals.

Since the goals of the organisation were not only economic, its achievements during our period cannot be assessed only in these terms, namely how much money was collected, how much land was bought in Eretz

Yisrael, and the like. The measures applied in organisational research can seemingly also be used to estimate non-economic organisational success as well: endurance, status, reputation, public sympathy and social support. Among the conventional measurement approaches for organisational success two should be noted: the achievement of goals and the values approach.

Achievement of Goals

This is the degree to which the declared goals of the organisation are achieved. This approach makes certain assumptions: the organisation has end goals (super-goals); the various goals are clearly defined and can be simultaneously realised; the organisation's progress towards achieving these goals is measurable. The declared super-goal of the JNF seems to have been 'the redemption of the land of Israel for the Jewish people'. Yet during the period under discussion, despite the JNF's great land redemption projects it lagged behind the private sector in the purchase of land, and by no means succeeded in redeeming all the land of Eretz Yisrael, nor even large sections of it. Nevertheless, these purchases were vital to the Jewish settlement process in Eretz Yisrael, whose borders were determined during this period according to the land purchased by Jews. Over the years, as we have shown in this study, the JNF leaders assumed additional goals for the organisation, among them that of 'bringing Eretz Yisrael closer to the hearts of the people'. To attain these goals the JNF departments of Propaganda and Education were developed, and these increased the organisation's capacity to realise its super goal. This steps were taken to allow the organisation to survive within its political area of activity. In this area the organisation undoubtedly had great success, which has remained engraved in the collective memory of Zionism: the JNF and its symbols have become synonymous with the redemption of Eretz Yisrael.

The Values Approach

This approach is based on subjective evaluation, in which the standards used to evaluate the success of organisations rest on the values of the evaluators themselves: no absolute standards exist for measuring the success of an organisation. In addition, at each stage the organisation will presumably have to grapple with various existential problems, so the standards for its success change according to its life cycle. An organisation coming into being has to display innovation, creativity, the acquisition of resources and environmental endurance. By contrast, a mature organisation has to grapple with the need to maintain stability and efficiency, to establish an internal regime and to control all the resources well.

Clearly then, no evaluation of JNF success is itself free of the values of the evaluators themselves. The conventional assessment of the organisation, as presented and legitimised in the historiography of the

Zionist movement, has been much influenced by the organisation's self-appraisal, and by those who wrote its history, namely members of the organisation or historians whom the JNF engaged for the task. These worked in complete cooperation, and without doubt received their guidelines from the people in the Department of Propaganda. These official texts glorified the organisation's deeds and magnified its successes in raising funds and in redeeming the land. As we have shown in this book, the propaganda and education machine—which till now has not received the attention it deserves—was the factor responsible for the fostering of the image of a successful organisation with splendid achievements. From this aspect the success of the JNF's Propaganda Department was enormous, possibly far greater than that of other information and propaganda bodies in the Zionist movement. The departments of Propaganda and of Education seem to be the bodies that greatly contributed to the survival of the organisation on the map of Zionist consciousness while other organisations virtually vanished from it. There is in this perhaps a victory in the battle that the JNF fought against its rivals for public awareness and image, in the first place the battle against Keren Hayesod.

This was an impressive victory for the JNF, which successfully operated an information and propaganda system that proved capable of converting material capital (land and contributions) into the symbolic and political capital of prestige, admiration and public standing; of producing landscape and human images, of contributing to the construction of many Zionist myths, and of influencing the behaviour of individuals and groups. The ceremonies, rituals, symbols and slogans that the JNF Propaganda Department created during our period still perpetuate the organisation in Israel's collective memory to the present day.

Postscript

After the establishment of the State of Israel (1948) room no longer seemed to exist for an institution whose goal was the purchase of land for the Jewish people for settlement in Eretz Yisrael. As described in the book, however, the JNF is an institution with a highly developed ability to adapt to and survive changing conditions, and this has continued to the present. The JNF goes on with its traditional activities such as afforestation and the preparation of hilly land; but it has also entered new areas such as water storage and the paving of roads. In addition, over the last several decades the JNF has become a major element in the Green movement, which operates in the area of preservation of Israel's environment: cleansing polluted rivers, stabilising sand dunes and arresting desertification in the south of Israel. The JNF is likewise developing a 'natural environment' for the integrated activities of human being and nature, and runs centres for recreation and activities in the forests.

These current activities of the JNF are the direct results of an agreement between it and the State of Israel. After the establishment of the state, a situation developed of parallel administration of national-public lands. On the one hand the State of Israel administered its lands (state lands), while there were lands administered by the JNF (lands of the Jewish people). This duplication had to be eliminated, and by an agreement signed in 1961 the JNF transferred the administration of its lands to the State of Israel (although the ownership of the lands remained registered in the name of the JNF). In exchange, the JNF was accorded the right to be the official institution that prepared land and forests for the government of Israel. Similarly the JNF was given a combined mandate by the World Zionist Organisation and the State of Israel to continue collecting funds for its needs and to operate an information network (propaganda) for children and youth. This clause gave the JNF's departments for Education and for Information new momentum to expand their activities in Israeli schools and Jewish educational institutes in the Diaspora. These departments in fact continue the tradition of propaganda established by Julius Berger and Nathan Bistritski; it has been adapted to contemporary matters such as the preservation of the environment. Still today the JNF continues to produce propaganda-information booklets, filmstrips and journals in many languages.

The JNF symbols devised about a century ago, such as the Blue Box and the stamps, continue to be distributed in the educational system in Israel and in Zionist education throughout the Jewish world. In practice the present green colour of the JNF's departments for Education and for Information is a cover for the continuation of the Zionist socialising activities in Israel and the Diaspora. The tradition established by Menahem Ussishkin for political and organisational reasons has made the JNF an instrument for the formation of a national identity through the territorial socialisation of Eretz Yisrael.

Notes

Notes to Preface

1. For those wishing to read more about propaganda, I suggest general sources which discuss the mass media, persuasion, and propaganda in all its aspects, for example, Garth Jowett and Victoria O'Donell, *Propaganda and Persuasion,* London, Sage Publications, 1986; Melvin DeFleur and Sandra Rokeach, *Theories of Mass Communication,* New York, Longmans, 1989; Charles Larson, *Persuasion: Reception and Responsibility,* Belmont, Calif., Wadsworth, 1989; Michael Sproule, *Channels of Propaganda,* Bloomington, Indiana University, 1994; Jaques Ellul, *Propaganda,* New York, Vintage Books, 1973.

2. Nazi propaganda made use of geography in schools during the 1930s and 1940s: see, for example, Henning Heske, 'The Entanglement of Geography and Politics: Geographical Education under National Socialism', *Internationale Schulbuchforschung,* vol. 13, 1991, pp. 77–85.

3. For a description of the history of education during the mandate period see Rachel Elboim-Dror, 'Focal Points of Decision in the Hebrew Education System in Eretz Yisrael', *Cathedra,* vol. 23, 1982, pp. 125–156 (Hebrew); '"Here He Comes: The New Hebrew Is Emerging from Out of Us": On the Youth Culture of the First Aliyot', *Alpayim,* vol. 12, 1996, pp. 104–135 (Hebrew). For didactic applications of values, see Abraham Cohen, *Education in Values in the Lesson,* Bat Yam, Noam Books, 1996 (Hebrew).

4. Yizhar Smilansky, *A Call for Education,* Tel Aviv, Sifriat Hapoalim, 1984, p. 35 (Hebrew). See also for this argument: Zvi Adar, *Education, What Is It?* Jerusalem, Magnes Press, 1969 (Hebrew).

5. Zvi Lavi, *Challenges in Education,* Tel Aviv, Sifriat Hapoalim, 1978, p. 364 (Hebrew).

6. For a detailed discussion on the Israeli collective memory, see David Ohana and Robert Shtrich, *Myth and Memory: The Metamorphosis of Israeli Consciousness,* Tel Aviv, Hakibbutz Hameuhad, 1997 (Hebrew). On the role of the JNF in the formation of the image of the native Israeli youth see Oz Almog, *The Sabra: A Portrait,* Tel Aviv, Am Oved, 1997 (Hebrew).

Notes to Chapter 1

1. See Zvi Shiloni, *The Jewish National Fund and Zionist Settlement 1903–1914,* Jerusalem, Yad Ben Zvi, 1993 (Hebrew).

2. Dr. Chaim Weizmann (1874–1952), a chemist born in Russia, who became a statesman, then president of the World Zionist Organization and later elected first president of the State of Israel.

3. For the political background of the twenties see Eviatar Friezel, *Zionist Policy after the Balfour Declaration 1917–22,* Efal, Israel, Hakibbutz Hameuhad, 1997 (Hebrew); Ben Zion Yehoshuah and Aharon Kedar, *Ideology and Zionist Policy,* Jerusalem, Zalman Shazar Centre, 1978 (Hebrew).

4. On the country's borders and the process of determining them in this period see Gideon Biger, *A Crown Colony or a National Home,* Jerusalem, Yad Ben Zvi, 1983 (Hebrew); Moshe Brawer, *The Borders of Israel: Past, Present, Future,* Tel Aviv, Am Oved, 1988 (Hebrew); Itzhak Galnoor, *Territorial Partition: Decision Crossroads in the Zionist Movement,* Sde Boker, Israel, The Ben-Gurion Heritage Centre, 1995 (Hebrew).

5. Menahem Ussishkin (1863–1941), born in White Russia; secretary of *Hovevei Zion* (Lovers of Zion) movement, head of the delegation committee and member of the Zionist Executive, a member of the Herzl-Weizmann group. On his life and personality, see Shalom Schwartz, *Ussishkin in His Letters,* Jerusalem, Reuven Mass, 1950 (Hebrew); Berl Katznelson, 'Menahem Ussishkin', in Nathan Agmon (Bistritski) (ed.), *The Earth Scroll,* Jerusalem, JNF Publications, 1951, vol. 2, pp. 109–18 (Hebrew); Yosef Klausner, *Menahem Ussishkin: His Story and Life's Work,* Jerusalem, JNF Head Office, 1952 (Hebrew); Adam Ackerman, *Menahem Ussishkin: Fighter for the Redemption of Eretz Yisrael,* Jerusalem, The Teachers' Council for the JNF, 1987 (Hebrew); Yossi Goldstein, *Ussishkin's Biography,* Volume 1: *The Russian Period, 1863–1919,* Jerusalem, Magnes, 1999 (Hebrew).

6. Getzel Kressel, *The Story of the Land: Chronicles,* Jerusalem, JNF Head Office, 1951, p. 91 (Hebrew).

7. One dunam equals 1,000 square metres; four dunams equal one acre.

8. Kressel, *The Story of the Land,* p. 91

9. Yosef Weitz, *Our Settlement during the Time of Turbulence,* Tel Aviv, Sifriat Hapoalim, 1947, pp. 11–27 (Hebrew).

10. Abraham Gotkovsky, *A Catalogue of JNF Stamps, 1902–67,* Jerusalem, JNF Head Office (stencil), 1966 (Hebrew); Arnon Golan, *Change in the Settlement Map in Areas Abandoned by the Arab Population on Which the State of Israel Was Established as a Result of the War of Independence, 1948–50,* Ph.D. thesis, Jerusalem, Hebrew University, 1993 (Hebrew). Golan points out that in December 1948, the state sold the JNF a million dunams of absentee landlord properties, and two years later an additional million dunams: pp. 330–34.

11. JNF, *Report to the Twenty-First Zionist Congress, 1928–29,* Jerusalem, JNF Head Office, 1939, p. 207.

12. Kressel, *The Story of the Land,* p. 124.

13. JNF, *Report to the Twenty-Second Zionist Congress, 1940–46,* Jerusalem, JNF Head Office, 1947 (Hebrew).

14. Emanuel Haroussi, 'Thoughts on Zionist Propaganda Problems', in Nathan Bistritski (ed.), *Kama—The JNF Yearbook on Issues of the Nation and Eretz Yisrael,* Jerusalem, JNF Publications, 1950, p. 410 (Hebrew).

15. The Blue Box Work: *Karnenu,* Year 1 (1924), no. 2, p. 5.

16. *Karnenu,* Year 3 (1926), no. 5–6, p. 5.

17. *Karnenu,* Year 4 (1927), no. 1, p. 6.

18. *Karnenu,* Year 1 (1924), no. 2, p. 5.

19. *Karnenu,* Year 3 (1926), no. 6, p. 82.

20. A good example of the publicity approach is the first publication of the names of donors, for example, in the reports to the Zionist congresses and later in the organisation's newspapers.

21. *Karnenu,* Year 3 (1926), no. 4–5, p. 1.

22. Klausner, *Menahem Ussishkin,* p. 67.

23. The self-imposed tax was collected by the JNF until the agreement with Keren Hayesod, which disallowed the JNF to raise funds in this way.

24. On the development of propaganda in Germany in the 1920s and 1930s see Harwood Childs (ed.), *Propaganda and Dictatorship,* Princeton, N.J., Princeton University Press, 1936; Jaques Ellul, *Propaganda,* New York, Vintage Books, 1973; Eugen Hadamovsky, *Propaganda and National Power: The Organization of Public Opinion for National Politics,* New York, Arno Press, 1972; Frederic C. Bartlett, *Political Propaganda,* Cambridge, Cambridge University Press, 1940.

25. *Karnenu,* Year 2 (1925), no. 1, p. 24. Julius Berger (1884–1948), born in Germany, immigrated to Eretz Yisrael in 1923, active in the Zionist movement. Nathan Bistritski (Agmon) (1896–1980), born in Ukraine, writer, playwright, immigrated to Eretz Yisrael in 1920.

26. Since there was no clear separation between the work of the propagandists and the Youth Department staff in their everyday work, in the following we treat them as a single group, which decided on the propaganda methods and was responsible for their implementation.

27. JNF, *Report to the Ninth Congress,* Köln, Bericht des Hauptbureaus des Jüdischen Nationalfonds, 1909.

28. Kressel, *The Story of the Land,* p. 70.

29. JNF, *Report to the Twenty-First Zionist Congress,* p. 8

30. *Karnenu,* Year 22 (1945), p. 11. From 1926, agreements were made in the USA to collect funds through the United Palestine Appeal and divide them between the JNF and Keren Hayesod. In 1939 this fundraising body entered into partnership with the United Jewish Appeal, and during the war period the JNF received about a fifth of the sum collected by the UJA. See JNF, *Report to the Twenty-Second Zionist Congress,* p. 103.

31. *Karnenu,* Year 3 (1926), no. 1–2, p. 10.

32. *Karnenu,* Year 1 (1924), no. 3, p. 8.

33. See report in *The New Palestine* of 5 October 1923.

34. See various reports in *The New Palestine* of 19 December 1924 and 23 January 1925.

35. Shoshana Sitton, *Education in the Spirit of the Homeland: The Educational Program of the Teachers' Council for the JNF.* Ph.D. thesis, Tel Aviv, Tel Aviv University, 1995, p. 36 (Hebrew).

36. *Karnenu,* Year 1 (1924), no. 2, p. 6.

37. Baruch Ben-Yehuda, *The Teachers' Movement for Zion and Its Redemption,* Jerusalem, JNF Head Office, 1949, p. 18 (Hebrew).

38. In due course cooperation developed between the organisations in work with young people and schools, resulting in the establishment by the Zionist Executive, the JNF, and Keren Hayesod of the Coordinating Committee for Youth Matters. This produced a variety of propaganda materials and dealt with informal educational activities.

39. On the reasons for the establishment of the movement and its educational character, see Ben-Yehuda, *The Teachers' Movement for Zion and Its Redemption*; Sitton, *Education in the Spirit of the Homeland.*

Notes to Chapter 2

1. For the development of the box and the collection of charitable funds see Yosef Shapira, The History of the JNF, Jerusalem, JNF Publications, 1976, p. 8 (Hebrew); Shaul Shtemper, 'The Adventures of the *Pushkeh*: The Funds of Eretz Yisrael as a Social Phenomenon', *Cathedra,* Vol. 21, 1981, pp. 89–102 (Hebrew); JNF, *Catalogue of the Blue Box Exhibition,* Jerusalem, JNF Head Office, Information Wing, 1991, p. 1 (Hebrew).

2. See, e.g., JNF, *Report to the Ninth Zionist Congress.*

3. For a photo of the banner see JNF, *Catalogue of the Blue Box Exhibition,* p. 17.

4. Photos of the box can be seen on the front page of the exhibition's catalogue: JNF, *Catalogue of the Blue Box Exhibition.*

5. For photo of the banner see JNF, *Catalogue of the Blue Box Exhibition,* p. 17.

6. See examples in the exhibition's catalogue, JNF, *Catalogue of the Blue Box Exhibition,* p. 3. In these years the European Central Office of the JNF was in Berlin.

7. Approach to Ruppin by the German office staff, 28 March 1911, Central Zionist Archives (CZA), Record Group: KKL 5 (= CZA/KKL 5), file 213.

8. *Karnenu,* Year 6 (1931), no. 2, p. 30.

9. Letter from the Head Office to the New York Office, CZA/KKL 5, file 231.

10. For this correspondence see CZA/KKL 5, file 232. At this time the Head office even prevented local manufacture in the USA. See CZA/KKL 5, file 4867.

11. Letter from Head Office to the National Committee in Poland, CZA/KKL 5, file 975.

12. For the reports from Warsaw to Jerusalem see CZA/KKL 5, file 4866.

13. For the memorandum see CZA/KKL 5, file 4865.

14. CZA/KKL 5; see also correspondence, files 6247, 6249.

15. Approach made by South Africa to the Head Office, 7 August 1935, and also instructions for the design of the map on the boxes made in the USA: CZA/KKL 5, file 6247.

16. JNF, *The JNF Box,* Jerusalem, JNF Head Office, 1921, pp. 3–4 (Hebrew).

17. *Karnenu,* Year 2 (1925), no. 6, p. 1.

18. See JNF, *Report to the Twenty-Ninth Annual Convention of ZOA,* New York, JNF, 1926.

19. Letter of 13 February 1924, CZA/KKL 5, file 231.

20. The Blue Box, booklet for JNF workers, number 6/96, CZA/KKL 5, file 7501.

21. Letter of 18 May 1928, CZA/KKL 5, file 2902.

22. Letter of 17 February 1932, CZA/KKL 5, file 4865.

23. Letter of 17 February 1932, CZA/KKL 5, file 4865.

24. See copy of the letter from the American National Committee of 28 January 1928, CZA/KKL 5, file 232.

25. CZA/KKL 5., file 231

26. If not noted otherwise, all data in this section are from Abraham Ulitsur,

National Capital and the Building of the Land: Facts and Figures, Jerusalem, Keren Hayesod Head Office, 1939, pp. 127–134 (Hebrew).

27. *Karnenu,* Year 12 (1935), no. 5, p. 70.

28. Ulitsur, *National Capital,* p. 129.

29. The source for data of 1902–47 is *Karnenu,* Year 24 (1947), no. 3, p. 14. Also Year 22 (1945), no. 3, p. 11. During this period E. Epstein was the editor of *Karnenu.* Eliyahu Epstein (1895–1958), born in England, lived in Eretz Yisrael from 1919, one of the leading JNF officials.

30. JNF, *Report to the Twenty-Second Zionist Congress,* p. 104. Despite the activity of the UJA, the absolute total of money collected by the JNF during this period rose.

31. Ulitsur, *National Capital,* p. 246

32. For a prior discussion and relevant data see chapter 1.

33. This figure is calculated from the ratio of the sum collected by the boxes to total JNF expenditure on land redemption in those years (£P 3.7 million) multiplied by the total area of land bought by the JNF in that period.

34. The area of Eretz Yisrael west of the Jordan River under the British Mandate was about 26,000 sq. km, so the direct sums of money collected by the Blue Boxes did not redeem more than 0.3 percent of that part of the land of Eretz Yisrael in those years.

Notes to Chapter 3

1. The classification of the stamps was according to the catalogue of Jay Kaplov, *Stamps Catalogue of the JNF,* New York, JNF & Society of Israel Philatelists, 1973. Additions and changes, mainly in regard to the Polish stamps, were introduced in the dates of issue of different stamps according to the findings in the files. According to the above sources, the Head Office in Jerusalem produced 266 different stamps from 1902–47, half of them between 1940 and 1947. The JNF national committee in New York published 243 stamps (1902–47), and in Poland 123 stamps were published up to 1939.

2. Donald Reid, 'Egyptian History through Stamps', *The Muslim World,* vol. 62, 1972, pp. 209–29; and 'The Symbolism of Postage Stamps', *Journal of Contemporary History,* vol. 19, 1984, pp. 223–49.

3. Robert Newman, 'Orientalism for Kids: Postage Stamps and Creating South Asia', *Journal of Developing Societies,* vol. 5, 1989, pp. 71–82.

4. Reid, 'Egyptian History'.

5. Henry Miller and Paul Terrell, 'The Charity Stamps', *Social Service Review,* vol. 65, 1991, pp. 157–67.

6. Abraham Gotkovski, *A Catalogue of JNF Stamps, 1902–67,* Jerusalem, JNF Head Office (stencil), 1966 (Hebrew).

7. It seems that the first announcement on the issue of the first JNF stamps was in *Die Welt* on 7 March 1902, p. 10. See Sidney Rochlin, *Handbook of the Issues of the JNF,* New York, JNF Department of Education, 1990, and Kaplov, *Stamps Catalogue of the JNF,* for a description of the stamps.

8. A report in *Karnenu,* Year 1 (1924), no. 3, p. 5.

9. Letter from the Head Office to Leopold Schen, 2 August 1926, CZA/KKL 5,

file 998. A stamp booklet was distributed. This was a small album in which a child who bought a stamp pasted it at the place showing the outline of that stamp.

10. See notices in *Karnenu*, Year 5 (1928), no. 4, p. 12.

11. Bloch's letter; see CZA/KKL 5, file 3552.

12. Letter from the Head Office to Sapoznikov, 2 December 1929, CZA/KKL 5, file 3552.

13. See the Head Office report, 7 January 1930, which was sent to the secretary of the Jerusalem Office, who at that time was in New York.

14. *Karnenu*, Year 6 (1930), no. 2, p. 31.

15. Circular from the Head Office to the national offices, 5 June 1930, CZA/KKL 5, file 3552.

16. From the Warsaw office to the Jerusalem Head Office, 3 May 1939, CZA/KKL 5, file 9012.

17. The Ziman report, 11 June 1936, CZA/KKL 5, file 7543

18. Levi Barkley, 'JNF Stamps Tell Their Story', *Yediot Lamoreh*, Nissan, 1944, vol. 6 (Hebrew).

19. Bistritski to the Youth Federation centres, 18 July 1934, CZA/KKL 5, file 6253.

20. Circular to the national offices, 4 December 1934, CZA/KKL 5, file 7547.

21. Letter to the national offices, 27 November 1936, CZA/KKL 5, file 7543.

22. Letter to the national offices, 15 February 1938, CZA/KKL 5, file 9012.

23. Head Office to the national committee in Tel Aviv, 19 March 1937, CZA/KKL 5, file 8077.

24. See, e.g., a letter from the Union of Insurance Companies to the Head Office, CZA/KKL 5, file 7547.

25. The text 'Stamp tax paid to the JNF' appears printed on the stationery of different institutions. See examples in CZA/KKL 5, file 7544.

26. Classification of the stamps shows that the 'Fathers of Zionism' (Herzl, Nordau, Weizmann) were the people most often represented. In the Diaspora they also preferred commemorating 'local figures' (Brandeis, Balfour), and in Eretz Yisrael the preference was for heroes (Trumpeldor or paratroopers). There was a preference for showing areas in the north of the country, where JNF lands were concentrated, as part of the programme to glorify its work. This is discussed later in the book.

27. Yaakov Keren, 'An Instrument That Educated a Generation', *Yediot Lamoreh*, vol. 4, Iyar 5706 (1946) (Hebrew).

28. Only rarely did Ussishkin call for decisions by the directorate to commemorate the memory of persons on stamps. The first case was the stamps in memory of Rothschild and Kremnitski (the directorate's decision of 26 November 1934, CZA/KKL 10, page 1159). For another case, that of Meir Dizengoff (1881–1936), a founder and the first mayor of Tel Aviv, see directorate meeting of 2 December 1936, ibid., page 1316.

29. The Tel Hai episode and its place in the Zionist ethos has been much researched. See, e.g., Anita Shapira, *Walking along the Horizon*, Tel Aviv, Am Oved, 1988 (Hebrew); Yael Zerubavel, 'The Politics of Interpretation: Tel Hai in Israel's Collective Memory', *American Jewish Society Review*, vol. 16, 1991, pp. 133–59.

30. Undated memo, probably August 1939, CZA/KKL 5, file 9012.

31. Reuven Tsederbaum of the Youth Department in Warsaw to the Head Office, 4 August 1938, CZA/KKL 5, file 9013.

32. Undated memo, apparently August 1939, CZA/KKL 5, file 9012.

33. See CZA/KKL 11, The Abraham Gotkovsky collection of JNF stamps, container 2.

34. See Kaplov, *Stamps Catalogue of the JNF,* pp. 126–28.

35. For the attitude of Hebrew education to the Diaspora, see Ruth Fuhrer, *Agents of Zionist Education,* Haifa, University of Haifa, 1985 (Hebrew).

36. Letters from the Eretz Yisrael national committee to the Head Office, 1 November 1936, 31 May 1936, CZA/KKL 5, file 8077.

37. Letter from the JNF Teachers' Council to the Head Office, 13 May 1938, CZA/KKL 5, file 9615.

38. Letter from the Eretz Yisrael national committee to the Head Office, 16 November 1941, CZA/KKL 5, file 11961.

39. Circular from the Head Office to the national offices, 8 June 1938, CZA/KKL 5, file 9012.

40. See document on these changes, 16 November 1943, CZA/KKL 5, file 11961.

41. Memo of the Propaganda Department, 28 May 1939, CZA/KKL 5, file 9012.

42. Circular of the Propaganda Department to the national offices, 1 October 1939, CZA/KKL 5, file 10728.

43. Letter to the Eretz Yisrael national committee in Tel Aviv, 9 December 1937, CZA/KKL 5, file 9012.

Notes to Chapter 4

1. For a report on this see *Karnenu,* Year 3 (1926), no. 4–5, p. 5. 'The subject of pictures and Zionist photography', reviewed by Ruth Oren, *Photographing the Landscape of Eretz Yisrael in Zionist Propaganda, 1898–1948,* M.A. thesis, Jerusalem, Hebrew University, 1994 (Hebrew).

2. An almost identical formulation for the policy of enlisting journalists and authors can be found in *Karnenu* ten years earlier, Year 1 (1924), no. 3, p.4.

3. For the ordering of songs and melodies, printing of songbooks, and their use for JNF propaganda with youth movements in Eretz Yisrael and the Diaspora, see Nathan Shahar, *The Songs of Eretz Yisrael and the Jewish National Fund,* Jerusalem, Institute for the Study of the History of the Jewish National Fund, Land and Settlement in Eretz Yisrael, 1994 (Hebrew).

4. For details of these games see *Karnenu,* Year 3 (1926), no. 1–2, p. 9.

5. *Karnenu,* Year 3 (1926), no. 4–5, p. 2.

6. Game file: see CZA/KKL 5, file 2378.

7. General newsletter about the game, undated, CZA/KKL 5, file 2519.

8. CZA/KKL 5, file 2378. The artist, Nahum Gutman (1898–1980), arrived in Eretz Yisrael in 1905 as a child, and immortalized in his art the way of life of the country, especially Tel Aviv.

9. Circular from Bistritski, 5 February 1935, ibid. Various entrepreneurs used the JNF's letters of recommendation to promote sales of their games. See CZA/KKL 5, file 7482.

186 Notes to Pages 61–66

10. The game's instructions, CZA/KKL 5, file 11945.

11. Correspondence, November 1944., CZA/KKL 5, file 12863. After the war the Head Office continued to encourage the production of games conveying messages about the JNF. See, e.g., circular dated 10 March 1946 about the game The Jewish Community in Eretz Yisrael, CZA/KKL 5, file 14124.

12. From the very beginning, Ussishkin supported the idea of the Youth Library and always ascertained that its work was done.

13. At first the booklets appeared in soft cover under the series title *The Youth Library*; later the series was reprinted in hard cover, and entitled *The Eretz Yisrael Library,* also published by Omanut and the JNF. The financial investment in the Youth Library in the budget allocated to the Schools Department was high, in some years amounting to one third of that budget. See CZA/KKL 5, file 3600.

14. See CZA/KKL 5, file 2458/1.

15. Bistritski to Yehuda Karni, 12 March 1928, CZA/KKL 5, file 2458/1.

16. Letter from Bistritski to Lifshitz, before he was asked to join the editorial board of the Youth Library, 13 March 1931, CZA/KKL 5, file 3644.

17. See CZA/KKL 5, file 2458.

18. Internal memo, apparently from June 1928: see CZA/KKL 5, file 2458/1.

19. Bistritski's report after the mission, 'Cultural-educational work done by the JNF', CZA/KKL 5, file 2458/1.

20. In the years 1929 to 1931, thirty-seven booklets appeared; 1932 to 1934, eleven booklets; 1935 to 1937, ten booklets; and in 1938 only three. For financial and distribution reports see CZA/KKL 5, file 9158.

21. Report on the sales and distribution of the books submitted by Omanut to the Head Office on 20 May 1932, CZA/KKL 5, file 4972.

22. Memo of M. Haezrahi, 10 June 1943, CZA/KKL 5, file 12010. At the beginning of 1944 four more manuscripts were at various stages of work: see minutes of the Youth Library editorial board of 9 April 1944, CZA/KKL 5, file 12945. Altogether 86 monographs were published in the Youth Library, some twice. The manuscript of the booklet on Ussishkin, written by Yosef Klausner, remained in the Head Office and was only published in 1952, not as part of *The Youth Library* series.

23. Monographs unrelated to the above-mentioned areas were *The Yemen Diaspora, Religion and State, Rome and Jerusalem, Rabbi Yehuda Halevi,* and others.

24. Yehuda Alkalai (1789–1878), a forerunner of Zionism who settled in Jerusalem and often preached for the return to Zion and the use of Hebrew as a daily language. The settlement Or Yehuda is named after him.

25. For the literary content, the Zionist consensus, and the political conflicts see Nurit Gratz, *Literature and Ideology in Eretz Yisrael during the 1930s,* Tel Aviv, The Open University, 1988 (Hebrew).

26. Haim Peles, 'Relations between the JNF and Mizrahi between the Two World Wars', Jerusalem, *Proceedings of the Eleventh World Conference on Jewish Studies,* part 2, 1993, p. 251 (Hebrew).

27. Letter from Berman to the JNF Youth Department, 30 January 1930, CZA/KKL 5, file 2487.

28. Ussishkin's appeal was made in a letter signed by Halperin on 7 February 1930, CZA/KKL 5, file 2487. Another interesting response, dated 31 January

1931, arrived from a Mr. Halala who lived in Aden. He asks that all the books published be sent to him for distribution in Aden, because when he read the book on the Dead Sea he could see, in his mind's eye, 'all the places, and this proves that there are now true authors who can write scientific books in our tongue and in language which is pure, sweet and clear and which illuminates knowledge': CZA/ KKL 5, file 2487. The JNF looked forward to letters of support like this from the Diaspora, which affirmed the necessity of the Youth Library.

29. Letter from Kook to Ussishkin, 3 April 1929, CZA/KKL 5, file 2487/1.

30. Ussishkin's letter to Kook, 7 April 1929, CZA/KKL 5, file 2487/1.

31. Letter from Kook to Ussishkin, 6 Nissan 5689, CZA/KKL 5, file 2487/1.

32. Rabbi Meir Berlin (Bar-Ilan) (1880–1949) was the general secretary of the Mizrahi World Movement, a member of the Zionist Executive, and editor of *Hatsofeh* newspaper. He was a member of the JNF directorate.

33. Since Rabbi Berlin was busy with so many concerns, E. M. Lifshitz took his place as the permanent censor on the board. E. M. Lifshitz (1879–1946), born in Galicia, educator and author; in 1920–21 he established the Mizrahi Teachers' Seminar in Jerusalem, which was named after him.

34. Letter from Bistritski to Aharonowitz, 16 March 1928, CZA/KKL 5, file 2481/1.

35. Ze'ev Jabotinsky (1880–1940), born in Russia; writer and essayist, founder of the right-wing Revisionist movement, and seen as controversial by the Zionist establishment at that time. For his feelings about this incident, the various interpretations, and its significance see, e.g., Nakdimon Rogel, *Tel Hai,* Jerusalem, The Zionist Library, 1994 (Hebrew); Shapira, *Walking along the Horizon*; Yael Zerubavel, 'The Politics of Interpretation: Tel Hai in Israel's Collective Memory', *American Jewish Society Review,* vol. 16, 1991, pp. 133–59. Yael Zerubavel, *Recovered Roots,* Chicago, University of Chicago Press, 1994.

36. Exchange of letters between those involved, November and December 1930, CZA/KKL 5, file 3641.

37. The Nili underground was a Jewish-British group in Eretz Yisrael during the First World War. Some opposed their activity, fearing Arab and Turkish reprisals. On the Nili episode see Yoram Efrati (ed.), *Aharon Aharonson's Diary,* Tel Aviv, Karni, 1978 (Hebrew); Yaakov Ya'ari-Polskin, *The Nili Affair,* Tel Aviv, Idit, 1952 (Hebrew).

38. Letter from Bistritski to Smilansky, 6 November 1929, CZA/KKL 5, file 3640–41.

39. Further interesting reactions sprang from various places after the monographs appeared in print. An example is protests from Keren Hayesod on the omission of its name from the booklet on settlements that it had established. see CZA/KKL 5, file 3636.

40. Report from Halperin to Bistritski, 24 January 1929, CZA/KKL 5, file 2458/1.

41. The Head Office, to a certain degree, concealed the failure of distribution. In an issue marking the Youth Library's anniversary in 1934, *Karnenu* reported that 'up till now about 150,000 copies have been printed. Close to 100,000 copies have been distributed to the public and the rest are steadily being sold': Year 12 (1934), no. 4, p. 61. Reports sent to the Head Office from Omanut publishers on the printing and distribution of the booklets revealed an entirely different situation.

42. See the letter of the New York Hebrew Teachers' Union to the Head Office of 16 May 1928, stating that the Hebrew of the first book to appear was difficult for the children; they suggest that the Head Office issue a textbook written in suitable language about the geography of Eretz Yisrael. In the 1930s several Youth Library booklets were translated into different languages, but this effort did not improve distribution and it was halted.

Notes to Chapter 5

1. For a discussion on this topic see Yosef Halahmi, *No Matter What,* Jerusalem, The Steven Spielberg Jewish Film Archives, 1995, pp. 21–25 (Hebrew). He points out that even at the beginning of the 1880s in the Hibat Zion movement in Russia, there is evidence of the importance of the use of pictures of leaders and their distribution amongst the Zionist community.

2. For Zionist photography and photographs of the Eretz Yisrael landscape at the beginning of the twentieth century (stills) see Yeshayahu Nir, 'Photographic Representation and Social Interaction: The Case of the Holy Land', *History of Photography,* vol. 19, 1995, pp. 185–200; Ruth Oren, 'Zionist Photography, 1910–41: Constructing a Landscape', *History of Photography,* vol. 19, 1995, pp. 201–209.

3. The original suggestion was sent to Herzl that same month, and the essence of it was published in the Zionist movement's paper in German. See Halahmi, *No Matter What,* pp. 43–45; Hillel Tryster, *Israel before Israel: Silent Cinema in the Holy Land,* Jerusalem, Steven Spielberg Jewish Film Archive, 1995.

4. The quotation comes from a response by Dr. Yaakov Kremer, 22 December 1899; see Halahmi, *No Matter What,* p. 39.

5. Ibid., p. 41.

6. This is Halahmi's appraisal.

7. See Ayelet Cohen, 'The Beginnings of the Cinema in Eretz Yisrael as a Reflection of the Ideas of the Times', *Cathedra,* vol. 61, 1991, pp. 141–55 (Hebrew); also Halahmi, *No Matter What*; Tryster, *Israel before Israel.*

8. Letter from New York to the office in Jerusalem, 7 December 1923, CZA./KKL 5, file 231.

9. For a description of the script see Tryster, *Israel before Israel,* pp. 86–87.

10. For the minutes see Nathan Gross and Yaakov Gross, *The Hebrew Film: Chapters in the History of Silent and Talking Movies in Israel,* Jerusalem, Mehabrim Publications, 1991, pp. 64–65 (Hebrew).

11. Representation of reality in films is a complex question with many facets, such as whether the films reflect reality (real life) or perhaps create a life of their own (reel life). Different researchers argue that even documentary films do not necessarily reflect actual reality but subjectivity—the values and ideological world from which they are taken. See, e.g., Christopher Williams, *Realism and the Cinema,* London, Routledge, 1980; Erik Barnouw, *Documentary: A History of the Non-Fiction Film,* Oxford, Oxford University Press, 1983; Paul Swann, *The British Documentary Film Movement, 1926–46,* Cambridge, Cambridge University Press, 1989; Stuart C. Aitken and Leo Zonn (eds.), *Place, Power, Situation and Spectacle: A Geography of Film,* Lanham Md., Rowman & Littlefield, 1994.

12. On this see the attempts by the Head Office between 1928 and 1936 to introduce domestic moving picture equipment (cinematographs) for use at assem-

blies of youth organizations and in schools. Several projection instruments were purchased, and in the winter of 1928, a special film was produced for this machine; Yechiel Halperin (1880–1942, a Hebrew educator who worked for the JNF Head Office from time to time) went to Warsaw to present it. See CZA./KKL 5, files 2386, 3495/1, 3488.

13. The heads of the JNF and Keren Hayesod as well as their propaganda officials were present at this meeting. See CZA/KKL 5, file 2379/1.

14. Agreement with Ben Dov of 21 February 1928, CZA/KKL 5, file 2379/2.

15. Letter from Epstein to Granowski, 26 September 1929, CZA/KKL 5, file 2379/1. There are also minutes of the discussion with the Paramount company representative.

16. Gross and Gross, *The Hebrew Film*, p. 411.

17. At this congress James Neil, a Christian Zionist, presented photographs he had shot in Palestine.

18. For full quotation, see Tryster, *Israel before Israel*, p. 13.

19. See Halahmi, *No Matter What*, p. 22. In the decision they also said that if the experiment succeeded they would go over to using a 'cinematographic description', namely moving pictures.

20. *Haolam*, 23 January 1921, no. 1, p. 19.

21. Letter from the Jerusalem Head Office to all the national offices dated 4 December 1930, CZA/KKL 5, file 3492.

22. The contemporary 'event experience' in mass communications is connected to the family television set but it also has experience components similar to those of the magic lantern, despite the gaps in technology and time. For a discussion on this see Paul Adams, 'Television as Gathering Place', *Annals of the Association of American Geographers*, vol. 82, 1992, pp. 117–135.

23. For an exchange of letters between the Head Office and Berlin about the filmstrips, as well as an internal report of the Propaganda Department about the filmstrips prepared and the state of their distribution up to 21 February 1927, see CZA/KKL 5, file 965/1.

24. Epstein's letter to Berlin, 28 November 1930, CZA/KKL 5, file 3489.

25. Yehuda Lapson's proposals for filmstrips, 1 December 1930, CZA/KKL 5, file 3488.

26. Example of an approach to Rabbi Binyamin, 7 July 1931, in which Epstein details his proposal for the preparation of a filmstrip on school life in Eretz Yisrael, as suggested by the American committee. See CZA/KKL 5, file 3489. Other approaches to writers are located here.

27. Epstein's letter from Jerusalem to Dr. Machner in Berlin, 4 January 1933, CZA/KKL 5, file 4809.

28. See the distributed booklets of the American Education committee in New York. CZA/KKL 5, files 6195, 3495/1.

29. For a list of the transparencies and the printed lecture, see CZA/KKL 5, files 2379/1, 2382/1.

30. In contrast to the patterns of presentation and the image of the American child in Hollywood films, the Hebrew child was presented in the JNF filmstrips and visual propaganda only in a positive way. For a comparison with the image of the American child see Kathy Jackson, *Images of Children in American Film*, Metuchen, N.J., Scarecrow Press, Methuen, 1986.

31. The above quotations were taken from the lecture under discussion. See CZA/KKL 5, file 2381/1.

32. Rachel Elbaum-Dror, '"Here he comes: The New Hebrew Is Emerging from Within Us": On the Youth Culture of the First Aliyot', *Alpayim*, vol. 12, 1996, pp. 104–135 (Hebrew).

33. A letter about the magic lantern light picture strips, 9 November 1936, CZA/KKL 5, file 7475.

34. The report was prepared by Harry Levin and passed on to the Head Office, 27 April 1937, CZA/KKL 5, file 7475.

35. The subject of the film on stamps was discussed even earlier and in the Joint Committee for Youth Affairs. The filmstrip and the accompanying explanatory material can be found in Yaakov Keren, 'An Instrument That Educated a Generation', *Yediot Lamoreh*, vol. 4, Iyar 5706 (1946) (Hebrew). The letter cited was written by the national committee to the Head Office in Jerusalem, 25 October 1939, CZA/KKL 5, file 11143.

36. For correspondence and a list of the filmstrips that were prepared at the beginning of 1944, see CZA/KKL 5, file 12861.

37. The memo is accompanied by a list of filmstrips including details of twenty-six filmstrips prepared abroad and in Eretz Yisrael between 1927 and 1944. Memo by Dr. Y. Man, 30 October 1944. CZA/KKL 5, file 12861.

38. See, e.g., a letter sent to Buenos Aires by the JNF, 7 June 1936, CZA/KKL 5, file 7476.

39. Epstein's letter to all the national offices, 14 December 1944, CZA/KKL 5, file 12861.

40. H. Barr's letter from the JNF's London office, CZA/KKL 5, file 14121.

41. The number of sixty filmstrips is drawn from the various inventories compiled after the Second World War in Tel Aviv and the Head Office, with the addition of details about the production of filmstrips from correspondence from the 1920s and 1930s. This is a small number, and there may have been filmstrips produced in New York and even in Berlin on which we have no reports.

42. Halperin's letter to Bistritski, 30 August 1928, CZA/KKL 5, file 2458/1.

43. On the subject of content presented in Hebrew films made during the same period see Ayelet Cohen, 'The Beginnings of the Cinema in Eretz Yisrael'.

Notes to Chapter 6

1. On the development of Hebrew culture in Eretz Yisrael see Itamar Even Zohar, 'The Crystallization and Growth of a Local Native Hebrew Culture in Eretz Yisrael 1882–1948', *Cathedra*, vol. 16, 1980, pp. 165–89 (Hebrew).

2. On the importance of the JNF in the popularization of the songs of Eretz Yisrael see Nathan Shahar, *The Songs of Eretz Yisrael from 1930 to 1950: Musical and Socio-Musical Aspects,* Ph.D. thesis, Jerusalem, Hebrew University, 1989 (Hebrew).

3. This social concept of *civil religion* was developed at the beginning of the 1960s, with reference to the case of Israel. See Eliezer Don-Yechiya, and Charles Liebman, *Civil Religion in Israel: Traditional Judaism and Political Culture in the Jewish state,* Berkeley, University of California Press. Some do not accept the term *civil religion* in the case of Israel, where there is no clear

separation of nation and religion, and they suggest using the term *civil culture*. See Maoz Azaryahu, *State Rituals: The Celebration of Independence and the Memorialisation of the Fallen in Israel, 1948–1956*, Sde Boker, The Ben-Gurion Heritage Centre, 1995.

4. Oz Almog, 'Monument to Israel's War Dead: A Semiological Analysis', *Megamot*, vol. 34, 1991, pp. 179–210 (Hebrew).

5. Azariyahu, *State Rituals*, pp. 8–9.

6. The source here is a booklet *Mipi Yeladenu* (From the Mouths of Our Children), a publication of the Head Office (1935?), p. 8. See CZA/KKL 5, file 7485.

7. This letter was published in Reuven Tsederbaum (ed.), *The Jewish National Fund and the Hebrew School*, Warsaw, JNF Head Office in Poland, 1939, p. 24 (Hebrew).

8. The above booklets appeared under different names: *Geulat Ha'aretz* (Redemption of the Land), *Geulat Hakarka* (Redemption of the Ground), and others. The planners used the same texts as well as uniform plates for the binding and photographs of the landscape of Jezreel valley. See CZA/KKL 5, file 7501.

9. See 'File for the Box Work' from 1927, CZA/KKL 5, file 2350.

10. See notes of the teacher Y. Mulzadezky, 'The Pupils' Boxes', in Tsederbaum, *The Jewish National Fund*, p. 23.

11. From reports of the Teachers' Council it seems that in the mid-1930s in 200 out of 340 Hebrew education schools in Eretz Yisrael, money was collected for the JNF.

12. For example, see Shoshana Sitton, *Education in the Spirit of the Homeland: The Educational Program of the Teachers' Council for the JNF*. Ph.D. thesis, Tel Aviv, Tel Aviv University, 1995 (Hebrew) on the importance of the JNF in the development of textbooks, and the determining of content in Geography and *Moledet* (homeland) studies. See Yoram Bar-Gal, *Homeland and Geography in the Century of Zionist Education*, Tel Aviv, Am Oved, 1993, p. 51 (Hebrew).

13. See her speech in JNF, 'The JNF in the Kindergarten', *Yediot Lamoreh* (Teacher's News), Teveth, 1944, p. 8 (Hebrew).

14. Sitton, *Education in the Spirit of the Homeland*, pp. 163–165.

15. Zvi Zohar and Baruch Avivi, *The Book of the Child in Second Grade*, Warsaw, New Education Publications, 1935, p. 192 (Hebrew).

16. Baruch Ben Yehuda, *The Teachers' Movement for Zion and Its Redemption*, Jerusalem, JNF Head Office, 1949, p. 94 (Hebrew).

17. Several studies describe the development of the ceremonies and the festivals of Eretz Yisrael and discuss the place of the JNF in this process: Shahar, *The Songs of Eretz Yisrael*, pp. 33–59; Gideon Efrat, *Land, Man, Blood: The Myth of the Pioneer and the Rite of Land in Plays of the Settlements*, Tel Aviv, Cherikover, 1980 (Hebrew).

18. From the end of the 1920s dozens of booklets were printed in different languages by the Head Office on the planning of different festivals; they included Bible passages, proverbs, and traditional resource material for the festival, together with suggestions on how to organize it in a fresh way.

19. Shoshana Sitton, 'The Contribution of the Teachers' Council for the JNF to the Planning of Zionist Festivals and Ceremonies', Jerusalem, *Proceedings of the Eleventh World Congress of Jewish Studies*, vol. 2, 1993, pp. 235–242 (Hebrew).

20. Shmuel Navon, 'The Festival in the Educational Work of the Jewish National Fund', *Shorasim*, vol. 1, 1939, pp. 19–24 (Hebrew). Also Sitton, 'The Contribution of the Teachers' Council', p. 11.

21. Baruch Ben Yehuda, *The Voice of Zionist Education,* Jerusalem, JNF Publications, 1956, p. 89 (Hebrew).

22. Shahar, *The Songs of Eretz Yisrael,* p. 53; Sitton, *Education in the Spirit of the Homeland,* pp. 13–14.

23. Tsederbaum, *The Jewish National Fund,* p. 20.

24. Baruch Ben-Yehuda, *Fundamental Approaches to Zionist Education in Schools,* Jerusalem, JNF Publications, 1952, pp. 43–73 (Hebrew).

25. Sitton, *Education in the Spirit of the Homeland,* pp. 189–95.

26. The recommended times for box-emptying were: *Succot,* the month of Teveth, *Pessah,* and the month of Tammuz. See JNF, *The JNF Box,* pp. 5–8.

27. On the Box anthem and the correspondence about it, see CZA/KKL 5, file 36251.

28. Zvi Zohar, *Eretz Yisrael in Our Education,* Jerusalem, JNF Head Office, 1940, p. 142 (Hebrew).

29. Ibid., p. 145. Also referred to by Sitton, *Education in the Spirit of the Homeland,* p. 188.

30. See, e.g., *Karnenu,* Year 4 (1926), no. 2, p. 39.

31. On the Redemption Flag competition in Poland, see Tsederbaum, *The Jewish National Fund,* p. 30. The scope of JNF activity in the Hebrew schools in Poland was large-scale, and in 1939 the national office in Warsaw was involved in activity in more than 400 schools. Ibid., pp. 28–29.

32. Details on the ceremony and quotations are from Ben-Yehuda, *The Teachers' Movement for Zion and Its Redemption,* pp. 116–117. Descriptions of this ceremony appear in other publications of Ben-Yehuda.

33. The subject of social symbols and their meanings is dealt with by many disciplines: Sociology, Psychology, Linguistics, Art, Philosophy, and others. A general discussion about the different approaches to symbols and their functional development can be seen in Shlomit Kreitler, *The Psychology of Symbols,* Tel Aviv, Papyrus, 1986, pp. 11–88 (Hebrew).

34. In the original discussion on the essence of holy times, Eviatar Zerubavel notes the great importance of the separation and distinction made between units of time in Jewish religious ceremonies; he demonstrates this with the Sabbath. Eviatar Zerubavel, *Hidden rhythms: Schedules and Calendars in Social Life,* Chicago, University of Chicago Press, 1981, pp. 101–138.

35. The significance of the vertical spatial dimension and its conversion into a holy space (e.g., a high mountain or a Gothic cathedral) is well known. For an important cross-cultural discussion on this see Yi Fu Tuan, *Topophilia: A Study of Environmental Perception, Attitudes and Values,* Englewood Cliffs, N.J., Prentice-Hall, 1974.

36. For a description of the script and details about the film, see Tryster, *Israel before Israel, Silent Cinema in the Holy Land,* Jerusalem, Steven Spielberg Jewish Film Archive, 1995, pp. 87–88.

37. Dov Kimhi (1889–1961) author, translator, and editor, born in Galicia, immigrated to Palestine in 1908, edited various publications for the JNF. The citations that follow are taken from Dov Kimchi, *The Blue Box,* Jerusalem, The Jewish National Fund Head Office, 1926 (Hebrew).

38. Zvi Zohar and Baruch Avivi, *The Book of the Child in Second Grade*, p. 15.

39. A critical discussion on the connection between the images of the woman and the land points out that this is not unique to Hebrew culture and grammar but has universal expression. See Val Plumwood, *Feminism and the Mastery of Nature,* London, Routledge, 1993, pp. 19–41.

40. For an example of the 'tax duty' see chapter 3. The JNF created an unofficial system of 'taxes' in Eretz Yisrael, the best known of which was called the 'self-tax'. It was a 'compulsory contribution' that the individual undertook to give at the beginning of each year. Much pressure was placed on those who tried to evade paying these 'contributions'.

Notes to Chapter 7

1. See mainly Alan Burnett, 'Propaganda Cartography', in David Pepper and Alan Jenkins (eds.), *The Geography of Peace and War,* Oxford, Basil Blackwell, 1985, pp. 60–89; Mark Monmonier, *How to Lie with Maps,* Chicago, University of Chicago Press, 1991. Mark Monmomier and George Schnell, *Map Appreciation,* Englewood Cliffs, N.J., Prentice-Hall, 1988; Denis Wood, *The Power of Maps,* London, Routledge, 1993.

2. For important articles on cartographic doctoring during the Second World War see John Wright, 'Mapmakers are Human: The Subjective Maps', *Geographical Review,* vol. 32, 1942, pp. 527–544; Hans Speier, 'Magic Geography', *Social Researcher,* Vol. 8, 1941, pp. 310–330.

3. On the 'truth' transmitted by maps and their hypnosis phenomenon, see Samuel Boggs, 'Cartohypnosis', *Scientific Monthly,* vol. 64, 1947, pp. 469–476.

4. On the hidden expressions of propaganda in everyday maps, see Yoram Bar-Gal, 'Ideological Propaganda in Maps and Geographical Education', in Joop Van der Schee et al. (eds.), *Innovation in Geographical Education,* Netherlands Geographical Studies 208, Amsterdam, 28th International Geographical Congress, 1996, pp. 67–79; Yoram Bar-Gal, 'Boundaries as a Topic in Geographic Education: The Case of Israel', *Political Geography,* vol.12, 1993, pp. 421–437.

5. For details about these maps see Zeev Vilna'i, *The Hebrew Map of Eretz Yisrael,* Jerusalem, Publication of the Society for Research into Eretz Yisrael and Its Antiquities and The Bialik Institute, 1944, pp. 42–43 (Hebrew).

6. The so-called *Jabotinsky Atlas* was also edited by Samuel Perlman and Zeev Jabotinsky (eds.), *Atlas,* London, Sofer Publications, 1926 (Hebrew).

7. See Getzel Kressel, *The Story of the Land: Chronicles,* Jerusalem, JNF Head Office, 1951, p. 101 (Hebrew).

8. For a detailed discussion on the establishment of the territory of Palestine (Eretz Yisrael) and the accompanying arguments, see Itzhak Galnoor *Territorial Partition: Decision Crossroads in the Zionist Movement,* Sde Boker, The Ben-Gurion Heritage Centre, 1995 (Hebrew).

9. For a discussion on Ussishkin's position as part of the continuum of Zionist political ideas, see Galnoor, *Territorial Partition,* pp. 166–168.

10. For the memorandum to the Committee for the Partition of Eretz Yisrael, Jerusalem, 23 Tammuz 5698, see Adam Ackerman, *Menahem Ussishkin: Fighter*

for the Redemption of Eretz Yisrael, Jerusalem, The Teachers' Council for the JNF, 1987 (Hebrew)

11. Circular from the Head Office to the national offices, 28 December 1925, CZA/KKL 5, file 984.

12. For additional details about these stamps see chapter 3.

13. In the period under study, maps of Eretz Yisrael were published for propaganda purposes by other Zionist bodies, as well as commercial companies that used the map of Eretz Yisrael for advertising. An example is the advertisement of the Palestine Land Development Co. of New York that appeared in the magazine *The New Palestine* on 14 April 1924.

14. Schen's letter to the Head Office, 13 November 1931, CZA/KKL 5, file 4827.

15. Epstein's answer to Schen, 27 November 1931, CZA/KKL 5, file 4827.

16. *Yediot Lamoreh,* 1946, Tishrei, p. 6.

17. For copies of the correspondence about this map see CZA/KKL 5, file 6212. It was reprinted from time to time in the 1930s (e.g., 1938), after the Peel Commission.

18. Yosef Azaryahu (1872–1945), born in Poland; lived in Eretz Yisrael from 1905. Educator; supervisor of high schools during the Mandate.

19. Azaryahu's letter to the Head Office, 15 April 1930, CZA/KKL 5, file 3503/1.

20. Avraham Ya'akov Brawer (1884–1975), born in the Ukraine, lived in Eretz Yisrael from 1911. Geographer and educator.

21. Letter from Brawer to the Head Office, CZA/KKL 5, file 3503/1.

22. See Bar-Gal, *Homeland and Geography* pp. 125–136

23. Response of the Head Office to the editorial board of *Haboker,* 3 November 1930, CZA/KKL 5, file 8966.

24. For details of the competition for the design of the box and its image, held in the mid-1920s, see chapter 2 above.

25. 'A New Box', *Karnenu,* Year 12 (1934), no. 9, p. 4.

26. Letter from the Austrian national office in Vienna, 15 January, 1935, CZA/KKL 5, file 6249.

27. Answer from the Head Office, 29 January 1935, CZA/KKL 5, file 6249. Several of these versions of the map on the Blue Box produced in Israel continue to appear on it still today.

28. Undated release by the Head Office, apparently summer 1931, CZA/KKL 5, file 3504.

29. Brawer's letter to the Head Office, 14 April 1930, CZA/KKL 5, file 3503/1.

30. Azaryahu's letter to the Head Office, 15 April 1930, CZA/KKL 5, file 3503/1.

31. Letter from Epstein to Brawer, 17 July 1931, CZA/KKL 5, file 3506.

32. *Map of Eretz Yisrael,* scale 1:500,000, issued by the JNF Head Office, Jerusalem, 1938.

33. A detailed report of this meeting was sent to Epstein who was in New York, 7 January 1930, CZA/KKL 5, file 3552.

34. These maps found on the stamps are from the Gotkowsky collection, CZA./KKL 11.

35. *Karnenu,* Year 24 (1947), no. 2, p. 10.

Notes to Chapter 8

1. Many studies have been written during the last few decades on this subject, both theoretical and empirical, and we refer to several: Yi Fu Tuan, *Topophilia*; Edward Relph, *Place and Placelessness*, London, Pion, 1976; Donald Meinig (ed.), *The Interpretation of Ordinary Landscapes,* Oxford, Oxford University Press, 1979; James Duncan and Nancy Duncan, '(Re)reading the Landscape', *Environment and Planning (D): Society and Space,* vol. 6, 1988, pp. 117–126; Kay Anderson and Fay Gale (eds.), *Inventing Places,* Melbourne, Longmans, 1992 ; Gerard Kearns and Chris Philo (eds.), *Selling Places: The City as Cultural Capital, Past and Present,* Oxford, Pergamon Press, 1993; David Gregory, *Geographical Imaginations,* London, Basil Blackwell, 1994.

2. In regard to Israel, see: Bar-Gal, *Homeland and Geography*; Zerubavel, *Recovered Roots*.

3. On the sanctification of spaces and the memorialisation of heroism in Eretz Yisrael, see Almog, *Monument to Israel's War Dead*; Maoz Azaryahu, 'Between Two Cities: The Immortalisation of the War of Independence in Haifa and Tel Aviv, a Study of the Fashioning of Israeli Memory', *Cathedra,* vol. 68, 1993, pp. 98–125, (Hebrew); Azaryahu, *State Rtuals*.

4. Years ago Eliezer Schweid (1979) discussed the links between Jewish tradition and the Zionist viewpoint on Eretz Yisrael. For a social approach to the subject see Shlomo Hasson, 'From Frontier to Periphery', in Arie Shahar (ed.), David Amiran Memorial Volume: Eretz Yisrael, Archaeology, History and Geographical Studies, vol. 22, Jerusalem, Publication of the Society for the Study of Eretz Yisrael and Its Antiquities, 1991, pp. 73–85 (Hebrew).

5. Examples of the JNF's visual representations, mainly posters of the time, can be found in three catalogues to exhibitions about Eretz Yisrael: Batia Donner, *Being the People of the Dream,* Tel Aviv, Tel Aviv Museum 1989 (Hebrew); Tamar Shatz, *From Land to Orange,* Jerusalem, Israel Museum, 1992 (Hebrew); Rachel Arbel, *Blue and White in Technicolour: Visual Images of Zionism 1897–1947,* Tel Aviv, Am Oved, 1996 (Hebrew).

6. The 'Golden Book' is the name given to the books containing the names of generous contributors to the JNF. See Arbel, *Blue and White in Technicolour,* p. 56.

7. See the quotation attributed to Ussishkin's recollection of his trip to Eretz Yisrael in a publication (no author named): JNF, *Emek Chapters: Twenty Years of Redemption in the Jezreel Valley,* Jerusalem, JNF Head Office, 1942, p. 3 (Hebrew).

8. This concept of preference for the country over the city in Zionist movement has been described by Erik Cohen, *The City in Zionist Ideology,* Jerusalem, Hebrew University, 1970. See also Hasson, 'From Frontier to Periphery'.

9. Yet there is also reference to JNF projects in cities, especially in films produced with their support. This can be seen in *Shavu banim ligvulam* (The sons have returned to their land), 1926, and *Aviv be'eretz yisrael* (Spring in the Land of Israel), 1926.

10. The afforestation work and the JNF's planting policy in the period under study has been described in a number of studies, mainly those by Yosef Weitz, e.g., Yosef Weitz, *Forests and Forestry in Israel,* Ramat Gan, Massada, 1970 (Hebrew).

11. The child-tree motif was very common in a variety of forms. See the collection of JNF posters in the Zionist archives.

12. From the JNF's proposal to plant a forest for the fallen from the Hebrew University, CZA/KKL 5, file 8413.

13. Shatz, *From Land to Orange*, p. 57. Erik Cohen, 'The Representation of Arabs and Jews on Postcards in Israel', *History of Photography*, vol. 19, 1995, pp. 210–220.

14. Menahem Ussishkin, *Last Concerns*, Jerusalem, JNF Head Office, 1947, p. 197 (Hebrew).

15. In the film *Aviv be'eretz Yisrael* (1928) the desolate landscape meant to portray the land of Tel Aviv before it was built is a desert, apparently part of the Judean desert.

16. See more details about the Lotto game in chapter 4. The source for the Lotto game document is CZA/KKL 5, file 6202.

17. David Ben-Gurion, 'The Burden of the Wilderness', in the collection of articles assembled by the JNF, *Nineteenth of Tevet, JNF Foundation Day*, Jerusalem, JNF Head Office, 1947, pp. 24–25 (Hebrew).

18. Ussishkin, *Last Concerns*.

19. Anda Pinkerfeld-Amir, *Collecting JNF Boxes*, Jerusalem, JNF Head Office, 1938 (Hebrew) (stencil). See also chapter 6 above on the personification of the box.

20. Much has been written about Jezreel valley and its redemption; on the draining of the swamps and settling the land see Yoram Bar-Gal and Shmuel Shamai, 'The Swamps of Jezreel Valley: Myth and Reality', *Cathedra*, vol. 27, 1983, pp. 163–174 (Hebrew). See also other articles written in response to this article in the following number of *Cathedra*. See also the collection of articles in Mordechai Naor (ed.), *Jezreel Valley 1900–1967*, Jerusalem, Yad Ben Zvi, 1993 (Hebrew).

21. The filmstrip's lecture booklet *Thirty Years of the JNF*, published by the JNF Head Office, 1932, CZA/KKL 5, file 4810.

22. Yehoshua Hankin (1864–1945), born in Ukraine, a Zionist activist and 'land redeemer' for Jews in Eretz Yisrael.

23. Arthur Ruppin, *Thirty Years of Land Building*, Jerusalem, Schocken, 1937, pp. 164–171 (Hebrew).

24. Nehemiah De Limah (1882–1940), born in Holland, economist and Zionist activist. On land purchases in the Emek and the JNF, see Zvi Shiloni, 'Land Purchase and Zionist Settlement', in Naor (ed.), *Jezreel Valley*, pp. 26–42, (Hebrew); Michal Oren-Nordheim, 'One Dunam and One More', in ibid., pp. 43–53.

25. The feeling that the JNF's existence was threatened because of Keren Hayesod was not unfounded. This is attested by the way the Zionist Organisation's institutions treated the two funds in *Ha'olam* (The World), its official organ. For example, in 1921, an announcement was published 'to all Jews' informing them of the establishment of Keren Hayesod and its goals: 'Aliya and settlement'. Its tasks accordingly were 'purchasing and preparing land, paving roads and streets, building a railway, ports and bridges, draining swamps, irrigation, afforestation, exploiting water power . education'. *Ha'olam*, Year 10 (1922), no. 10, p. 1.

26. These six pictures in the magazine perhaps augur the pattern of visual propaganda for the Emek. See *Ha'olam*, Year 11 (1923), nos. 11–12, (28 March), pp. 224–225.

27. See Zionistischen Organisation, *Stenographisches Protokoll der Verhandlungen des xii. Zionisten-Kongresses in Karlsbad,* London, 1924. See also the Congress information sheet about this meeting.

28. The script of *Eretz yisrael hamitoreret* was written in August 1923, after the film had been re-edited by Ettinger. See CZA/KKL 5, file 966. Remains of the film are in the Spielberg Archives; they consist of the second part, devoted to Haifa and the Emek.

29. See David Gefen, 'William Topkis's Diary, 1923', *Cathedra,* vol. 13, 1979, 72–94 (Hebrew), for many biographical details. William Topkis (1878–1925) was an American Zionist entrepreneur who was an enthusiastic supporter of private enterprise. He decided to go to Eretz Yisrael to spend time with his family there in 1923. He travelled around the country, and, among other things created a company for Hebrew tourist services and guided tours to Jerusalem. In the spring of 1923 Ettinger approached him to produce a propaganda film for the JNF since Topkis was also involved in the American film industry. I wish to thank Hillel Tryster for drawing my attention to this diary.

30. On 6 June 1923 Topkis wrote that Schweig and Ettinger wanted 'only the Jewish National Fund in the film' so they were re-editing it. See Gefen, 'William Topkis's Diary, 1923', p. 91. Akiva Ettinger (1872–1945) was an agronomist, one of the founding fathers of Hebrew settlement in Eretz Yisrael. Yosef Schweig (1903–84) studied film in Vienna and performed much film work for the JNF, immortalising the ethos of Jezreel valley. For details about him and his work see Ruth Oren, 'Zionist Photography 1910–41: Constructing a Landscape', *History of Photography,* vol. 19, 1995, pp. 201–209.

31. In the film only a few scenes show drainage work and digging canals in Nahalal. By that time, spring 1923, most of the drainage work at Nahalal had been completed.

32. See Tryster, *Israel before Israel,* pp. 87–88.

33. Letter from Yehiel Halperin: see CZA/KKL 5, file 2487/2.

34. On the delegation to Poland in 1925 see Shmuel Dayan, *Nahalal,* Tel Aviv, Massada, 1961, pp. 113–119 (Hebrew).

35. Shmuel Dayan, *The Village of Nahalal,* Tel Aviv, The Book Fund, 1926, pp. 30–32 (Hebrew).

36. See, e.g., JNF, *Nineteenth of Tevet, JNF Foundation Day,* p. 13; JNF, *Emek Chapters,* p. 15.

37. Henry Nir and Baruch Ben-Avraham, *Studies on the Third Aliya: Image and Reality,* Jerusalem, Yad Ben Zvi, 1995, p. 44 (Hebrew).

38. Nurit Gratz, *Literature and Ideology in Eretz Yisrael during the 1930s,* Tel Aviv, The Open University, 1988, chapter 2 (Hebrew).

39. Nurit Gratz, 'Social Myths in Literary and Political Texts during the Periods of the Yishuv and the State', in N. Gratz (ed.) *Point of View: Culture and Society in Eretz Yisrael,* Tel Aviv, The Open University, 1985. p. 275 (Hebrew). For an example of this type of writing, See Yosef Aricha, 'Swamps in Jezreel', *Hapoel Hatza'ir,* vol. 24, 1931, pp. 2–6 (Hebrew).

40. For an evaluation of the description of the Emek in literary works see Avner Holzman, 'A Country Charged with Vision and New Wine', in Naor (ed.), *Jezreel Valley,* pp. 204–227.

41. For examples of these see Shatz, *From Land to Orange,* pp. 9–11.

42. See a photograph of the stamp in Naor (ed.), *Jezreel Valley,* p. 45. For a comparison of the illustration by Hershkowitz, see Shatz, *From Land to Orange,* p. 11.

43. See the above illustration in Zohar, *Eretz Yisrael in our Education,* p. 196.

44. Tamar Katrieli, 'To Tell of Eretz Yisrael: Ethnography of the Museum of the History of Settlement', *Several Words,* vol. 2, 1997, pp. 57–78 (Hebrew).

Notes to Conclusion

1. Walter Powell and Paul DiMaggio (eds.), *The New Institutionalism in Organizational Analysis,* Chicago, University of Chicago Press, 1991; Richard Scott, *Organizations: Rational, Natural and Open Systems,* Englewood Cliffs, N.J., Prentice-Hall, 1987.

2. Ulitsur, *National Capital and the Building of the Country.*

Bibliography

Ackerman, *Menahem Ussishkin: Fighter for the Redemption of Eretz Yisrael,* Jerusalem, The Teachers' Council for the JNF, 1987 (Hebrew).

Adams, Paul, C., 'Television as Gathering Place', *Annals of the Association of American Geographers,* Vol. 82, 1992, pp. 117–135.

Adar, Zvi, *Education, What Is It?* Jerusalem, Magnes Press, 1969 (Hebrew).

Aitken, Stuart C., and Zonn, Leo (eds.), *Place, Power, Situation and Spectacle: A Geography of Film,* Lanham, Md., Rowman & Littlefield, 1994.

Almog, Oz, 'Monument to Israel's War Dead: A Semiological Analysis', *Megamot,* Vol. 34, 1991, pp.179–210 (Hebrew).

———, *The Sabra: A Portrait,* Tel Aviv, Am Oved, 1997 (Hebrew).

Anderson, Kay, and Gale, Fay (eds.), *Inventing Places,* Melbourne, Longmans, 1992.

Arbel, Rachel, *Blue and White in Technicolour: Visual Images of Zionism 1897–1947,* Tel Aviv, Am Oved, 1996 (Hebrew).

Aricha, Yosef, 'Swamps in Jezreel', *Hapoel Hatza'ir,* Vol. 24, 1931, pp. 2–6 (Hebrew).

Azaryahu, Maoz, 'Between Two Cities: The Immortalization of the War of Independence in Haifa and Tel Aviv, A Study of the Fashioning of Israeli Memory', *Cathedra,* Vol. 68, 1993, pp. 98–125 (Hebrew).

———, *State Rituals: the Celebration of Independence and the Memorialization of the Fallen in Israel, 1948–1956,* Sde Boker, The Ben-Gurion Heritage Centre, 1995 (Hebrew).

Bar-Gal, Yoram, *Homeland and Geography in a Century of Zionist Education,* Tel Aviv, Am Oved, 1993 (Hebrew).

———, 'Boundaries as a Topic in Geographic Education: the Case of Israel', *Political Geography,* Vol. 12, 1993, pp. 421–437.

———, 'Ideological Propaganda in Maps and Geographical Education', in Van Der Schee, Joop, et al. (eds.), *Innovation in Geographical Education,* Amsterdam, *Netherlands Geographical Studies* 208, 28th International Geographical Congress, 1996, pp. 67–79.

Bar-Gal, Yoram, and Shamai, Shmuel, 'The Swamps of Jezreel Valley: Myth and Reality', *Cathedra,* Vol. 27, 1983, pp. 163–174 (Hebrew).

Barkley, Levi. 'JNF Stamps Tell their Story', *Yediot Lamoreh,* Nissan, 5704 (Vol. 6, 1994) (Hebrew).

Barnouw, Erik, *Documentary: A History of the Non-Fiction Film,* Oxford, Oxford University Press, 1983.

Bartlett, Frederic C., *Political Propaganda,* Cambridge, Cambridge University Press, 1940.Ben-Gurion, David, 'The Burden of the Wilderness', in *Nineteenth Tevet, JNF Foundation Day,* Jerusalem, JNF Head Office, 1947, pp. 24–25 (Hebrew).

Ben-Yehuda, Baruch, *The Teachers' Movement for Zion and Its Redemption,* Jerusalem, JNF Head Office, 1949 (Hebrew).

———, *Fundamental Approaches to Zionist Education in Schools,* Jerusalem, JNF Publications, 1952 (Hebrew).

———, *The Voice of Zionist Education,* Jerusalem, JNF Publications, 1956 (Hebrew).

Biger, Gideon, *A Crown Colony or A National Home,* Jerusalem, Yad Ben Zvi, 1983 (Hebrew).Boggs, Samuel, W, 'Cartohypnosis', *Scientific Monthly,* Vol. 64, 1947, pp. 469–476.

Brawer, Moshe, *The Borders of Israel: Past, Present, Future,* Tel Aviv, Am Oved, 1988 (Hebrew).Burnett, Alan, 'Propaganda Cartography', in Pepper, David, and Jenkins, Alan (eds.), *The Geography of Peace and War,* Oxford, Basil Blackwell, 1985, pp. 60–89.

Childs, Harwood (ed.), *Propaganda and Dictatorship,* Princeton, N.J., Princeton University Press, 1936.

Cohen, Abraham, *Education in Values in the Lesson,* Bat Yam, Noam Books, 1996 (Hebrew).Cohen, Ayelet. 'The Beginnings of the Cinema in Eretz Yisrael As A Reflection of the Ideas of the Times', *Cathedra,* Vol. 61, 1991, pp. 141–155 (Hebrew).

Cohen, Erik, *The City in Zionist Ideology,* Jerusalem, The Hebrew University, 1970.

———, 'The Representation of Arabs and Jews On Postcards in Israel', *History of Photography,* Vol. 19, 1995, pp. 210–220.

Dayan, Shmuel, *The Village of Nahalal,* Tel Aviv, the Book Fund, 1926 (Hebrew).

———, *Nahalal,* Tel Aviv, Massada, 1961 (Hebrew).

Defleur, Melvin, and Rokeach, Sandra, *Theories of Mass Communication,* New York, Longmans, 1989.

Donner, Batia, *Being the People of the Dream,* Tel Aviv, Tel Aviv Museum, 1989 (Hebrew).Don-Yechiya, Eliezer, and Liebman, Charles S., *Civil Religion in Israel: Traditional Judaism and Political Culture in the Jewish State,* Berkeley, University of California Press, 1983

Duncan, James, and Duncan, Nancy, '(Re)Reading the Landscape', *Environment and Planning (D): Society and Space,* Vol. 6, 1988, pp. 117–126.

Efrat, Gideon, *Land, Man, Blood: The Myth of the Pioneer and the Rite of Land in Plays of the Settlements,* Tel Aviv, Cherikover, 1980 (Hebrew).

Efrati, Yoram, (ed.), *Aharon Aharonson's Diary,* Tel Aviv, Karni, 1978 (Hebrew).

Elboim-Dror, Rachel, 'Focal Points of Decision in the Hebrew Education System in Eretz Yisrael', *Cathedra,* Vol. 23, 1982, pp. 125–156 (Hebrew).

———, '"Here He Comes: The New Hebrew Is Emerging From Within Us": On the Youth Culture of the First Aliyot'. *Alpayim,* Vol. 12, 1996, pp. 104–135 (Hebrew).Ellul, Jaques, *Propaganda,* New York, Vintage Books, 1973.

Even Zohar, Itamar, 'The Crystallization and Growth of a Local Native Hebrew Culture in Eretz Yisrael, 1882–1948', *Cathedra,* Vol. 16, 1980, pp.165–189 (Hebrew).

Friezel, *Zionist Policy after the Balfour Declaration, 1917–1922,* Efal, Israel, Hakibbutz Hameuhad, 1997 (Hebrew)

Fuhrer, Ruth, *Agents of Zionist Education,* Haifa, University of Haifa, 1985 (Hebrew).

Galnoor, Itzhak, *Territorial Partition: Decision Crossroads in the Zionist Movement,* Sde Boker, The Ben-Gurion Heritage Centre, 1995 (Hebrew).

Gefen, David. 'William Topkis's Diary, 1923', *Cathedra,* Vol. 13, 1979, pp. 72–94 (Hebrew).Golan, Arnon, *Change in the Settlement Map in Areas Abandoned by the Arab Population in Which the State of Israel Was Established as a Result of the War of Independence, 1948–1950,* Ph.D. thesis, Jerusalem, Hebrew University, 1993 (Hebrew).

Goldstein, Yossi, *Ussishkin's Biography*. Volume 1: *The Russian Period, 1863–1919*, Jerusalem, Magnes, 1999 (Hebrew).

Gotkovsky, Abraham, *A Catalogue of JNF Stamps, 1902–1967*, Jerusalem, JNF Head Office (Stencil), 1966 (Hebrew).

Granowsky, Abraham, *The Land Regime in Eretz Yisrael*, Tel Aviv, Dvir, 1949 (Hebrew).

Gratz, Nurit, 'Social Myths in Literary and Political Texts During the Periods of the Yishuv and the State', in N. Gratz (ed.), *Point of View: Culture and Society in Eretz Yisrael*, Tel Aviv, The Open University, 1985, pp. 271–283 (Hebrew).

————, *Literature and Ideology in Eretz Yisrael during the 1930s*, Tel Aviv, The Open University, 1988 (Hebrew).

Gregory, David, *Geographical Imaginations*, London, Basil Blackwell, 1994.

Gross, Nathan, and Gross, Yaakov, *The Hebrew Film: Chapters in the History of Silent and Talking Movies in Israel*, Jerusalem, Mehabrim Publications, 1991 (Hebrew).

Hadamovsky, Eugen, *Propaganda and National Power: The Organization of Public Opinion for National Politics*, New York, Arno Press, 1972.

Halahmi, Yosef, *No Matter What*, Jerusalem, The Steven Spielberg Jewish Film Archives, 1995 (Hebrew).

Haroussi, Emanuel, 'Thoughts on Zionist Propaganda Problems', in Bistritski, Nathan (ed.), *Kama: JNF Yearbook on Issues of Nation and Eretz Yisrael*, Jerusalem, JNF Publications, 1950, pp. 408–417 (Hebrew).

Hasson, Shlomo, 'From Frontier to Periphery', in Shahar, Arie (ed.), *The David Amiran Memorial Volume, Eretz Yisrael, Archaeology, History and Geographical Studies*, Vol. 22, Jerusalem, Publication of the Society for the Study of Eretz Yisrael and Its Antiquities, 1991, pp. 73–85 (Hebrew).

Heske, Henning, 'The Entanglement of Geography and Politics: Geographical Education under National Socialism', *International Schulbuchforschung*, Vol. 13, 1991, pp. 77–85.

Holzman, Avner, 'A Country Charged with Vision and New Wine', in Naor, Mordechai (ed.), *Jezreel Valley, 1900–1967*, Jerusalem, Yad Ben Zvi Publications, Idan Series, 1993, 204–227, (Hebrew).

Jackson, Kathy M., *Images of Children in American Film*, Metuchen, N.J., Scarecrow Press, Methuen, 1986.

JNF, *Report to the Ninth Zionist Congress*, Köln, Bericht des Hauptbureaus des Judischen Nationalfonds, 1909.

JNF, *The JNF Box*, Jerusalem, JNF Head Office, 1921 (Hebrew).

JNF, *Report to the Twenty-Ninth Annual Convention of ZOA*, New York, JNF, 1926.

JNF, *Report to the Twenty-First Zionist Congress 1928–1929*, Jerusalem, JNF Head Office, 1939 (Hebrew).

JNF, *Emek Chapters: Twenty Years of Redemption in the Jezreel Valley*, Jerusalem, JNF Head Office, 1942 (Hebrew).

JNF, 'The JNF in the Kindergarten', *Yediot Lamoreh*, Teveth, 1944 (Hebrew).

JNF, *Report to the Twnety-Second Zionist Congress for 1940–1946*, Jerusalem, JNF Head Office, 1947 (Hebrew).

JNF, *Ninteenth of Tevet, JNF Foundation Day*, Jerusalem, JNF Head Office, 1947 (Hebrew).JNF, *Catalogue of the Blue Box Exhibition*, Jerusalem, JNF Head Office, Information Wing, 1991 (Hebrew).

Jowett, Garth, and O'Donell, Victoria, *Propaganda and Persuasion*, London, Sage Publications, 1986.

Kaplov, Jay I., *Stamps Catalogue of the JNF,* New York, JNF & Society of Israel Philatelists, 1973.

Karnenu (Journal, 1924–1962), Jerusalem, JNF Head Office.

Katrieli, Tamar, 'To Tell of Eretz Yisrael: Ethnography of the Museum of the History of Settlement', *Several Words,* Vol. 2, 1997, pp. 57–78 (Hebrew).

Katznelson, Berel, 'Menahem Ussishkin', in Agmon (Bistritski), Nathan (ed.), *The Earth Scroll,* Jerusalem, JNF Publications, 1951, Vol. 2, pp. 109–118 (Hebrew).

Kearns, Gerard, and Philo, Chris (eds.), *Selling Places: The City As Cultural Capital, Past and Present,* Oxford, Pergamon Press, 1993

Keren, Yaakov, 'An Instrument That Educated a Generation', *Yediot Lamoreh,* Vol. 4, Iyar 5706 (1946) (Hebrew).

Kimchi, Dov, *The Blue Box,* Jerusalem, JNF Head Office, 1926 (Hebrew).

Klausner, Yosef, *Menahem Ussishkin: His Story and Life's Work,* Jerusalem, JNF Head Office, 1952 (Hebrew).

Kreitler, Shlomit, *The Psychology of Symbols,* Tel Aviv, Papyrus, 1986 (Hebrew).

Kressel, Getzel, *The Story of the Land: Chronicles,* Jerusalem, JNF Head Office, 1951 (Hebrew).Larson, Charles U., *Persuasion: Reception and Responsibility,* Belmont, Calif., Wadsworth, 1989.

Lavi, Zvi, *Challenges in Education,* Tel Aviv, Sifriat Hapoalim, 1978 (Hebrew).

Meinig, Donald W. (ed.), *The Interpretation of Ordinary Landscapes,* Oxford, Oxford University Press, 1979.

Miller, Henry, and Terrell, Paul, 'The Charity Stamps', *Social Service Review,* Vol. 65, 1991, pp. 157–167.

Monmonier, Mark, *How to Lie with Maps,* Chicago, University of Chicago Press, 1991.

Monmomier, Mark, and Schell, George, *Map Appreciation,* Englewood Cliffs, N.J., Prentice-Hall, 1988.

Mulzadezky, Y., 'The Pupils' Boxes', in Tsederbaum, Reuven (ed.), *The Jewish National Fund and the Hebrew School,* Warsaw, JNF Head Office in Poland, 1939 (Hebrew).Naor, Mordechai (ed.), *Jezreel Valley, 1900–1967,* Jerusalem, Yad Ben Zvi Publications, Idan Series, 1993 (Hebrew).

Navon, Shmuel, 'The Festival in the Educational Work of the Jewish National Fund', *Shorasim,* Vol. 1, 1939, pp. 19–24 (Hebrew).

Newman, Robert, S., 'Orientalism for Kids: Postage Stamps and Creating South Asia', *Journal of Developing Societies,* Vol. 5, 1989, pp. 71–82.

Nir, Henry, and Ben-Avraham, Baruch, *Studies on the Third Aliya: Image and Reality,* Jerusalem, Yad Ben Zvi, 1995 (Hebrew).

Nir, Yeshayahu, 'Photographic Representation and Social Interaction: The Case of the Holy Land', *History of Photography,* Vol. 19, 1995, pp. 185–200.

Ohana, David, and Strich, Robert, *Myth and Memory: The Metamorphosis of Israeli Consciousness,* Tel Aviv, Hakibbutz Hameuhad, 1997 (Hebrew).

Oren, Ruth, *Photographing the Landscape of Eretz Yisrael in Zionist Propaganda, 1898–1948,* M.A. thesis, Jerusalem, Hebrew University, 1994 (Hebrew).

———, 'Zionist Photography 1910–1941: Constructing a Landscape', *History of Photography,* Vol. 19, 1995, pp. 201–209.

Oren-Nordheim, Michal, 'One Dunam and One More', in Naor, Mordechai (ed.), *Jezreel Valley, 1900–1967,* Jerusalem, Yad Ben Zvi Publications, Idan Series, 1993, pp. 43–53 (Hebrew).

Peles, Haim Y. 'Relations between the JNF and Mizrahi between the Two World Wars', Jerusalem, *Proceedings of the Eleventh World Conference on Jewish Studies,* Part II, 1993 (Hebrew).

Perlman, Samuel, and Jabotinsky, Zeev (eds.), *Atlas,* London, Sofer Publications, 1926 (Hebrew).Pinkerfeld-Amir, Anda, *Collecting JNF Boxes,* Jerusalem, JNF Head Office, 1938 (Hebrew) (Stencil).

Plumwood, Val, *Feminism and the Mastery of Nature,* London, Routledge, 1993.

Powell, Walter, and Dimaggio, Paul (eds.), *The New Institutionalism in Organizational Analysis,* Chicago, University of Chicago Press, 1991;

Reid, Donald, 'Egyptian History through Stamps', *The Muslim World,* Vol. 62, 1972, pp. 209–229.

———, 'The Symbolism of Postage Stamps', *Journal of Contemporary History,* Vol. 19, 1984, pp. 223–249.

Relph, Edward, *Place and Placelessness,* London, Pion, 1976.

Rochlin, Sidney, *Handbook of the Issues of the JNF,* New York, JNF Department of Education, 1990.

Rogel, Nakdimon, *Tel Hai,* Jerusalem, the Zionist Library, 1994 (Hebrew).

Ruppin, Arthur, *Thirty Years of Land Building,* Jerusalem, Schocken, 1937 (Hebrew).

Schwartz, Shalom, *Ussishkin in His Letters,* Jerusalem, Reuven Mass, 1950 (Hebrew).

Schweid, Eliezer, *Homeland and Its Country,* Tel Aviv, Am Oved, 1979 (Hebrew).

Scott, Richard W., *Organizations: Rational, Natural and Open Systems,* Englewood Cliffs, N.J., Prentice-Hall, 1987.

Shahar, Nathan, *The Songs of Eretz Yisrael from 1930 to 1950: Musical and Socio-Musical Aspects,* Ph.D. thesis, Jerusalem, Hebrew University, 1989 (Hebrew).

———, *The Songs of Eretz Yisrael and the Jewish National Fund,* Jerusalem, Institute for the Study of the History of the Jewish National Fund, Land and Settlement in Eretz Yisrael, 1994 (Hebrew).

Shapira, Anita, *Walking along the Horizon,* Tel Aviv, Am Oved, 1988 (Hebrew).

———, *Sword of the Dove,* Tel Aviv, Am Oved, 1992 (Hebrew).

Shapira, Yosef, *The History of the JNF,* Jerusalem, JNF Publications, 1976 (Hebrew).

Shatz, Tamar, *From Land to Orange,* Jerusalem, Israel Museum, 1992 (Hebrew).

Shiloni, Zvi, *The Jewish National Fund and Zionist Settlement, 1903–1914,* Jerusalem, Yad Ben Zvi, 1993 (Hebrew).

———, 'Land Purchase and Zionist Settlement', in Naor, Mordechai (ed.), *Jezreel Valley, 1900–1967,* Jerusalem, Yad Ben Zvi Publications, Idan Series, 1993, pp. 26–42 (Hebrew).

Shtemper, Shaul, 'Adventures of the *Pushkeh*: The Funds of Eretz Yisrael as a Social Phenomenon', *Cathedra,* Vol. 21, 1981, pp. 89–102 (Hebrew).

Sitton, Shoshana, 'The Contribution of the Teachers' Council for the JNF to the Planning of Zionist Festivals and Ceremonies', Jerusalem, *Proceedings of the Eleventh World Congress of Jewish Studies,* Vol. 2, 1993, pp. 235–242 (Hebrew).

————, *The Teachers Council for the JNF: Encounter between Hebrew Culture and British Colonial Culture*, Jerusalem, Institute for Research into the History of the JNF, Land and Settlement in Eretz Yisrael, 1994 (Hebrew).

————, *Education in the Spirit of the Homeland: The Educational Program of the Teachers' Council for the JNF*. Ph.D. thesis, Tel Aviv, Tel Aviv University, 1995 (Hebrew).Smilansky, Yizhar, *A Call for Education*, Tel Aviv, Sifriat Hapoalim, 1984 (Hebrew).

Speier, Hans, 'Magic Geography', *Social Researcher*, Vol. 8, 1941, pp. 310–330.

Sproule, Michael J., *Channels of Propaganda*, Bloomington, Indiana University Press, 1994.Swann, Paul, *The British Documentary Film Movement, 1926–1946*, Cambridge, Cambridge University Press, 1989.

The New Palestine (Journal, 1919–1989), New York, Zionist Organization of America.

Tryster, Hillel, *Israel before Israel: Silent Cinema in the Holy Land*, Jerusalem, Steven Spielberg Jewish Film Archive, 1995.

Tsederbaum, Reuven (ed.), *The Jewish National Fund and the Hebrew School*, Warsaw, JNF Head Office in Poland, 1939 (Hebrew).

Tuan, Yi Fu, *Topophilia: A Study of Environmental Perception, Attitudes, and Values*, Englewood Cliffs, N.J., Prentice-Hall, 1974.

Ulitsur, Abraham, *National Capital and the Building of the Land: Facts and Figures*, Jerusalem, Keren Hayesod Head Office, 1939 (Hebrew).

Ussishkin, Menahem, *Last Concerns*, Jerusalem, JNF Head Office, 1947 (Hebrew).

Vilna'i, Zeev, *The Hebrew Map of Eretz Yisrael*, Jerusalem, Publication of the Society for Research into Eretz Yisrael and Its Antiquities and the Bialik Institute, 1944 (Hebrew).

Weitz, Yosef, *Forests and Forestry in Israel*, Ramat Gan, Massada, 1970 (Hebrew).

————, *Our Settlement during the Time of Turbulence*, Tel Aviv, Sifriat Hapoalim, 1947 (Hebrew).Williams, Christopher, *Realism and the Cinema*, London, Routledge, 1980.

Wood, Denis, *The Power of Maps*, London, Routledge, 1993.

Wright, John K., 'Mapmakers Are Human: The Subjective Maps', *Geographical Review*, Vol. 32, 1942, pp. 527–544.

Ya'ari-Polskin, Yaakov, *The Nili Affair*, Tel Aviv, Idit, 1952 (Hebrew).

Yehoshuah, Ben-Zion, and Kedar, Aharon, *Ideology and Zionist Policy*, Jerusalem, Zalman Shazar Centre, 1978 (Hebrew).

Zerubavel, Eviatar, *Hidden Rhythms: Schedules and Calendars in Social Life*, Chicago, University of Chicago Press, 1981.

Zerubavel, Yael, 'The Politics of Interpretation: Tel Hai in Israel's Collective Memory', *American Jewish Society Review*, Vol. 16, 1991, pp. 133–159.

————, 'The Historic, the Legendary, and the Incredible: Invented Tradition and Collective Memory in Israel', in Gillis, John, R. (ed.), *Commemorations: The Politics of National Identity*, Princeton, N.J., Princeton University Press, 1994.

————, *Recovered Roots*, Chicago, University of Chicago Press, 1994.

————, *Between History and Legend: The Phases of Israeli Consciousness*, Tel Aviv, Hakibbutz Hameuhad, 1997 (Hebrew).

Zionistischen Organisation, *Stenographisches Protokoll Der Verhandlungen Des XII Zionisten-Kongresses in Karlsbad*, London, 1924.

Zohar, Zvi, *Eretz Yisrael in Our Education,* Jerusalem, JNF Head Office, 1940 (Hebrew).

Zohar, Zvi, and Avivi, Baruch, *The Book of the Child in Second Grade,* Warsaw, New Education Publications, 1935, p. 192 (Hebrew).

Index

210 *Index*

The Jewish National Fund [JNF] is the executive body established by the Zionist movement in 1902 to buy land in Palestine for the Jewish people. Very quickly, however, it became an international organization and soon had branches in many countries throughout the world. One of the tasks of these branches was to mediate between the central office in Jerusalem and the millions of Jews who donated money to buy land. The organization, which is still active throughout the Jewish world, concerned itself with "the marketing of ideology": the dissemination of symbols, knowledge and ideas to the masses of the Jewish people, and converted them into money and real estate property.

In the memories of much of World Jewry the JNF is linked with memories of their childhoods and the forming of their identities. The memory was, in fact, fashioned by the Propaganda Department of the JNF which worked through the mass communications media in the Jewish world and made its presence massively felt in the Jewish education networks in many countries. Among the most remembered items are "the Blue Box," the flagship of the organization, and the stamps distributed to schools, which were miniature posters making political declarations. Up until today there has been virtually no research carried out on these aspects of Zionist propaganda which helped to fashion this collective memory and left its mark upon Jewish culture in Israel and the Jewish Diaspora.

Yoram Bar-Gal is Professor of Geography at Haifa University in Israel.

Lightning Source UK Ltd.
Milton Keynes UK
UKHW010009260820
368819UK00001B/55